I WILL

I WILL

*How Four American Indians
Put Their Lives on the Line
and Changed History*

SHERON WYANT-LEONARD

Arcade Publishing • New York

First Edition

Arcade Publishing books may be purchased in bulk at special discounts for sales promotion, corporate gifts, fund-raising, or educational purposes. Special editions can also be created to specifications. For details, contact the Special Sales Department, Arcade Publishing, 307 West 36th Street, 11th Floor, New York, NY 10018 or arcade@skyhorsepublishing.com.

Arcade Publishing® is a registered trademark of Skyhorse Publishing, Inc.®, a Delaware corporation.

Visit our website at www.arcadepub.com.

10 9 8 7 6 5 4 3 2 1

Library of Congress Cataloging-in-Publication Data is available on file.

Cover design by Erin Seaward-Hiatt
Cover photo credit: Getty Images

ISBN: 978-1-951627-76-8
Ebook ISBN: 978-1-951627-77-5

Printed in the United States of America

Four members of the American Indian Movement took a stand for Native Rights, and what happened next changed history forever. They were Dorothy Ninham, Herb Powless, Leonard Peltier, and Dennis Banks.

Some dialogue has been imagined to be consistent with events. Language and expressions are consistent with the periods depicted. Some of the names in the story have been changed to protect the guilty. This story was inspired by a series of interviews over more than two decades.

Contents

"Man does not weave this web of life. He is merely a strand of it. Whatever he does to the web, he does to himself." —Chief Seattle

PART ONE: DETERMINED

PART TWO:
"AND THEN THINGS GOT HEAVY"

PART ONE

DETERMINED

CHAPTER 1

Leonard Peltier, Inmate #89637-132, Lompoc, California
July 20, 1979

Agarish light rotating between two guard towers reveals the tall chain-link fence, topped by razor wire, that encloses the main cell block. As the moon begins its rise over the Santa Ynez mountains, the sun's last orange rays dip into the Pacific Ocean. At the main entrance of the prison, the squeaky new metal doors are sliding open, alerting the night staff to the changing guard. Rules govern the opening and closing of these doors: any outside visitor must be stamped and IDed, checked, and then stamped and IDed again. Then come the metal detectors.

Off in the yard, a gray stone tower stands in black sand like an ugly muted lighthouse. Its turning lights offer a glimpse of thick brushland beyond the fence. Oddly, no one is on watch as the giant mirrored spotlights move slowly across the complex and the grotesque shadows of late afternoon begin their dance. Light put in place to protect darkness.

Inmates can be seen closing up shops and padlocking doors, putting away rakes, farming tools, and other work implements with an exhausted air that says they are glad to see another evening arrive.

The sounds of preparation for the last meal of the day float across the yard from an open kitchen window. Voices lifted in an awkward harmony blend with the static of a rock hymn playing out of an old transistor radio. A truck bumps through the gates, carrying a bedload of prisoners. They are headed in from some farmer's field where their labor has been rented out. One prisoner drives a tractor, others gather up wheelbarrows; none are attended by guards. At Lompoc, low security really means low security. That said, prison is still prison.

To the east lie the Coast Range and the fertile San Joaquin Valley with its Mediterranean weather, terrain to which Leonard Peltier, then age thirty-four, is no stranger. His dark good looks are owing to his Chippewa and Miniconjou ancestry. Like many other inmates, he is in top condition. Already gifted with speed, when not outside working hard, he runs up the ladder to his top bunk and back down again as fast as possible to train his muscles and equilibrium. What is he training for? What else but escape?

Looking through the prison bars to the east, Peltier hopes to be walking there one day, and not on work detail. This view becomes a prisoner's best friend, a relative, a place to hope. The natural world renews his spirit, birds and invisible thunder beings take his prayers up to the sky. All are prayers for one thing: freedom. A young guard can be seen peering out to the same sand dunes looking just as lonesome, as his days are robbed by watching captured men.

Peltier has recently come to Lompoc from America's highest-security prison, USP Marion in Illinois. Lompoc is luxurious after Marion, where containment units house men where they can barely walk nine feet, coffin size. He has been in the prison system since his capture in 1976, and in the spring of '79 he is utterly surprised to be sent to this relatively new prison. His attorney is the most surprised of all.

Almost every inmate and guard at Lompoc is aware that Leonard Peltier has managed a few impossible escapes before. Just four years prior, after a battle with federal agents on the Pine Ridge Reservation in which two FBI agents and an Indian friend were slain, Leonard, along with a dozen or so other Indians, outran 250 agents. They combed through all fifty states, and still he alone escaped and crossed into Canada. *The FBI don't always get their man*, the story often pointed out, and Peltier's legend grew by leaps and bounds—made a little better every time it was told.

Peltier had been wounded during his cross-country flight, and he could have hidden anywhere under Indian protection. Despite the price that could be paid for hiding him, many did so. He would call out a warning as he approached a new site—the only decent thing to do—"You know the trouble I'm in?" On some reservations, you could be fired from your job for just mentioning his name, but nevertheless he was usually greeted with "Yes, yes! What took you so long to get here? We've been waiting for you!" Food, water, and blankets were left out in barns or at back doorsteps just in case he came by. The moccasin telegraph asked every day: did he make it? Is he still in the wind? How did he ever get away? Ceremonial prayers were lifted across the United States praying for Canada to hide him if he made it there.

When he was given asylum in Canada, the Native people there protected him and announced boldly, "When it comes to Indians, *we do not recognize these borders*." Such boldness was born of the fact most Canadian Indians were still on their original land. They were Indian all the way and could harbor whomever they liked. But no real Indian stays away from home long—both Sitting Bull and Crazy Horse risked their lives when returning from Canada to their ancestral land in the States. It was both a weakness and a strength, depending on who was looking at it.

Peltier spent short stays at two other dreadful high-security prisons before being sent to Marion (known for its harshness as "the end of the line"). Then, mysteriously, he was up and transferred to Lompoc.

Leonard now soaks in the warm weather; it is just as much a relief as the low security after not having seen a sunset while inside Marion's three stories of cement underground. He feels as if a large snake had swallowed him and then just up and decided to spit him back out. In California he could walk outside daily in the bracing sea air, but it is still prison. If his plans go right, he will soon be out of the system altogether.

A few nights before the planned escape, inmate Bobby Castillo, a young Chicano who had a great interest in Peltier, exchanged a look with him in the chow line. How was it, Castillo wondered, he'd ever been captured? Why not sport a tipi in the Kamloops and never be seen or heard from again? But Peltier had stayed close to the Canadian border, and many said he'd even gone back and forth regularly to see his family. This surprised no one who knew him.

Leonard wanted his people. He once told a friendly guard, "It's not that I hate you, brother, it's just I love my own!" He was familiar with the reservation blues, and those isolated, unforgiving landscapes had their problems, but the communal belief was *If you're one of us, you're with us.* That was why Leonard joined the Movement, to protect Indians' right to be left alone.

Leonard's story was the topic of ongoing debate both inside and outside prison. The inmates would argue over it at length—it was better than checkers. "Who did he protect? Where are they now, and would they help him?" Now, over four years later, all that was knowable was that Leonard was in Lompoc, still alive, and Indian people would go to great lengths to help him if he escaped again.

Bobby Castillo thought none of Peltier's situation made sense. Just how, he wondered, could Peltier, of all federal prisoners, be in low security? Did they want him to escape? If so, why? If anybody was likely to pull off an escape, this dude might. It made Bobby curious. Maybe others had plans, too. What Castillo could not know at the time was that an Indian prisoner recently transferred to Lompoc had persuaded Peltier he was not safe, in fact that his life was in jeopardy. Escape seemed his only remedy.

Seizing his chance in the chow line, Bobby called out to Leonard in Spanish. Peltier looked a little Mexican to Bobby's eyes, with his coffee tan and almond-shaped eyes. Leonard looked over and shook his head. "*No habla.* I don't speak the language, bro." No one in Canada mistook him—they knew at a glance he was Indian. It only happened in the States. The name Peltier was French from a trapper who had married into his Indian family long ago, a common enough affair.

Bobby was in Cell Block C and Peltier was in A, so they couldn't talk long. But before they headed in their separate directions, Peltier called out, "Come to the sweat tonight. Just use my name, tell them I invited you. You're just a Yaqui Indian after all. Come sweat!"

Bobby smiled. "What is it? Sweat?"

Peltier smiled back. "Whadda you care? Got a better engagement tonight? Come inside it and find out! They let us build our lodge right in the prison yard, willow branches and all, and we can invite who we say. It'll be good for you!"

"What do they do in there?"

Leonard replied over his shoulder, "Pray."

"Gracias," Bobby said, though he thought he wanted nothing to do with that shit. After years of church, he gave up life on his knees. But he did want this new friend, so he decided to go. He had no idea something was about to redirect his life forever.

Hours later, guards escorted Bobby Castillo to his first sweat lodge. Damned if it wasn't built right in the middle of the prison yard by Indian prisoners. *What a trip!* Castillo thought, thinking his eyes deceived him. Bobby called out to Peltier, "Thank you, brother!" Peltier answered, "Thank Jimmy Carter!" referring to the recent American Indian Religious Freedom Act, just a year old.

Archie Fire Lame Deer was the medicine man who came in from outside for the sweat. Even the willow poles had to go through the metal detectors, and the forty-four-year-old medicine man was strip-searched and told he couldn't bring in his staff topped with horsehair. Even Lompoc was not that casual. The warden was furious about the sweat lodge in the yard, and as always, the prison was understaffed. Guards argued that they'd stand watch outside the lodge, but damned if they were going inside. The prison chaplain also refused; let the warden roast if he wanted to. So no one went inside but the Indians. Once cross-legged on the dirt floor of the lodge, Archie Fire, as Leonard called him, untwined medicine and horsehair from his own hair, and re-topped a staff.

Following the sweat, Indians shadow Peltier through the prison. Bobby Garcia and Dallas Thundershield walk beside him, other men in front and behind working as an inmate form of security. Garcia, a wiry young part-Apache Chicano, and Thundershield, a Lakota Indian from Standing Rock Agency in North Dakota, are Leonard's close friends at Lompoc.

In a curved breezeway between cell blocks A and B, Leonard drops suddenly to one knee and appears to straighten his shoe. The Indian inmates know the drill and quickly form a circle around him as Leonard takes a medicine bundle from his waistband and slips it over his head and inside his T-shirt. Thundershield has squatted next to him to ask a question, and

Leonard answers brusquely, "No, little brother, you're not going. Getting out is one thing, staying out is another. Once over that fence we're all on our own. You don't have long to serve, so don't do it."

Dallas says, choking back tears, "I can't stay in here without you, Leonard. I just can't. Besides, I may be of some use. I'd take a bullet for you, and you know it."

"I do know it, and it's exactly what I don't want," Leonard answers.

Bobby Garcia whispers, "Close your jaws, brothers, you're getting attention."

"Then close yours, brother, and let me up," Leonard stands and starts heading for his cell at a fast clip. He looks forward to doing this soon for the last time.

Two days later, just minutes after final count for the night, a full moon riding high over the California sky, a rattlesnake coiled not far from the fence, three figures whisk across the prison yard. Peltier goes first, then Bobby Garcia, who had masterminded the escape plan, takes lead in front of him. The young Dallas Thundershield is right on their heels. Garcia proceeds to cut the wire at the top of the first fence as Peltier holds his legs.

At 10:00 p.m., Bobby Castillo hears a noise before anyone else on his cell block. Shuffling feet and a slamming door tell him something is not ordinary. There is never a peaceful setting, even following the nine o'clock final count, the one where you better be in your cell, sitting up and wide awake. Another count came at midnight, but that followed lights-out. Again, never silence. Funny how even in noise, there are noises you know, and those you don't. Just before the fire alarm and the sirens start, there are noises that Castillo doesn't know.

Unusual noises after count wake one up in a particular way. For a second or two there is a quick analysis, as an unexpected noise meant something bad. Bodies turn over in beds, lights switch on in faraway places, then off again. Even the sounds from the rugged terrain outside the windows seem to stop and question for a second, searching, listening. Usually the noise halts and the soft hum of insects and night rhythms return, a distant coyote tunes up again. But not this night.

Peltier unrolls the green wool army blanket he carries under his arm, throws it quickly over the cut wire opening, and disappears onto the other side. Dallas goes over next, but a slip of his blanket lets the wire gash his arm, and he is bleeding profusely by the time he comes to stand at Leonard's back in the space between the first and second perimeter fences. This second fence is closer than it looked from the yard and unexpectedly higher than the first, leaving no way to get a running start. Peltier doesn't hesitate and tears his way up the fence, again appearing to do it almost effortlessly. Young Dallas freezes, and is neither so swift nor so lucky. For one, he ran behind Peltier, instead of beside him. Brave, if not smart. A shot breaks through the ambient racket.

Bobby Castillo springs from his cot so fast his thin gray mat slides out with him. Quickly he's crouched to the left of his cell and joins a system of communication as cellies whisper, passing words from corner to corner.

"They're out! God dammit they-are-out!" shouts the celly three cells down.

"Who's out?" Bobby returns, the words almost fading on his lips, because, my God, he knows who! "Did they make it, are they over?"

He hears, "Ahhh, dammit, they got Garcia in the yard. Damn him, he gets out and is right back in before it starts, every time. Always grabbed first! It's not fair, man." In fact, Garcia had been pulled by the legs from a sewage ditch as he detoured. Maybe sensing the inevitable, he became a decoy.

Just minutes earlier, over in a separate building, a janitor is awakened in his bed. A guard who looks both strained and terrified tells him to get up, they need everyone, they are short-staffed. He plops a handgun into the startled janitor's lap. The janitor hops out of bed, knocks over a full mop bucket, pulls on his boots, and runs out behind the guard, still in his nightclothes.

In the hall, a guard grabs a ringing phone, listens, and answers, "Sir. No, sir, we don't know yet, sir."

In his cell, Bobby strains his ears, asking in a panic, "Peltier? Did he make it over? *Goddamn!*" The air is now riddled with gunshots, three so close to Bobby's window he drops into a squat, hugs his knees, and begins to pray. Then he jumps up and shouts, no longer bothering to whisper, "Peltier!"

Penetrating flashes of white light roll like a wave across the ceiling as if desperate to stop his next question. "Is he . . .? Did he make it out?"

A whisper echoes back to Bobby's ears, the words he's been waiting for.

"Peltier—*on the run.*" As the guards' nightsticks bang along the iron bars to cease the exchange, all coil back to their bunks.

Dallas Thundershield, they'd learn later, was shot in the back by the armed janitor and bled to death with no one to administer aid or comfort. When the janitor leaned over Dallas, he asked, "Are you the Indian they're all looking for?"

"Yes," the boy gurgled up, using his last breath to try and buy Leonard some time.

CHAPTER 2

The Chumash Cop,
Santa Maria, California
July 21, 1979

A Lompoc guard would note in the prison log: "12:15 a.m. One capture, Robert Garcia, captured at sewage ditch, #3 location, one, Dallas Thundershield, expired at fence outside guard tower road, and one, Leonard Peltier, on escape status."

All night long they counted the inmates in their cells instead of the usual lineup, as there were only a handful of guards not on the chase. They'd confirm they were one inmate number short, and in disbelief kept calling out, "Number 89637-132? Number 8-9-6-3-7-1-3-2!" Bobby Castillo wondered if they thought if they kept saying it, Peltier would somehow materially reappear. He was out!

The warden stood in the yard waving men and volunteers into private cars and trucks, as there were not enough prison vehicles. He decided to jump into one himself while others loaded rifles and chains and dogs into its bed. It was bedlam, with deafening sirens and phone calls demanding attention, and if the cells hadn't been on auto-lock, the whole prison population could have walked out. *All over one damn Indian*, thought the warden. *And now I am likely suspended.*

Leonard Peltier moves into a dead run to put some space between him and the close bullets of his pursuers. He knows the guards will have to turn back soon, and the farther into the brush they chase him, the farther they'll have to go back to get to their vehicles. With the expert ears of an ace mechanic, he knows half the state trucks leaving the prison yard each day aren't up to tackling the terrain ahead. Not quickly. He glances to the sky and smells the dense air and knows the authorities will soon speed over wet, sandy ruts—even better. By that time, he will be far off any road. He quickens his pace.

Minutes later, he drops to a squat inside some tree cover to draw a breath and get his bearings. He can still hear the disruption carried over from the prison yard, though two miles away. He tears out again, making noises more like those of a large, frightened animal than a man. Survival makes such sounds.

He leaps over dry gullies and through gulches and into a helpful layer of fog. He runs along rows of lettuce toward the nearest high ground. Noticing a parallel road that's too damn close, he darts in another direction. On that road is a barnwood sign that reads Entering Chumash Land. A metal street sign announces Lompoc, California, the garden seed capital of the world! EST. 1888.

Peltier scrambles up a large hill, occasionally slipping on loose sediment. At the summit he surveys his surroundings and assesses the sky, then dips his cupped hands into a small, fresh spring. He slurps the cool water, splashes some on his neck and face, and wets his red wind band. Though in a squat, he does not take his eyes off the sky. The starlight is telling him something. He wrings out his bandana and ties it back tightly around his forehead.

Through a small clump of trees, he spots a road and can tell by the distant glow of neon that he's nearing a small town. He takes off toward it. Mountains to his back now, open fields out front, he is in a full sprint in the darkness when he is surprised by the sight of yards. *Out here?* he thinks. *Where did this housing development come from?* It wasn't on the map.

The new suburb sprang up practically in the middle of nowhere as part of a newly planned Jewish community. The first finished house was already occupied by the county's new prosecutor. Five ornate, freshly bricked homes stand behind a stone entrance flanked by palm gardens and a small pond. Extravagant for a dryland community. Peltier can do nothing but duck low and run fast behind it.

Only the prosecutor has moved in, and he is busy filling a large trash can when he hears a dog bark in an unfamiliar way. He listens for a second and then goes back to the trash. Leonard does not slow down. A streetlamp casts a beam across his face, moving him sideways. His breath stops for as long as he can hold it.

The town can be seen in the distance now, and Leonard sprints through an open field, chest heaving, eyes frantic but focused, as this poses the greatest risk of his journey. The suburb surprised him, and he'd have to alter his planned route and run through farmland, hoping the crops were tall enough to hide him and his footprints would mingle with others and not leave a trail. The misty fog would help, and the strong and permeating smell of manure would likely fool any dogs.

The police searched everywhere in the sleepy town, trolling through the streets, some banging on doors in the predawn hours. Strained voices shouted over radio transmitters. They had no direction or plan or leads; they simply had to cover all possible ground and quickly, like a squeegee. The escape was already hours behind them, and morning approached. They knew things were always trickier the day following an escape.

By first morning light, a lone Indian woman with a baby in her arms approached an empty Laundromat. She looked around carefully before snatching down a wanted poster from a bulletin board, glimpsing Peltier's dark eyes before stuffing it quickly under her baby. Others scouted out telephone poles, a bus station bulletin board, or anywhere else there might be a poster and bravely and methodically pulled them down. Buying time was the only hope they had for the young Indian they'd all been told about. Every hour that passed was a blessing.

Many endeavored to help. A rock star of note, who lived on a ranch nearby and had recently held a concert for Peltier's legal defense, unlocked his large metal security gate. He, too, was risking to give harbor. *Not likely*, he thought, *but he might run this way. He just might.*

By dawn's full light Leonard spots the expected watermelon fields and passes out of the city limits. He's made a good run but doesn't relax or slow down. He does, however, punch his fist into a melon and bring up a juicy red handful, which he eats while he speeds on. He must pass into Santa Maria's city limits, though his destination is nowhere near. Workers start to fill the empty roads, both in vehicles and on foot. A cock crows off in the distance; a truck backfires.

A good ten miles behind Leonard, a young cop has pulled out a tape measure to check the span of some deep and recent footfalls, impressions across a gully. "Holy Moly! Almost ten feet across, we're after a damn Olympian!" he announces with a wide smile, which quickly fades as he sees his superiors standing on a ledge above him. Two FBI agents have appeared at their sides. A *Santa Maria Times* reporter snaps a quick shot and then scribbles down the young cop's comment.

A police cruiser carrying a Chumash Indian police officer, Eddy Light Horse, and his superior, a white sheriff, has pulled over an old jalopy truck packed with about twenty migrant farmworkers headed out to the fields. Light Horse knows the sheriff can't distinguish a Chicano from a Chippewa Indian; as proof, the frustrated man has just drawn his pistol and is waving it around and shouting, "If you are Leonard Peltier, stick your hands up right now or I will start shooting all of you!"

More cops drive up and hop out of their cars. One of them flings open the truck's passenger door, two others draw down on the men in the bed. Everyone knows the sheriff's bluffing—everyone but the migrant workers.

Light Horse rolls his eyes at the scene; a quick scan tells him Peltier is not present. He, too, knows the sheriff is bluffing—he has been riding with the man for hours and knows he's full of it. As the sun rises higher, Light Horse also knows the coming heat will not help calm things down, and Peltier will likely be in custody by nightfall. The area is too populated to hide for long or run far, and the heat and brush are merciless.

In the truck cab, one skinny old Indian man in a worn straw hat slowly shuts his eyes and raises one hand. Then all the men in the truck raise their hand as well. Great, Eddy thinks, *the poorest, hardest working men in America but today they're Spartacus.* The sweating sheriff finally lets out a loud huff, crams his gun into its holster, and leaves the truck. Light Horse is a tall man, and as he lowers his head to get back into the driver's seat, he is trying to stifle a giggle. It'd only make things harder if he is caught laughing at the county sheriff and likely hardest on the farmworkers. His smile dissolves at the thought. He'd seen things get out of hand before, and law enforcement is feeling the heat coming from all sides, both inside and outside the department. Everyone knows why.

The sheriff leaves the state patrollers behind to handle the scene, and once he is out of sight, they quickly wave the men back onto the road. The state patrol has already worked a night shift, and the men are anxious to get home, though that is unlikely until there's a capture. But Peltier is far outside the farming district by now, and the young Chumash cop likely knows it.

Miles away, Peltier breaks into a wild sprint as he reaches a small basin where the trees are taller and provide a little cover. He walks up to a drainage ditch, sees the large metal pipe inside it, and squats down. He's flooded with relief when he sees a colorful, finely woven Indian blanket rolled up on a pile of rocks. Pulling it out gently, he unrolls it to reveal a rifle—without checking, he knows it's loaded. A roll of bills is rubber-banded to its stock, and there's a snakebite kit and some clothes. He unrolls his prison-issue green army blanket—now badly ripped by razor wire—and checks something within it, then rolls it back up.

He dresses, stuffs the snakebite kit and cash into his pocket, then squats to roll the Indian blanket into a tight bundle. He lifts his pants legs to reveal ankles now raw from poison oak, and notices bloodstains where his toes have bled into his torn prison slippers. He looks around, but there are no shoes. Smiling, he shakes it off as he stands and slings the rifle onto his back. He positions the roll under his arm and squats again, his back up against a tree, facing the mouth of the basin.

15

He'll stay hidden there until night brings better cover and cooler air. Doing nothing will prove a challenge, but it is one he is used to. Many say take one day at a time, but few have had to live it, hour to hour. Leonard closes his eyes, and his own breathing lulls him into a deep sleep. He can't choose the danger he's facing, but he's determined to choose how he lets it affect him. Leonard Peltier is a man of considerable self-discipline.

The day is half over as the sheriff and the Chumash cop bounce down a dusty farm road with the windows partly open, though the hot breezes don't bring relief. If the air conditioner runs too long, the engine will overheat. Sacrifices of one kind or another come in expected ways in a dryland life.

There hasn't been a single sign of Peltier. How could anybody be that lucky in such a compact area and given the unforgiving terrain?

"Did he head to Mexico?" the sheriff asks out loud, and then answers himself. "Nah, and no way he's made it to mountain cover yet." The police radio pumps out nonstop information about the escaped convict, as it has been doing all day.

"A rez Indian could make twenty miles in a day," Light Horse observes.

"He's a city boy, you don't know that? Are you an Indian or ain't ya?"

"Historically. You kept our history, just got rid of us."

"I don't understand a damn thing you say," the sheriff says as he turns up the radio.

Eddy Light Horse has a hunch and he tries to direct the sheriff, who rarely listens to him until there is no alternative. Eddy wants to survey the new Sun Dance grounds. Reaching to turn down the police radio, he says, "If Peltier is headed anywhere, away from town would be where he'd go. He's likely traded stories and seen maps." The older man's eyes are closed, a cigar hangs from between his lips, and he's acting like he isn't listening.

Officer Eddy knows many Lompoc inmates are local boys, with Indians in population. They probably spent weeks trading ideas and covering the area with Peltier. Passing along an idea isn't breaking the law, if not caught doing it.

Eddy continues, whether the sheriff is listening or not. "Look, they talk inside, for example, one inmate could say in passing, there sure are some pretty low hills out there, isolated small farms, or mention watermelons were picked today, we went west of the main road, etcetera. They could lay out a whole map of the area that way. When you say armed and dangerous every minute, it just scares you in the end, and everybody freezes. Or shoots at the wrong thing. All them farmers are armed. This guy has no violent history or infractions from inside—"

The sheriff cuts in with his usual rhetoric, ignoring any facts. "What'd ya call killing those agents?! Cop killer, son, 'most dangerous man alive.' Anyone who'd do that—"

If he did do it, Eddy thinks as he cuts the sheriff off. "Dangerous to a cop maybe. Besides, I heard he went over that fence without a weapon. He'd have shot to protect his friends."

"'Scapee's got no friends! Heard? What else you hear, mister?" the sheriff barks, turning officious.

"He took his pipe out with him. They tossed his cell, and many others, it wasn't there. You smoke a pipe or a gun, but not both." Eddy knows a sacred pipe can't be carried alongside a weapon.

"Bull! This is not a religious individual!"

Eddy nods and knows not to pursue it. But he knows his source is real. He'd fail if he tried to explain the difference between a religion and a way of life. *Why bother?* He points the truck off the beaten path and jolts into the low hills.

A few empty hours later the two men spot patrol cars from three different counties parked haphazardly. A few engines are still running, meaning the occupants exited quickly. They'd found something.

Several radio frequencies led them to the spot. The sheriff hollers, "Why in hell is our radio down? Turn it up, nitwit!" On a higher hill a group of spectators has also gathered, mere shadows with the late afternoon sun at their backs.

Two ranchers are also on-site, their drawn guns pointing to the ground. The sheriff and Light Horse jump out and bust into the circle to see what the curiosity is all about. Up on a high hill Eddy spots the remnants of a recent Sun Dance, marked with thin strips of faded cloth, prayer ties still hanging from nearby tree limbs. The soft wind lifts them. Nightfall is approaching.

A washed-out handwritten sign on a fence post reads No CAMERAS, NO ALCOHOL, NO DRUGS, NO FIREARMS, NO RECORDING DEVICES OF ANY KIND. The drainpipe the cops have surrounded is nearby, but the mouth of the drain is outside the ceremonial grounds. Eddy turns full circle, observing.

The sheriff holds out his badge, but it is Eddy who waves everyone to back up, thinking, *What in hell are they aiming at, a snake bed? Is there a man inside that drain?* Something green is on top of the rocks piled at the entrance in full view. It appears to be an army-issue wool blanket.

The sheriff points with his gun to direct a county cop to pull it out. "What in hell? Why'd he leave his blanket? Everyone knows it gets cold come nightfall."

As the cop pulls at the blanket, it unrolls and a delicate wooden pipe stem rolls toward them onto the ground. The sheriff jumps as if it were a snake. It's clear to Eddy that its stone pipe bowl is tied inside a fine leather pouch beside it. Before anyone gets a chance to kick at it, he picks up the pouch, then gently lifts the wooden stem as well. Nobody stops him; nobody wants to.

He studies the pipe's burned markings a moment before turning toward the vast sandy landscape with the soon-to-be enveloping darkness. Maybe Peltier is hurt out there. Maybe he's rolled up in another blanket in a back seat halfway to Canada. If they don't get him soon, he's gone.

The sheriff, suddenly alert, waves the other men back into their vehicles, then turns in frustration and kicks hard at the drain's rock pile.

The wind begins to kick up and with it a familiar howl. Without taking his eyes off the landscape, Eddy Light Horse tells the sheriff, "Now, you can say he's armed."

CHAPTER 3

The Chicken Coop,
Oneida, Wisconsin
Winter 1951

Ten-year-old Dorothy Ninham was a good ice skater, and in 1951 on a Wisconsin Indian reservation it was the only fun recreation available. Her tribal Indian land was hard up against Lake Michigan, a stone's throw from Green Bay, and a two-hour trek into Milwaukee. The Canadian provinces of Manitoba and Saskatchewan and Ontario are as familiar names to the Oneidas as Green Bay is to their brothers and sisters to the north. The little girl had managed to find a pair of worn skates two sizes too big and stuffed them with old socks and newspaper and made them fit. She was determined, resourceful, and skated at a remarkable speed. Small and lean, she loved the movement, the call to be fearless, and especially she loved speeding through darkness. She liked to sneak out at night, hit the ice, and feel alive as the freezing air hit her face.

A Wisconsin winter meant real ice. Moving water was hard to freeze and took longer—often it didn't freeze through but appeared to have done so. Locals knew what was safe. Dorothy skated by the light of the moon and stars and was headed to a small pond she knew, an offshoot from Duck Creek.

Her mother, Melinda, hated it when she found her daughter's cot empty, but the little girl preferred the outdoors to the noisy cabin. And after the day's chores had ended, why not play? A mother had to trust her daughter, but she knew that with winter drawing to a close the frozen waters could be unsafe. The natural world could help you—clear, clean water and fresh, bracing air could refresh you after working in an overheated cabin for hours—but the water could drown you, too. One had to always be aware of the water spirits, especially a mother. Dorothy had a rare, brave spirit herself and one she'd likely need later, so her mom let it rise inside her and would caution her but rarely stop her. Still, you'd think having almost drowned at age five would have kept anyone away from that pond forever. Not her Dorothy.

One morning five years earlier, Dorothy had stopped only long enough to put on her worn red mitts and ragged coat before she ran out to follow her brother to go skating with cousins. They didn't want a five-year-old tagging along, so they ran to get out of her sight. She knew her brother, Tawit, would be crossing the bridge, named for De Pere, Wisconsin. Locals knew of it; merchants just thought of it as a reach beyond the big apple orchards outside of Green Bay.

And there was always little Strawberry Island, where she enjoyed swimming. She was a good swimmer. Though in the Land of Lakes, there was no lake near the Ninham cabin, just arctic weather and one wide, curvy, very long creek. Dorothy knew its curves like the lines on her hand, but now she was on land, chasing her brother's voice and running almost as fast as she skated. Wisconsin girls knew about the possibility of thin ice under the snow and were taught to read the waterlines before they could walk, but Dorothy was so determined to catch up with Tawit that she just didn't look or care.

Jumping a small pond, with her heavy skates over her shoulder, she fell straight through the snow into an ice hole that had been cut for a milk cow to drink from. Her piercing scream reached her brother and he decided to turn back, just in case (there would be many *just in cases* in Dorothy Ninham's life; this was the first). Backtracking, he caught a glimpse of her red mitten sticking out above the hole.

The water had been so cold it knocked her plumb out, or so she was told, but afterward she didn't recall anything but the sound of the ice water. She woke to the crackling of flames inside the cookstove and her mother rubbing her vigorously to bring her back to life. Dorothy's thick black lashes lifted a fraction, and she noticed that her brother was crying. She had no memory of having seen him cry before. How in all Wisconsin had he gotten her home? He was only three years older.

She recovered and went skating the very next day. Such were the little pleasures afforded to her on the rez. Each day her mother made the long walk to town to search for work, any work, just to earn a nickel. She'd offer to sew or babysit or wash or clean. It was Dorothy's job by age ten to get her brother and two sisters off to school. Make their breakfast and make their lunches.

Before sunrise, she would fill a metal milk jug nearly as big as she was with water from the well at the bottom of the hill, lug it inside the house, and start to wash the day's corn. The one pleasure in washing corn before daylight was watching the stars, which she never thought of as three sisters or a big handle, as her Mormon teacher referred to them. Those were not their names to an Oneida. Her mother recalled some of the Oneida language and she called them the star nations. They were beautiful and far away and they were watching over Dorothy.

After the corn, she'd swipe three biscuits with a thin ribbon of lard, wrap them in newspaper, and put them in her siblings' coat pockets—school lunch. She had to prepare the noon meal of corn soup before leaving for school, so she lagged far behind the others. Likely she'd have to pass old Luther on her way, a leering drunk who often managed to be sitting on the ground near her school. If a Mormon had caught him, she'd be lucky, but usually there he sat, always calling out the same thing, "Remember that we were People of the Standing Stone, and *we were a fierce people!*" He was a war veteran and she tried to honor his words, but mainly she honored her pulse that said to get away fast.

He always seemed to start a conversation, if you could call it that, just as he pulled the tab on his Milwaukee beer, corn of another kind, with a smell and effect that Dorothy thought were awful. For the rest of her life that familiar hiss when a beer was popped open would be a bad omen. It meant ill will and a broken life, that was all she ever needed to know about it. She only wanted to be away from it, and one day she knew she'd get her chance. She wouldn't stay a child forever.

Dorothy's mother heard her say that once and warned, "You want to give your children what you don't have, but don't forget to give them what you do!" Dorothy asked her mother what she thought she had that was so darn good to give them, and she would always remember her reply. Lifting her daughter's chin with her forefinger and looking her in the eye, Melinda said, "You're a good girl, Dorothy, and you have character. It is the most important thing to have."

There came a day for Dorothy when the morning started out as always, but by afternoon everything had changed. She got the other children up and dressed. Like the others, she had two sets of clothes, one for summer and one for winter; one worn pair of underclothes served both seasons.

There were mitts and old ill-fitting coats, and that was all. As she dressed, she heard old Luther come up to the door loudly looking for breakfast. This was a rare annoyance; even when drunk out of his mind, he knew to stay clear of her mother, though he would harass her brother and sisters something awful. So Dorothy sent them off running and proceeded to beat at Luther with a broken broom handle. He got hold of the end of it, but she jerked it back and beat around his head so hard he lost his bearings and rolled down the hill till the stone well casing stopped him. At this point, the other kids came to her aid, but she yelled at them to go on to school, she'd take care of it. "Grab a biscuit!" she added.

After tiptoeing close enough to smell the stink of malt and see that Luther was breathing, she ran back to the cabin to grab her coat and stuff a biscuit in her own pocket. Then she paused at the cabin door, ran back inside, and grabbed an old blanket to throw over Luther. She didn't know if he could get up and catch her, but she wasn't tempting fate, so after that she ran the full two miles to school.

Though she loved the books and enjoyed the company of the other girls at school, she was always glad at the end of the day to be out of the hands of the Mormons and back at the cabin. But approaching it today, she saw her mother sitting at the end of their road by a stack of their few belongings.

She came closer and leaned over to look into their one metal pot, which should have held the corn soup for supper. It was as empty as her mother's eyes. Out of respect she let her mother speak first.

"We're going to our new house, and we have to walk fast. Go get your sisters. I sent your brother back to school to see if he can sleep on the headmaster's porch for just the night, then we will go get him."

"You sent Tawit off?" If there was trouble, they'd need him. If there wasn't, they'd still need him.

"Dorothy, move. We will have to hurry. We have a ways to walk."

"To where? Do we have a place?"

"Of course we do!" her mother answered in a false tone.

Dorothy scurried the younger girls out of the cabin and all began to walk quickly, though their mother's long stride made it hard to keep up. Fear helped, and Dorothy wouldn't breathe lightly till she saw this "place" her mother spoke of.

Hours down the road, her mother stopped suddenly, told her daughters to wait, and darted into the woods. She returned to say excitedly that she had found a cabin, and it was empty. Dorothy went in first. The single window had a tree limb growing through it, and cobwebs and dust were everywhere. She asked, softly, "Whose cabin is this?"

"Ours," her mother replied with finality.

The wind was starting to blow snow outside. Melinda used some store of inner strength to pull at tree limbs and break them with her foot until they had a little firewood. There was no stove, so they made a fire on the packed-earth floor and huddled around it. Dorothy felt a kind of fear she'd never known; it came from shame. Any minute the cabin's owner would open the door. It was just a matter of time.

After a few days of squatting there, they begin to walk again. Her mother had a cousin, June, who had married a Mormon. She was not wealthy by any stretch, but maybe she had a barn they could sleep in for a bit.

They arrived at June's road just at nightfall with the smell of impending snow thick in the air. Melinda was not exactly on great terms with her "Aunt June," so she sent Dorothy and her sisters to the back door. The youngest could cry on a dime, and they could make use of her tears.

Begging was not in Dorothy's nature. She knocked and could smell food being cooked. After the long, cold day that aroma lodged forever in Dorothy's memory, and she would never afterward take a bite of anything if the person next to her was not also able to do so. But this wasn't new, as she had always been the last to eat.

Aunt June looked put out as she came to the door, then tried to peer down the road, but it had grown too dark. The barn, she explained, was crammed with their threshing equipment and winter store. Not an inch to fit a single soul into it.

She scrutinized the girls' dirty clothes, then looked back at her husband, who was already grousing at anything that interfered with supper time. "Is your mother drinking?"

"No, ma'am!" Dorothy said, quite defiantly. It was pretty clear that if her husband got a word in, it would be no. Dorothy started to leave, but she couldn't fail her mother, and so she pleaded, "We will take anywhere, Aunt June, just for the night. Please."

June finally said okay and explained that the chickens would just have to move over, or they could move out to the run, so the girls could have their coop for the night. She mentioned before shutting the door that she had a little space heater she could run out and a few blankets. Melinda Ninham had already started up the road, leaving their belongings in a heap behind her. They could see after them later.

Melinda acted as if they'd been given the prized hallway in a sanctuary. Dorothy spoke up to her for the first time in two days and said, "Momma the smell is unbearable. We can't, we just can't!"

"Shhh, girl! It's somewhere. I have to get out of the snow."

"We'd be better off in the snow! I'll make a woodfire in the pot, Momma, and we can huddle together, at least it's clean."

"I have to get out of the snow now, right now. I'm gonna have a baby."

Feeling like the breath had been knocked out of her, Dorothy reached over to pull back her mother's shawl. "When, Momma? When are you going to have a baby?"

"Tonight."

Hours later, Dorothy watched softly floating snowflakes start to catch on the tiny eyelashes of the newborn sister sleeping in her arms. She pulled her mother's shawl closer about her shoulders and covered the baby's face with it. Her mother was asleep on a rack inside the awful coop with Dorothy's coat covering her. Earlier, Dorothy had found a small axe and cut low pine boughs to make a bed for them all in the coop and borrowed a little hay from the barn. They had snuggled close together to provide some warmth before Dorothy got up to go outside with the infant. Auntie June's small space heater didn't do them much good.

June had also brought them a cloth napkin with four biscuits, a slab of honey, and two cold chicken legs. Melinda Ninham didn't take a nibble, and Dorothy didn't want to eat until she saw that her mother could. But it was a fine feast for the smaller girls. What was available in abundance was the feeling of love, and there was no greater gift at such a family time. Even their sadness communicated love, and the small sustenance of food and a little warmth did, too. They were still together, and that was about it. It was always enough.

Dorothy had assisted in an event that in her limited experience was beyond describing. When the serious moaning started, she no longer had to beg the stubborn chickens to leave. As Dorothy started to panic and dart for the main house, Melinda pulled her in close and assured her she had done this four times already and nature would help. Dorothy stayed to her side. When the worst was over, but the cord not yet cut, her mother pulled her face close and whispered, "Thank you, my good girl." And then she passed out.

Dorothy brought snow to cool her mother's fever, and soon she was awake and feeding the baby. She told Dorothy to heat some snow to a boil and wash whatever she'd cut the pine limbs with and bring it to her. The baby cooed while she did this and had not cried more than once. She was already cooperating with her new family, Dorothy thought. How good of her new baby sister to help her out in her first hours here.

Hours later, standing in the light snowfall with the baby in her arms, Dorothy thanked the Creator that both her mother and sister had lived through it. She sang and investigated the smallest face she'd ever seen and whispered the name her mother had chosen. Always of a mind to show gratitude even in the most unlikely of circumstances, she had named the little infant June.

With daylight, Aunt June would learn what had transpired and immediately take mother and baby into the house. Not until morning, though. And just them.

Much later, Dorothy would ask her mother about her own mother for the first time. That subject was never discussed, and Dorothy had never known why. In all hurtful situations, it is the one harmed who needs to be the first to do the talking. Melinda shared the one and only thing she knew about her mother, which was that she had died giving birth to her.

A few years after June was born, Melinda was walking to work on that same long road they'd taken after the eviction when a drunk driver hit her and pinned her against another car. Dorothy, not sixteen, was told she was not old enough to visit her in the hospital. Tawit, who was always at their mother's bedside, tried hard to find a way to get his sister inside to say goodbye.

Dorothy told him that it was not to say goodbye, but so she could heal her. She knew she could. Tawit explained that every bone in her body had been broken and she was just holding on to say goodbye, holding on hard. The hospital, however, stuck to its cruel policy.

Tawit delivered Melinda's last words for Dorothy: "I will visit you from the stars, my girl. If you ever need me, just look up. Please take care of my children for me. You have always been my brave girl, the rock on which I could rest." With that, Melinda Ninham entered the sleep from which no one ever awakes.

Dorothy left the cement hospital stoop with her brother and set out to face her uncertain future, determined to keep the family together as her mother had asked. Tawit seemed to be in deep thought as his young sister carried a burden too big for her small broken heart. Still, she asked, "Did anything else happen in that room?"

"Yes. It did," her older brother answered, his eyes not meeting hers. "Mother kept calling to her mother; she said she was in the room with us."

This gave the young Dorothy a small momentary comfort that she, too, one day, might see Melinda Ninham again. "Old ones comment on that all the time, their mother coming for them. Soldiers do, say it happens even on battlefields."

"Yes, they do. But our mom never saw her mother or heard her voice. How did she know it was her?"

CHAPTER 4

Wahpeton Indian Boarding School, Wahpeton, North Dakota
September 1941

Dennis Banks lived with his mother and sisters in a nice, clean cabin. His father had come home from the war and married another woman, and Dennis had seen very little of him in his young life. An old man gave him a stick of candy once outside an old hotel on his town's main street, and said with a laugh, "Don't say I never gave ya anything." Dennis used to pretend that was his father, but likely it was just a kind Indian elder. Maybe one who knew his circumstances.

His mother, Bertha, was pretty, quiet, and a good homemaker, though they had little. They were Ojibwe people on Leech Lake, Minnesota. She threw her nets out with the menfolk, and when he got old enough, Dennis did, too. The family had a motto: "If you can walk, you can fish." His ma had only made one mistake with him that he knew of, but it was a big one. She noticed his clothes were getting raggedy and before making him a school outfit from a flour bag, she decided to go to the Indian agency. It had an allowance for clothes, and she needed it, so why not ask? He recalled the long walk into town, over ten miles, and it felt like a walk around the world to a boy. He recalled the agency worker's harsh words and his mom ushering him out of her office to sit on a stoop and then going back in. He could still hear her raised voice. Then they made the long walk home.

The next day a sheriff knocked on their door. That very social worker was with him and insisted on checking the kids' wardrobes. There were none. With a glimmer of satisfaction, Bertha thought this assured that she'd get the help that was owed. Yes, owed. When they moved to take Dennis, his mom pulled back on his arm so hard he thought it'd pop off. Then the sheriff said, "Don't you want your boy to have clothes, good meals, and books and things you can't never provide?" The next thing Dennis knew, they were dragging him, and the other kids, into a bus, and he was shocked to see his mother inside it helping to pull him in. This broke his heart, and he stopped resisting, not knowing her heart was breaking, too. His first school was Pipestone, in Minnesota, at barely the age of four.

Dennis Banks would be in more than one Indian school over many years, and his second was Wahpeton, in North Dakota. The school had a rather large population of Sioux Indians, ushered in out of the local Sisseton Sioux Agency. That meant he knew a lot of Lakota early on in life. He was eleven.

He stood in a big hall for morning roll call. He didn't like seeing that loud microphone at the podium; he decided at a young age that public speaking was never going to be his calling. He would be wrong about that. The mic hissed like a snake and roll call began.

Students' names like Standing Elk, Two Shoes, or any name ending in Eagle or Bear smacked of totems and idolatry to the ears of Miz Winters, the schoolmistress and superintendent's wife, and she expressed her disapproval. Poor innocent Angela Dog Skin had been made to think her name was despicable. Every day "Old Lady Winters," as the kids secretly referred to her, openly winced when she had to say traditional names out loud.

Young Dennis, very observant, began to notice that his simple, pronounceable name earned him recognition, and so he stopped mentioning his grandpa Drumbeater, especially to Miz Winters, "the lady with the false smile." She wore rolled-up hose that always managed to stay just below the hem of her hand-sewn dresses, and she smelled of talcum and denture fixative. She was strict and cold and in charge. If you went into town for a movie, ate a piece of pie, or learned a prayer, it was under her aegis and approval. Mister Winters spent his days mainly with the dairy farm on campus, as they had a good one. Students spent half their academic days working the farm, the other half, dead tired, in what existed as classes. The school years were long and visits from loved ones rare.

Many years later, Dennis Banks would learn that this was one of the easier schools. The activities at others were unbearable and often unmentionable, though it would not always stay that way. Many had graveyards in the woods full of little gravestones, and some read "Unknown." Unknown (or unrecorded) names, birth dates, causes of death. Some students simply never returned home, and families were informed well after the fact, if at all.

Though their languages had disappeared for these Indian children, one reason the traditional names had not was that too much government paperwork and too many rules were tied to them. They might be John or Angela, Mary or Sam, but if they were also still Bear Runner, they were still Kit Fox ("Kit Fox" or "tokala" was Lakota that meant brave young man of good repute). Determined though the prevailing culture was to erase Indians, in this they had to acknowledge a small defeat.

Commodities were also tied to the government rolls, as well as land leases and tribal government budgets and head counts and teachers'—and the dean's—paychecks. So the names stayed, the wincing stayed, and something of what was left of these children's Indian heritage stayed. At roll call every sunrise, Dennis was transported back home by the sound of those splendid names. Roll call was one long word of Indian-speak. "Yeah, they hated that," Dennis later mused with an impish grin. "But I loved it!" It was a secret place he thought that only he could go, until he met young Anita Harjo and found others loved it, too.

He initially saw Anita's name the first time he was taken under the auditorium stage to carve out his own. Only a select few dared do this. It set you apart.

Then too hard to carve his full name with an instrument too awkward for his hand, Dennis managed a small *d* and a large *B*. A few others had had the guts to carve their last names, which was tantamount to self-incrimination. When caught, Dennis had admitted to it, and so he got the same whipping as the named carvers. Old Lady Winters stood over the boys and told them she'd teach them the price for destroying government property.

Dennis had learned early on how to stand up for himself. Indian school was the real school of hard knocks. No one was going to do it for you, not in this life. No one ever seemed to notice—not then, and not for the rest of his life—that Dennis was not a big fellow. The fight inside him was bigger than he was.

During the whipping Dennis drew the attention of a girl, but not just any girl. From somewhere near Anadarko, Oklahoma, Anita was a high school freshman when Dennis was just eleven. She was famous at the school and read to the younger kids once in a while and was a kind of mother to some of them, though Dennis did not view her that way. Because she had no family, she did not go home during the school year and had no visitors on visiting days. Neither did he.

Visitation took place under a big tree, not in a room. Cars pulled up to it twice a month on Sundays, and picnic lunches were unwrapped from newspaper or Sears and Roebuck catalog pages. These were fun to read or look at the funny pages, as it was the only contact from the outside world. School friends shared more than the funny pages with Dennis; occasionally they said their relatives were his as well, and he joined their families under the tree. Often, Dennis said, letters were not passed on from his mother. He'd spent years thinking she'd never written, and it was hard to reverse his feelings on this when he found out differently.

Dennis would spend visiting days with Anita and a few others when he could manage to get away from his dorm and over to theirs. He managed often. Anita was called an orphan by the Wahpeton teachers, and they thought of her as something of a black sheep. She had come from the farthest away and likely belonged at another school in another territory, but her adoptive parents were white Indians, mix bloods as they were called, from out of the plains. For some reason they had left her—car accident maybe, drunkenness, or death. No one knew why. She didn't. The school didn't say.

The Great Depression had something to do with it. Anita came out of the dust bowl, she said, and she imagined a big tunnel of dust spitting her out and rolling her to a stop at the foot of the Indian school door. She had no memory of parents. She was a dust baby. Whenever she saw dust on something, it reminded her that that was her people. Until Wahpeton.

As she grew older, she acquired a treasure trove of Indian history and was a regular outlaw at sharing it. She'd learned that dozens of tribes were crammed into Oklahoma. *Oka* meant red, in some Indians' language, and the rest of the word meant home. Why she would be so enthusiastic about this, none of them knew, but a strange world where she just might fit in began to draw her in. She became practically a savant, gathering any information she could about any and all tribes. For instance, her last name. Turned out, when making the government rolls, many southern plains Indians ended up with the name Harja or Harjo. Anita was told it was the word for *hard fighter*. It became a common name. Unless she was caught, which tended to be often, she "talked Indian" to the other students, and later to a few teachers to boot.

No number of switches could make her give it up. Anita had become her own version of a teacher, self-appointed in a school whose teachers hated what she was teaching. She was threading something, gathering a little bit here and there. Old Lady Winters liked her and called her Miss Contrary. Young Dennis thought it sounded like "Miss Cherries," and it suited. The Oklahoma girl became expert at hiding knowledge and knew just when to spill it.

Anita Harjo was a beauty, too, which meant she could get away with a lot. She used that currency as a sort of hypnotism, and it worked on Dennis Banks, who, though quite tough for one so young, could fall under Anita's spell.

She was brown-skinned, pink-cheeked, and had silky black hair that the teachers cut and cut, but it grew back fast. Once she started keeping it in a tight knot, they seemed to forget it was long. She always let it down when she was sharing stories, making the younger boys plain dizzy at the sight of its tumble.

Dennis would skip a meal to hear her speak, as their rest periods and lunch periods were at different hours. This didn't help the fact that he was already really skinny, and the skinny kids were put through an awful regimen of worming treatments. They were told that worms were eating them up inside and were made to swallow castor oil and worse remedies if they didn't gain weight.

The first time he saw poor tortured Angela Dog Skin up close, both were getting the treatment and under threat of also getting an enema if they didn't swallow the ghastly medicine. The minute Old Lady Winters forced it into her mouth, Angela would spit it out. Then Anita walked up and gently took the spoon from the hateful old woman, who gave it over with that false smile. Walking over to Angela, Anita whispered something to her, and the sad girl gulped the spoonful down fast and chased it with water from a cup in Anita's other waiting hand. Mercy was a beautiful thing, young Dennis thought, and so was rescue.

Dennis realized that a mother was the most beautiful thing on earth. They were the life-bringers and protectors, just as Anita always said. Most all Indian ceremonies re-created this for their people in some form or fashion. It all meant the same thing: honor life and the mother that brings it.

Once, catching Dennis missing his mealtime, Anita took half a sandwich from her pocket and handed it to him without missing a beat in her lesson on the Apache. All Dennis could focus on now was the touch of her hand and that she had singled him out. Maybe he'd go on a hunger strike at the ripe old age of eleven. He followed Anita to their favorite spot.

Young Dennis Banks loved the river and loved the woods, and it was under a clump of trees they sat, in Anita's "classroom." Wahpeton was on the Red River where it borders Minnesota and flows into Canada, way out on the edge of the plains. Another river, the Ottertail, was nearby and he thought he could hear the running water from their hiding place. The sereneness of the great mystery around him lulled him into a childhood nap, so much so he'd missed the slamming of the heavy metal school door and here came the "lady of the switches" as Miz Winters was steaming toward them, her face red as a beet, a stick in hand.

Moments alone with his own had been worth it, the small boy thought. Something was making choices for him, something forged out of this pain, born of his lost youth. It instilled in him that which couldn't be taken away. Anita had been talking of soldiers, right before the old witch showed up, and mentioned one had been kind to an Indian girl, whose name sounded like *Too-Mah-Quah*. Out of his dreamy haze, he spoke up to her now and said, "They were never kind, not to them!" She looked over at him with a grin as she tapped her finger on the end of his nose and said, "Them? Who do you think *them* are?" He was beginning to think Indians were separate, their doings related to someone else, no longer himself. Well, if Anita was proud to be one, he was, too. He was thinking that just as Old Lady Winter's switch hit him. He acted out of instinct and ran.

Dennis would leave Indian boarding school and go straight into the air force as planned. The year he did, Leonard Peltier arrived at Wahpeton. Leonard, too, would be dragged from his home and into a government vehicle. He arrived from Turtle Mountain along with his little sister, Betty Ann, and a cousin, Pauline. It was the first time he ever saw his grandmother lose a fight. She argued so loudly with the government driver in their yard that day that it brought young Leonard out from hiding in the woods to see to her rescue or to help in the fight.

Hours later the government driver offered his weeping little sister a sandwich while on the way to Wahpeton. When she went to refuse it, Leonard reached for it and stuffed it into his pocket. He figured they'd need it later, out in the woods when they'd all escaped this car. He watched out the back window for four hours trying to memorize the turns until he realized there was no finding his way back home when traveling this far. He was heartsick, but resolved they'd get away later, no matter how far they'd come.

At Wahpeton he was separated from Betty Ann and didn't see her again until some three days later, in the chow hall. She hadn't eaten one bite until she saw her big brother again, and seeing him, she ate so fast she was almost sick. Leonard was trying to slow her down when a matron came over. He thought the woman was there to help, but she had come to separate them again. Siblings were not allowed to be together. Betty Ann began to cry.

Later, Leonard Peltier would escape from Wahpeton and trek through a long wood, then try to run across an ice floe. Hours later, wet and cold, he just gave in and walked right up to the people out hunting for him. He was infamous for that daredevil attempt that ended in his having to decide whether to freeze to death or surrender. For hours, Leonard Peltier was almost the boy who got away.

Dennis Banks later recalled, when sharing his story of Wahpeton, that he could always hear some child screaming down a hall at nighttime, the sound haunted him for years. He thinks the child was him.

Wahpeton is an Indian word that means "the edge of the woods." Upon learning the definition, Dennis found it ironic that he had hated the school's name for many years. He wondered if the name itself had once, in some small way, reached out to him and sheltered him with another meaning. Something had made choices for him, something forged out of this hardship, born of his loss. It instilled in him that which could never be taken away.

He would run into Anita Harjo again, many years later, but she would be so altered by that time that he would not even recognize her.

CHAPTER 5

Herb Powless,
a Chain Gang in South Carolina
Summer 1956

Herb Powless worked in the heat, slept in it, and his body got adjusted to it. He was used to new circumstances and long waits, even though he was just twenty-one. Back when Herb, still underage, was heading for the marine recruiting station, his father had advised, "Son, situations you get in? If you find yourself in hell soon, don't even bother looking for a way out. Instead, just look for a water source."

The insects bothered him the most, but he'd gotten used to them, and to his captors' disrespect (he knew they saw him as something lower than any four-legged creature). Knee-deep in a Carolina swamp, he raised his wet hoe handle, his hard hands bloody with blisters, and spotted a familiar slithering motion not far away. A soft-bellied creature letting him know whose domain it really was. He wished it'd bite him, but somehow it must have known he'd bite it back.

He imagined he was a POW and not in his own country. It wasn't too far from the truth, even if he'd just survived Korea. An Indian boy who heard that his homeland was under attack would always grab a weapon and run to do battle. In all US wars, Indians had joined first. Herb had joined at age fifteen. *Never needed no draft letter*, he thought. He'd shipped out for Korea from a marine training base—now just visible beyond the prison fence—and told himself from day one that he'd get through it and one day soon feel the breeze off little Strawberry Island. He felt the same way about his current situation.

They could send him to one place after another, but he'd always recall home in his memory when he got there, never missing the last place he'd been. None of them counted. They weren't real to him. He watched Korean fishermen cover their lanterns with paper fans and throw out their nets in the morning fog and in his mind, he saw his own fishermen, Chippewa brothers from back home with night lanterns in their longboats on Lac Du Flambeau, *his* lake. He'd close his eyes and conjure the smell of the subtle fragrance of Oneida apples, state blossom of Wisconsin, as he saw the blue herons in chevron flight.

He missed his mother, though he knew she did not miss him; maybe his sisters did. *Can't think on that now*, he thought, or *I'll turn soft-bellied, too, but with no fangs to defend myself.* The squatty horseman guarding them looked to be holding his rifle more like a trophy than a weapon, and Herb wished the guy would turn on him. It'd be the last thing that man ever did in this life. For now, he gave himself a reminder that this was a system better lived through than fought. Herb preferred a good fight.

He daydreamed about meeting up with Mister Boss Man somewhere else. Carrying this chip on his shoulder helped him get through the swamp and the days that followed with hard work, hate, and his own brand of silence.

One day soon he would dare anyone who noticed that chip to try and knock it off.

He saw the yellow snake slither by again. Indians believed all that moved had a spirit and therefore deserved respect. He let it pass.

The water moved, the grass in the wind, the trees, and this damn snake. Respect was one thing, but mercy was another, meaning if it went to bite, it'd meet with the sharp end of Herb's hoe. It'd be the snake's fault for not showing this traveler a little mercy. *He'd spit me back out, I'm so full of poison*, Herb thought, without so much as a grin.

Only alcohol could push back down the kind of anger that filled Herb Powless. He never wondered why he didn't pass on a bottle; it was the only relief from his own fury he could get. He had only been stateside three days before he walked, drunk, right through a glass door and into an old white lady's dry cleaners. The last thing he saw before passing out was a big clock on the wall chiming ten o'clock. The next thing he remembered was the big clock on the station chief's wall as they booked him to go to court.

Herb stayed a little inebriated through the whole proceeding, and he damn sure didn't speak one word the whole time. The judge seemed to intentionally bang the gavel a little harder than usual, maybe checking to see if Lance Corporal Herb Powless was deaf. His loud clanging didn't cause Herb to so much as blink, so maybe he'd just have to wonder if he was a hearing man. He sure didn't care; Herb was certain of that.

The lawyer assigned to Herb leaned over in a waft of cologne and said the judge would automatically charge "midnight burglary." An invasion, even just one minute before midnight, got three months. At one minute after, you got three years on a prison gang. If you had a dark complexion, you automatically got midnight burglary, whatever the hour. "Likely," the lawyer whispered to Herb, "the judge don't know what you are." Herb knew this man didn't, either, unless maybe he'd seen the words "Oneida Reservation" in his military record.

They never know what we are, and don't want to, Herb thought. *If they did, they might have to put themselves on trial.* The whole damn town was named after invaders. Except the waterways outside, which mostly carried Indian names.

He got three years on a chain gang in South Carolina and was still in his marine uniform when they hooked up the belly chains. The hot sun reflected off his medal from the Battle of the Chosin Reservoir, bouncing light onto the courthouse clock as they walked him down the back steps. No point in upsetting any residents milling around out front. A marine uniform was common in this town, even if the looks of Herb Powless were not.

Herb endured the three years of what might have broken any other man and put it behind him as quickly as the wind pushed his old Chevy past the greatest of American lakes toward his old homestead. He placed South Carolina, and the time he'd been separated from home by the war, into the same bad deck and cast them out of his memory.

Herb's body was strong, but his mind was weary. Carrying an emotional tote of a lifetime of hardship and then adding on the horrors of war and pressing it all down inside, only to have it explode later—this was to define the men of Herb's generation. Herb, always of strong will and character, didn't need much excuse for that burden to rise up again, but for now he was sober and loving the fine sunrise and the prospect of being back home with his sisters in De Pere.

A few days later, some friends took him out to nearby Oneida, and he found himself leaning against a wall at a community hall dance—swarthy, disinterested, and ready to raise hell. He spotted Dorothy Ninham right away. She was small and quick and a pretty little thing, Herb noted. She was readying the tables for the Ho Yun festival—a holiday that was like Halloween by way of New Year's Eve—with her sisters. Indian kids went door to door, but not likely they saw candy, maybe a wrinkled apple wrapped in a newspaper, a treat to them.

Herb could tell the young Oneida girl in his gaze was the hardest worker there as she lugged an iron pot of chili to a folding table. It smelled good, and he suspected she had made it. She laughed easy, like a girl should, until she caught him looking at her. She'd noticed him back. He asked around and found out she was one of the Ninham girls. She already knew he was a Powless. Everyone there knew a Powless.

Instinctively she knew his stare, though sober, was hard. He didn't have his uniform on but wore a beret and had struck quite an impressive pose. She barely raised her eyes before looking quickly away. Then she surprised a young boy who was trying to spike a few cups of Kool-Aid by flinging a handful of ice water in his face. *Yeh, she's an Indian girl all the way*, Herb thought. The boy scurried off, just wet enough to douse his collar and his pride.

When she came back to the table with a tray of corn bread, she looked around for Herb. He caught her glance and laughed, making her face go pink. Herb figured that meant she was innocent and modest as well, and a little mad. Yeh, Indian girl all the way. Though not a big man, Herb was all man, and Dorothy had enough instinct to spot that. For all her hard work and obvious lack of fuss about her appearance, she couldn't hide her beauty, and Herb had never seen better.

Dorothy Ninham did not dwell long on the handsome Powless, as she and her girlfriend turned up their Dr Peppers and took a swig. After all, she was leaving the next day for Milwaukee and would likely not see him again, or so she thought. A friend from school had secured them both jobs at a fancy big hotel making beds, for fifty cents a bed.

In Milwaukee, she wasn't more than an hour into turning the heavy sheets over when she went to straighten her ponytail in the reflection of the large plate glass window overlooking the pristine white lawn down below. Standing dead center in it was a familiar shape. *My goodness*, she thought. It was Herb Powless staring up at the building. Her cheeks turned hot. *How dare he follow her!* She ran straight down the six flights of stairs to confront him.

The confrontation lasted only minutes, as she was a dependable worker and got right back to her post, but not before agreeing to meet him later. On that very first night, he'd finally found someone he could talk to. Dorothy was destined to be his. There was a lot he hid from her, but eventually she knew more about him than he shared with anybody else alive. Having one person to burden with that much trust was enough.

Herb and Dorothy would soon find themselves living permanently in Milwaukee, facing a rough and gritty urban life, while Indian culture was in danger close to home, with Wisconsin's Menominee Indians under a state of termination.

Herb Powless had already seen enough and had enough. All while feeling the love from under the branches of Wisconsin apple trees and the breeze off little Strawberry Island.

CHAPTER 6

Okaerinasai!
US Air Force Base in Occupied Japan
Spring 1958

Most days the high winds across the airstrip made Old Glory stand straight out from its flagpole. But today the still air hangs heavy, and the deafening buzz of cicadas cuts through the smog drifting across the bombed-out Japanese island.

Airman Dennis Banks leans his back against the Quonset hut where he sits in a squat almost every day. The hut serves as shelter and provides the only shade. He stubs out another Camel cigarette on a concrete block and counts the small white dots on the filter, refusing to let the boredom take him. But still, it takes him.

Dennis can't be mistaken for any other airman on base. His high cheekbones and the almond-shaped eyes of his Anishinaabe ancestors just get him accused of being part Japanese. Or of the *Nihon* people, which means *people of the sun's origin*. His new young wife is all of that—Japanese, that is—but he is an American Indian from Leech Lake, Minnesota, whatever called.

He is quite handsome but rarely smiles unless off base or at home leaning over his new baby girl. He feels undistinguished in either of his new roles, but as is usual with the US government, the choices are all theirs.

Two years earlier, to his shock and dismay, and later maybe relief, his whole platoon got lined up one day without explanation. His hateful, mean-tempered sergeant walked down the line tapping each man's shoulder, or on occasion just pointing with his thumb and forefinger in the shape of a gun, saying, "Japan, Texas, Japan, Texas, Japan, Texas . . ."

Later that day, a colonel who Banks was seeing for the first time showed up and hollered, "Men, we have received orders that you will report en masse to Foster Airfield for advanced training, and then you will jump off to the Republic of Japan! Get your affairs in order and wait for your new orders!"

Like in a child's game, and over in just minutes, it would land Dennis on a weather-hot island tarmac for eight months out of the year. Other men in his company stayed stateside, but at this time in his life, Dennis was very patriotic, and it was a relief to remain on active duty.

Dennis had spent more than half his life so far in an institution, three different Indian boarding schools, and now the military was just a continuation. Both had prepared him for boredom, as well as for words such as chow hall, commissary, visiting room, and disciplinary action. Boredom was a good motivator to teach escape, letting him delve daily into his own keen mind. He was very curious about the Japanese people and observed them closely. Too close for the air force.

Relentlessly daydreaming, Dennis sits against the hut and peers out into a rice paddy. He imagines the grand house that he plans to build back home in Minnesota, near his lake, for himself and Machiko and their new baby daughter. All around him are the sounds of farmers and families and the bustle of country life, and it makes him lonesome for his own village at Leech Lake.

He's been designing his house in his mind since he was eleven, facing the endless boredom of farmwork at Wahpeton boarding school. He shakes off that memory, never wanting to go back there, not even in his thoughts.

Military service came soon after school ended. He had been determined to be a general, running the whole Second Air Force, and couldn't wait to get to the recruiting office after his mother finally agreed to give her permission. He was only seventeen and one hundred percent devoted. But now, the only allegiance he feels strongly about is to his wife and child. He wants out.

He'd learned at Wahpeton that a human can wait out anything. And now he's found himself waiting again. He is not a draftee but a volunteer. Come to that, almost every Indian he ever met in service had done the same. Happy to volunteer, maybe due to the harsh poverty back home or glad to finally feel useful at something they were good at. They were good at fighting. Or good at volunteering. Communal-minded.

Second Lieutenant Walter White Bear suddenly plops down beside him and tells him he may get his wish for a break in the monotony. White Bear is from Pine Ridge, South Dakota, and despite his young age is already a decorated Korean War vet and in the air force for life. He's enjoying peacetime for now in Japan. White Bear looks as *skin* as Dennis does, as they refer to themselves, so they hang together when possible. Fraternizing between ranks is frowned upon, but out in this field, nobody notices. White Bear offers his usual salutation, "How's it going, Horse Thief?" No one else on base better say it, but between them it's an intimacy.

"Rumor is," White Bear says, "a civilian mob is organizing in town and coming soon to object to the runway our US Air Force is forcing on the locals." The runway would disrupt an important set of rice paddies and homes, possibly even burial grounds that are nearby.

"Civilians?" Dennis asks. "Whole goddamn country is a burial ground. What is a Japanese civilian? They hate us, but aren't likely to raise a fist, not after the ass whippin' they just got."

"Hah, hah. Wait till you see them come at ya! You know what a *civvie* is? A man with nothing left to lose, that's what. And you don't want to mess with him."

"What in hell are we doing here, anyway?" Dennis asks with an uncertain laugh.

"Think stateside is better, brother? You'll know soon, wontcha, and wish you were back here!"

"No I won't. If they don't let my wife go home with me, I'm not going anywhere but A-W-O-L. Legally we don't have to fight any wars unless they're fought on our soil. That's Minnesota for me, pal. Korea is not my soil, this island isn't, and last I looked we sure don't own Vietnam, but too soon to worry about that," he said, hopefully. "They don't hate all of us. My wife's dad called out *Okaerinasai!* when he met me."

"You went into a Jap's home. Shit for brains."

Dennis is used to Walter's humor.

"He bowed. It was different that I was an Indian from America. Machiko told me later that her father said words used to say I was of equal value. When does that happen in my own country? I'll tell you who's shit for brains."

"What brainwash shit are you talkin', Airman Banks? Who cares who they hate? Don't make me knock you down to do some pushups. That's how I met you, remember. You are sworn to protect one thing, the U.S. of A."

Dennis is half listening to Walter as he recalls the moment of meeting his wife's father. The instant respect was euphoric, and all in his eyes! He'd wanted to be a pilot, he told his new father-in-law, but mostly gets assigned to cleanups. He didn't share that. The locals made holes behind their homes, commodes, installed so they could ultimately carry them off and use the contents to fertilize the farmland. It's great fertilizer. These people wasted nothing, not even their waste. Smart people. On that note, Dennis knows he himself is wasting away here.

"Today we get a fight; that's good," Dennis says. "Makes me feel useful, because today, you're gonna have a worthy opponent."

"Better bring out that little bit of karate you learned in training, my friend, and you're about to see what a little bit actually is. Better yet, hang close to me today." Walter pours everything he has into being the best, and he has succeeded. He is better than his superiors at all their games—chess, drinking, cards, girls, even their war games when it comes to that. He'd been invited along when a Japanese admiral led their first servicemen into the Korean Islands. Why take a Japanese admiral into Korean waters? Only one who knew the way and could get them in.

Walter hops to his feet, lightly for a man of his weight, and saunters off.

Dennis kept pushing the base's bureaucrats about his wife. After all, he had a perfect record. Institutional life came naturally, and he hadn't had to make many adjustments to excel at military life. So why couldn't the brass extend a little courtesy, and one so desperately requested?

The brass didn't budge. So when it came to love, to the little bit of family Dennis Banks had, rebellion came just as naturally to him as conformity.

He had studied with work in Intelligence and it led to higher opportunities and got him permanently out of latrine duty. Things were looking up for his service record, until . . . love.

Dennis took to Shinto and was drawn into the language. He was pulled towards the mystery of their primeval woods and mountain monasteries where monks lived back on high cliffs. His wife would translate the stories of a great people for him, and he found that he never wanted to fight them again. Hell, why would he want to shoot at someone who looked like his own grandfather? Dennis had learned in even earlier training from his grandpa, Drumbeater: "Creator made four races of man, not one, and we all come from ancient civilizations and the truth of who we are has traveled on our blood."

Airman Banks started to concoct the idea to go AWOL if they tried to keep his wife from him. It was his only option, but he would need a plan for how to hide out in a country that was not his. He knew he could adapt, hadn't Indians always had to do that? They were pushing him to it.

"I learned early on in life," Dennis said to his father-in-law, "that there are rules and laws, but the universal law was that you can get away with anything you were man enough to get away with." The number one rule, on and off base, was no personal association with Japanese people. Well, they found out fast how well that didn't work. All any airmen on base did was wait around all day until they "worked" or "played" with them.

Then he met sweet, beautiful Machiko. "*Watashi wah anata-o-aishitei-ma-su!*" she called out. She was proud of him, a reflection of the way that Japanese people commonly cared about indigenous people. She was smiling when she said it, and he knew he'd remember that smile for the rest of his life, even if he never saw this young girl again. He learned later the words were a declaration of love at first sight. Loved for who he was, no longer in spite of it. The feeling was mutual.

Suddenly he was surrounded by people who were eager to meet him. It was intoxicating because it was not only genuine acceptance, but all so instantaneous. He felt pride well up. Without a word to them, they already knew what he was, and they liked it, too. And it definitely wasn't the uniform.

Dennis only relaxed socially when around GIs like himself. He met two from California, both of Chinese ethnicity, and a few Native brothers, and there was Daniel Ivory, a Black man saddled with that name. Dennis watched their handlers make a field day out of it any chance they got. And there was White Bear, but his attitude was different. Though constantly surrounded by whites, he didn't meet them with the usual downcast eyes that characterized most back home. He didn't seem to be ashamed of anything and actually walked through the world as if he were white and was daring anyone to challenge it. This rarely happened, but those who did quickly wished they hadn't.

Then in a single day Dennis was suddenly not just equal but was apparently perceived as exceptional. He was way too inexperienced to put it together that after losing a war, he was facing people occupied by the same mentality that occupied him. Ancient ways and beliefs scoffed at. The color of one's skin scoffed at, one's eyes, hair, mind, language. And yet they were equally exceptional. Talk about *waste*.

Dennis Banks had learned the hard way, as he always did, that if you followed the prevailing culture's plan for your life, you thrived, or you could follow your own and suffer. He made his own plan, to make a place to hide out, and simply to get home somehow, get a good job, and be a civilian. Build that dream home in Minnesota and raise his family.

The Japanese civilian protestors begin gathering before sunup. Contrary to Walter White Bear's warning, most are unarmed, though some of the farmers carry bats and sticks. Unless their drums counted, and they should count, Dennis thinks. He's never heard such a penetratingly deep and terrifying sound, both beautiful and intimidating. The drummers lead the protestors. There are many Buddhist monks and nuns in odd garb, looking somehow ominous and not at all Western. Others have closely shaved heads and white face paint. Their singing is a high-pitched monotone that causes a wave of sound—not singing, more like movement.

There are so many of them, a few thousand or more by the time they are done gathering. Dennis had taken to their language quickly and can read some of the signs. Walter pulls out his handbook of five easy lessons in Japanese and is struggling to interpret. Then the Japanese police arrive in their new American-manufactured jeeps. Clearly, the airmen and American guard patrols are on-site to support them.

Then the Japanese police unleash their dogs on the monks and nuns. Faces and necks are savaged, and police batons rain down on the monks' heads. Dennis has a weapon, of course, and Walter looks poised to begin an all-out one-man military assault. Unfortunately for him, he is about to rain it down on his own unit, on those that are pointing to the civilians. If one knew Walter, this action was unthinkable. Everyone freezes that can see his stance, which saves Walter White Bear and the assailants, and just confuses the officer in charge. That newly minted second lieutenant was Walter White Bear! One monk looks up at him with pity on his blood-stained face and then he begins to disperse; the rest follow.

The protestors take a while to break up as there are so many of them. But their point has been made, and the nonviolent religious sect seems to lose interest in pursuing it further. They have curled up and taken their blows, never striking back, not one of them. The farmers have been as tough as any fighter Dennis ever witnessed . . . except for maybe their feral dogs. The occupiers have made their point, too, and likely the airstrip will still go in. Definitely it will.

Dennis is deeply affected by this day and will never forget it. These religious indigenous, with their drums and songs and language, have a right to protect their homeland, the farms that feed their families. No war is bigger than that idea, no intruder. Their drums had not stopped, so they had not stopped.

Dennis discovers a personal patriotism that day that has been inside him all along, and with time it will only grow stronger. As Grandpa said, the truth of it has traveled on his blood.

Before heading home to Minnesota, the unthinkable happened—his commander threatened to send him stateside without his family—and so he'd next be doing his daydreaming from inside a stockade for desertion. The more Dennis experienced, reflecting on both home and abroad, the more he began to understand that freedom, real freedom, was uniquely an American *Indian* idea. The words *Okaerinasai!* would reverberate in his head whenever he had anything heavy to face. White Bear was struck that day by an unexpected change, one of the heart. He'd strived hard in uniform to bring about a change to his life, to be superior in every way. *Show the bastards!* He was unaware that the change coming to him would come from within. Only Walter knew it was the nonviolence that struck him through. He knew well these men were great masters, skilled at hand-to-hand combat, out of monasteries or not, they could really fight and yet, they came out this day *not to fight.* Here they stood with barely any shoes on and wouldn't have gone up against a military force except for the fact they were desperate and forced to. The fight they brought was defense. The word karate itself meant *empty* hand and the idea was to protect without permanently harming. This was a fight that would change Walter White Bear forever. A real warrior protects, and not always in the way thought. Dennis found out the Japanese expression his father in-law first said to him, simply meant "welcome home." As for Dennis, what was to come next would happen closer to his own backyard. A Movement was coming across Indian land. And when it did, he would be at civilian level. He and Walter White Bear would see each other again years down the road, outside another small village fighting to protect its land and sacred burial place, an outpost marked on a South Dakota map as Wounded Knee.

CHAPTER 7

Leonard Peltier,
Turtle Mountain Reservation,
North Dakota
Winter 1961

Leonard Peltier peered into the cracked mirror of the dirty Gulf station bathroom and struggled to force his shiny black curls into a ducktail. His hair was so jet black it cast a navy-blue sheen from under the yellow light of the dirty bulb. And for all the VO5 gel, his curls kept popping back. He traded his oil-stained parka for his prized but well-worn black leather motorcycle jacket. During the workday, he hid it with his other valuables in a rusty drum in the shop. Pulling it on, he headed out to hop onto the tailgate of the last departing truck.

If he'd missed it, he'd have to walk across the frozen Turtle Mountain rez at night, and though he had a pass to go into town to work, it did not extend past dusk. All Indians better be carrying that pass if stopped, and they would be stopped, if only for just being Indian. The Turtle Mountain Agency where Leonard was born is a desolate and windswept outpost on the North Dakota plains less than thirty miles from Manitoba, Canada.

Leonard huddled in a tight squat to make room for others getting into the truck. Once they were deep into the rez, there was some talk about taking a six-pack to the gravel pit, a common place to drink, smoke, and meet girls. A gravel pit girl could stick on you and make life even more complicated. For his part, Leonard had a better idea, and when the old jalopy of a truck came to a stop, he leaped over the side to the ground and headed toward Jermain's cabin. She was reputed to be the prettiest girl on the rez, due in part to her green eyes. She was a gentle spirit, sweet natured, quiet, and vulnerable. Unlike the other girls, she didn't try to act tough.

Though just seventeen, Leonard had the stride of a full-grown man, and hard living went into every step. Always alert for danger, eyes vigilant, he was nevertheless high-spirited and hopeful. Finally of an age when he could work with the men, there'd be no more chasing after scraps. He was a hard worker, and he was unafraid. Both were gifts.

He felt no bitterness about anything and often summed it up this way: what had happened to him had happened to all Indian people; what they were made to face, he'd face, too, without complaint. *Where did complaining get ya?* was his thinking. He zipped his prized jacket up. The still-wet ducktail already had little icicles forming on it. Jermain would probably laugh when she saw it, though that was not the kind of humor young Peltier appreciated.

Leonard had a great sense of humor, but never much took to anyone laughing at him. Jermain was the first girl he ever seriously noticed. She had hair as black as a raven's wing, and those hazel green eyes, framed by lashes so dark it looked like they'd been drawn on to mimic those society women on the magazine covers in the shop. But Jermain's came naturally. Her hair may have been as black as Leonard's, but not her coloring. He could never hide who he was, but her soft brown skin revealed pink cheeks.

For all her beauty, Jermain was a sad girl, in part because her momma had taken to the bottle. She and Leonard had that in common, though he never mentioned it or took anybody home to see it. Jermain, however, clung tightly to her shame like the ratty shawl around her shoulders. Leonard liked the challenge of making her smile, and he'd spend this evening at her place facing that challenge. The gravel pit would have to wait.

Leonard notes from far off that Jermain's modest little cabin has no smoke lifting from its chimney. Likely that means her mother is bundled up inside and there's no wood stacked next to her. He can see Jermain pacing outside; she must have spotted him coming. She laughs without making a sound as she plucks an icicle off his ducktail first thing.

"What? I use those to make ice cream." he says.

"It's too cold for ice cream."

"Ahh, it's never too cold for that. Rich people eat it all year. Christmas, they chop up candy canes in it, seriously. Saw it in a magazine. Got any sugar? I'll show you."

"Oh, sure. I keep it right next to the petrol," she laughs, then adds, "We can't go inside."

Leonard jumps into action gathering twigs. While he pulls some larger limbs together, she turns over an old rusted-out metal drum and rolls it toward him. There are only two precious matches left in his matchbook and he strikes both at the same time, coaxing cardboard into a small flame and quickly adding dried sticks, then wood, until they have a warm fire. He'd grab a branch to light a fire inside the cabin before too long. Always mindful of womenfolk and elders.

Jermain's old dog, a large hound named Digger, comes close for the warmth. Eyeing a nearby piece of cardboard, probably once used to block a broken window, Leonard finds some rope, pulls out a small knife, and fashions a makeshift sled. Laughing, he fastens the rope around Digger's neck.

"No! You'll choke him!" Jermain yells.

"No, I won't, it's not on tight enough. Come on!"

"Heck no, I'm not getting on that thing!"

"Why? It won't go fast. Why have a big ole dog if ya never do anything with him? He don't hunt!"

"He can't help it, Leonard. Loud guns spook him."

"Coward. Come on. The hill will do all the work!"

He coaxes the dog to the top of a small snowy hill, sits alone on the cardboard, and slaps the reins. Digger tears straight down the hill at a gallop and shoots between two small trees, swiping Peltier into the snow and loping away.

Jermain is laughing hard as Leonard drags the slobbering hound back up the hill and sits on the cardboard sled once again. The performance repeats itself. This time, Leonard rolls several times before stopping, laughing at himself now.

When Jermain runs to his rescue, he grabs her, shawl and all, and tussles with her in the soft new snow before just hugging her to him, gently but firmly. It's the first feeling of love he has ever known.

"Ya gonna chase Digger again, wise guy?"

"Nope. My daddy says, chase a coward but never catch him. Digger's long gone anyway, and he mighta got choked just a little. Run, dog, before an old man eats ya!" They laugh together and snuggle close again.

Later, when the fire glows white-hot through rust holes in the drum, Leonard reaches into his pocket and draws out a prize he's been hiding there all day, a piece of Wrigley's spearmint chewing gum. He holds it up to the firelight for her to see, then hands it to her. Unwrapping it as if it were a fine treasure, she folds the tinfoil liner and slides it into her skirt pocket, then tears the gum in half and presents him with his share. He leans down and takes it between his front teeth, then folds it into his mouth. Jermain smiles as they chew.

"A customer gave it to me when I ran out into the snow to pump up her tires. She didn't have to; she was the fifth car that morning that I filled. It's just air; gauge is tricky to work though, don't work half the time so you better be a good guesser. Too low or too high you can ruin your tires. Gotta change your oil regular, too. It's twenty-nine cents a quart now! They say in California gas might top a dollar. Who can believe that? Twenty-five cents here and a dollar there. Oil is oil. Thieves. Mainly robbing workingmen, they the main ones depend on it."

Jermain looks solemnly at Leonard. It's not right to meddle, but she wants to know something badly enough to speak plainly. "Why ya care what costs are in California, Leonard? I heard about the rumor that your grandmother might be headed back to Seattle."

"You know that lawyer robbed her over in Grand Forks—robbed Tommy really, my cousin. Hell, ya rob one of us you rob us all. Thieving bastard! Tommy was coming into the first money any of us ever known, and the damn lawyer spent it, every dime. It was Tommy's dad put that lawyer in charge. Ya know Tommy's dad was white? I knew the minute that lawyer asked me to leave his office and wait in the car it was rigged. He just wanted to talk to

Grandma and Tommy alone. He officed near the Indian agency downtown, just to rope in poor Indians. Said he'd make it up to Tommy and my grandma and then handed him five hundred dollars to pay for taking thousands from a land lease left for Tommy. I'd a thrown it back in his face!"

"You would have! Five hundred dollars is a fortune!"

"Yeah, well, wrote his name down, Hawthorn. I won't forget it, either, he told Tommy he knew all the lawyers in town and the judge, and they couldn't do nothing about it, but he'd pay it back a month at a time, best he could. Guess any money is better than no money, I reckon. I'd of handled it different.

"I had to pull potatoes for months after that, and I saved enough for a bus, but if my Uncle Billy is going back, I can drive him. I have to, honey, don't ya see? Make some money any way I can. Potatoes don't pay more than a dollar a day, and them Norways over there hate us and work us hard and cheap. Dirt goes up your nose and mouth, down your throat. You cannot wash it off.

"Boarding school didn't train us in anything that paid. Might as well have just thrown all the books out and handed us a hoe and a bag. I can get a city job. I'm a trained mechanic now, and I can drive anything with wheels . . ." His voice trails off.

Jermain knows her worst nightmare has just been spoken out loud. She's getting robbed, too—of him. It's real.

People leaving the rez is the most common talk in these troubled times. It was happening almost every day, it seemed. It was not in their way to be so talkative and less in their way to leave home. But leave they must, those that could, if they wanted to live. New policies to relocate Indians to the city were promising a lot.

"If you're gonna go, ya just go, not talk about it all the time," Leonard goes on. "Nobody needs all this notice, then it becomes just talk. Instead you just ought to hop in a car and that's it! If ya don't wanna say goodbye or too many is asking to go, my Uncle Billy says, 'Just go out for the milk.'"

"Go for what?"

"Milk. You're going out for the milk and then you hop in the car and stay gone. They figure it out when ya don't come back."

At the thought that she cares when he'd come and go, his heart quickens, and his cheeks feel a warm glow that's not from the fire. He dares to put his arm around her shoulders and pull her closer, saying, "I'll always come back,

Jermain, I give you my word I will." Leonard was never one to break his word, and this was a solemn oath coming from a pure heart.

"Seattle, Leonard? That has an ocean, why would anybody come back? It's so cold here."

"I don't mind the cold. It's home. Jermain, listen to me now . . . *it's home.* Ya never have another. After Wahpeton, I ain't ever leaving home again. If I go to Seattle I'm coming back. Hell, send an Indian to the moon!"

"What?"

"They are always trying to decide who to send to the stupid moon. Do we send a chimp or a man or a Russian? Hell, send an Indian. Ya know why? He'll always find a way to get back home."

She laughs, then turns sad eyes toward the cabin then to the rising moon. "She's not stupid, Leonard, she's beautiful, ya know?"

Leonard pulls her chin toward him and kisses her softly—two innocents.

"Go with me!" he blurts. "We'll jump in that warm ocean together! I'll build us a cabin near it with indoor heat! Hah, what Indian ya ever saw had that? Only heat inside any building here is at the BIA jail. So, okay, I will stay cold and happy then. I already felt jail at the boarding school, not doing that again ever. Waiting all month for a family just to have a visit under a tree, and mine couldn't afford to come more than once."

"Why didn't you run out of there? Wahpeton is not that far."

"Hell, it is four hours by car! I paid attention to that when they took me, and I was just nine. I knew I'd have to plan my escape if I was gonna get me and my sister out, and my cousin Pauline, couldn't leave without them. More people, ya gotta plan it. And getting out's one thing, staying out is another. You gonna be hunted by people that know how to hunt." He pauses a moment, remembering.

"They captured me in three days; hell, I think I was walking toward them so's they'd notice, I was that hungry and lost and cold. It was harder to be back the second time. Don't really like remembering it. That's behind me. Nobody's locking me up anywhere ever again."

They sit quietly for a bit and he kisses her again, this time deeply. He hugs her closer as she whispers, "I knew when your Uncle Billy bought that new car . . . They said then your cousin got the five hundred dollars from that lawyer over in Grand Forks."

"New? A '53 Chevy, only a hundred thousand miles on her, so yeah, for us she's new. Going over Wolf Pass, we'll see how new her brakes are. Coming over from Portland I couldn't wait to see Donner Pass, 'cause Uncle Billy scares hell out of us telling us about these people that ate themselves. Their Indian scouts left some family members with them, too, and when they get back they say they were just gone, had wandered off. Bullshit, they ate them for sure, first! Well, I say I don't believe it, but we don't ever get to this Donner Pass, 'cause it is near Nevada, not nowhere near where we are. But I speed up, ya see, playing a joke, and wake up Uncle Billy and Grandma says—don't stop, not for nothin' or nobody, they might eat us!" They laugh out loud the way the young do. "I said it ain't nothin' there, I got ya! But we will go over it if we head back by way of California."

"California," she says, wistfully.

"Not me. I'd go straight over to Oregon, no matter what snow or mountains was in the way. Uncle Billy has some family to see, that's all. Hadn't met up with them in a long while."

"You get to see all those places. Say, remember that hall meeting I first met you at?"

"The government one? Sure, I remember."

"We were all scared to death then, too, and you said you were just there for the fry bread. I thought you were brave; you weren't nervous at all."

"My grandpa Bunches was mad, and he kept calling out one word: fight! Interruptin' the government man. My other grandpa Alex was there, too, he's more of a peacemaker, like Pop."

"Grandpa Bunches? Where'd he get that name?"

"He's French, that's where. Fight!" He hugs the girl close.

"Even Momma sobered up for that meeting. I'll never forget that word long as I live—*terminate*. Well, it didn't happen, but it still could."

"No, it can't. We fought it and won, and if it comes up again, we will win again. Nobody wants it, and when you really don't want it, you will not sell out. Seriously, let's head out to Washington together. They got other Indians out there, we'll make out. What others can do, we can do."

Jermain's head droops, "Who will take care of my mother?"

"Who's taking care of her now? Hell, people take care of people, always have."

"No, they don't, not anymore, Leonard, too many to look after and the old ones just die."

"Your momma's not old. Okay, okay. I'll come back then, for the both of ya." He says this without adding his oath. He knows as she does that the odds are greatly against returning once gone; all your energy is needed for staying. He wouldn't want to intentionally get caught up in breaking a promise; that would make it a lie.

His grandmother had a special reason for coming home and sold everything she had, planning to stay once here. Tommy promised her a house from money he'd never get, now she was on a cot staying with relatives. Uncle Billy would return, and this is Leonard's only chance to get back. He'd likely not be coming home to Turtle Mountain for quite a while. He kisses her again, and likely for the last time. She knows it, too. Her sadness can be felt in their kiss.

Leonard would soon leave for Seattle and not be able to come back to Turtle Mountain again, though he'd spend many years trying. He would hear, years later, that Jermain married a white man and left the reservation.

CHAPTER 8

The Wagon Burner

An old American scripture centered on the words "self-reliance," and President Richard Nixon loved those words. A plan began to circulate in Washington to quiet it all back down, "it" being the new Indian problem. "Let's get these people off the dole and standing on their own! The plan worked wonders for all the other immigrants, didn't it?" "Immigrant" meant anyone other than themselves. Vietnamese boat people were immigrants, but not the descendants of colonists, or the Irish or Italians, Russians or Germans or Poles. Washington especially hated and wanted to be rid of that one little unreviewable word, *treaty*. If it were reviewed it might remind people that they weren't dealing with an immigrant problem, or an ethnic one, either. Civil rights marchers wanted a fair seat at the table, in a classroom, in representation in Washington. Herb Powless wanted a survival school, and the Menominee woods given back to the Menominee in Wisconsin. And he was self-determined, all right, but not the way they planned. He and Dorothy had grown up on the Oneida Reservation, and under great hardship; still, they had neither been sent to an Indian government school or suffered Indian relocation. It instilled in them a certain amount of defiance when they began to gather with the "relocated Indians" that had suffered that fate. Dorothy and Herb were independent-minded.

Once the Indians were out on that long, unforgiving road heading away from their reservation in a rickety old automobile, there was no going back. They'd be stuck somewhere else when the dust settled, surrounded by strangers.

Well, Washington thought, *hadn't it worked out beautifully for their own ancestors when they came to Indian land?* Just reverse the reservation system, and once they were in a city, the Indians could make do according to their individual worth. The American way! Their family was depending on it. The communal life was a few hundred miles behind them now, which was the idea. Government men hated the word communal, which conjured up *reds*.

When Indians like Herb Powless and Dennis Banks first got back from Asia, they thought the government scheme was a pretty good offer, and they planned to do pretty well. They'd soon realize that they were listening to the same damn promises that had lured them into active service. They promised the Indians housing that turned out to be pretty awful, if it existed at all, and jobs that nobody wanted, if they existed at all. Some did end up living the American dream this way, but for them and many like them, Indian relocation became the American nightmare. A new term was coined: red ghetto.

Dennis was ambitious, and after the air force he eventually landed an accounting job at Honeywell, where his ride was better than for most; but for someone with a dark complexion, the ever-present low ceiling existed. He just couldn't adjust to that, and like Herb Powless, by 1970 he had seen enough and had enough. Herb went union, first Iron, then Auto Workers. He got a new car, and with Dorothy beside him, he didn't complain. They started a family.

Dennis had made good on his threat to go AWOL if the air force held firm to the policy that wouldn't let his Japanese wife and daughter into the States. He was captured and given a stint in the stockade, then forced to return stateside alone. He'd have to wait too long to return to Japan, and when he did, it was too late. His daughter would one day have to find him. The worst thing that could happen to this man had happened—he'd lost his family for a second time.

His desertion was now on his permanent record, and troubles were accumulating. Forced to leave his wife and baby stranded in another country, his corporate job a failure, he began to know desperation. He managed to put this shame and sorrow to good use.

One night in the late sixties, when walking home in his red ghetto of Minneapolis, Dennis sees an Indian man being dragged from his car and beaten by a cop, while the cop's partner just watches. Dennis ducks behind a building and yells, "I see everything you're doing, Officer, and I'm calling for help!"

The one cop pauses, looks around, and then both draw their guns. But after looking again, they just leave. Dennis helps the Indian, who says he'd done nothing other than just get pulled over, so Banks gets him back into his car and rides home with him. That night they start a neighborhood alliance with others. Anytime an Indian man is seen walking alone or is pulled over, a dozen Indian men would follow and watch.

A white friend of Dennis comes along, too. Pretending to be a reporter, he snaps pictures. Some will become evidence later, but they also persuade those doing the pulling over to head on down the road. Dennis would remind the cops that they can't arrest them all, they'd need dozens of cars and explanations for that. Good words that work—not always, but often. There is strength in numbers, in just being present and being in the right. *For now, anyway*, thinks a young Dennis Banks.

Now he's onto a new path; if he can't help himself, maybe he can put his energy into helping his people. This is a profound insight. As the sixties wane, he joins like-minded Indian men and women in the streets of Minneapolis and St. Paul as a new urban Indian movement is born.

After patrolling with other Ojibwe Indians, Dennis and the group go through a few names, "Concerned Indians of America" and the like, Red Power movement all the way, as the 1970s roll him and another Ojibwe, Clyde Bellecourt, into the first chapter of the American Indian Movement. Clyde, like Dennis, is handsome, direct, and self-determined, made from the fabric of good leadership. Another asset is his size. Some that started out with them head into other directions and strengthen their academic backgrounds or spiritual and traditional roots. Dennis dons a red beret and stays to the street. After a year of guarding Indian people, he is looking more like a young Indian police officer himself, with his leather beret and nightstick. He and Clyde decide that they need to broaden their scope. A bundle of arrows wrapped together cannot be so easily broken as a few. Working security for the streets of Minneapolis taught them this.

Dennis and his new friends collect a caravan of old Indian cars with loud mufflers and start attending speaking engagements at universities. AIM would just show up and join in—sometimes invited and sometimes not. Dennis's shameless good looks and charisma make him a standout, and he soon discovers that he feels at home on a microphone—and the press is listening. He goes from being hopeless to standing ten feet tall, in the Movement.

On their way to a college event in downtown Milwaukee, the AIMers in their caravan notice an Indian bar, the Thunderbird Tap Pool Hall, and they decide to stop in. They are using every opportunity to recruit.

Herb Powless is sitting inside having his usual Schlitz beer after his hard day at the union hall. It is then that he notices a wiry Indian and his beautiful Indian girlfriend sitting at the bar. Something tells him they aren't locals. Always a man to mind his own business, even around other Native people, he puts his eyes back down on his sweating glass of beer.

A burly Indian who looks seven feet tall to Herb bends over a pool table and is inebriated enough to be causing a stir. With two Indian gals hanging on his arms, he's trying to make a good shot. Then pop, he shoots the ball right off the table. *Can't hold his brew,* Herb thinks, knowing he's not one to judge that.

The phone beside the bar rings and rings, and finally, the good-looking Indian gal sitting at the bar answers and says, "Yes, yes. No, stay right there if you're shorthanded, we will send someone to you!" The man with her—Herb will soon learn he is a Lakota named Floyd Red Crow Westerman—makes an odd whistle to the large guy at the pool table, and several other Indians at the bar come to his side. Two of them head to the alley. Herb, curious, looks up and asks the wiry Indian what the phone call was all about, and Floyd answers, smiling, "Oh that? Some distributor asked if we wanted their case of liquor delivered or did we want to come get it? My gal said we'd come get it, and we sure are!" Dennis walks over and introduces himself to Herb.

"Go with us, we're going over to an 'Indian education' meeting at your local college."

"I already got an Indian education, but I might see ya over there." Dennis is hard to turn down, even for Herb Powless.

"What makes you think those kids will listen to ya?" Herb asks.

"You're listening to me."

At that moment the big guy from the pool table walks over and is introduced to Herb as Clyde Bellecourt. "He's our main speaker," Dennis comments. *If he can still stand by then*, Herb is thinking.

An hour later they are in the new setting. Herb notices the hall is full to overflowing, and many of the skins are too old to be college age; they are seasoned red-ghetto age.

Before the education begins, Floyd Red Crow Westerman takes the stage with a guitar and begins to sing Indian songs. He warms up the crowd. Herb has never heard such lyrics before; they are about them. A professor, a distinguished-looking Indian, introduced as Professor Deloria, speaks first.

Another Indian, a local Oneida boy Herb recognizes as a kid called Charlie Hill, is about to try out his new comedy act. He just played a real club earlier in the week, a white one in Chicago, and every Indian in Milwaukee is talking about him. Herb overhears Dennis say they are all headed to Los Angeles next to raise funds.

Herb is impressed. Indians reaching far out, indeed.

Charlie Hill takes the mic before this large, mixed audience of Indians and a lot of white students. He is quite handsome and has the longest hair of all of them.

"I just came from Chicago, and all these cities are starting to look alike to me. I think you all look alike to me. Except in Los Angeles, man, that place is diff-rent! I didn't plan on being a comic, I wanted to be an actor, right? A movie star, right!" The kids applaud and laugh. He wags a finger at them. "You know! I watched every Western they made, and there's all these Indians in them, so why not me? Only they look pasty-faced in this reddish makeup they wear and kinda stupid looking, and I don't see any Indians back home that look like whatever this damn tribe is they're using, you know. So, me and a bunch of guys from the community center go try out, and they cast us all!" The hall grows quiet.

"Gonna really pay us to be Indians, man! One problem though, first day, they want me on this horse, yeah. Big ole beautiful palomino paint, and I say 'hell yeah.' But I'm thinking, *shit, bro, all I ever rode in my life was a skateboard. Man, I'm from Milwaukee, bro.*" Charlie catches Dennis's eye and he is laughing right out loud, getting his meaning. "So, I climb up on this big sucker, standing in this creek and this beautiful hippie chick is holding the rein and staring up at me, and I try to look all stoic and badass, right? And then boom! This loud-ass gun goes off and this director yells 'cut'! And he comes over to me all pissed, and says, 'Ya didn't fall off!' *Fall off?* I'm thinking, *where, in the creek, bro, hell there's some serious rocks down there. Shit, don't they have a mattress or something for these things? I could get hurt, man.*" The whole hall lifts with laughter.

"Director gives me this mean-ass shit expression, damn, he is one disagreeable dude, and says, 'Are those your friends over there?' He means the other Indians, and I'm thinking *I just met these guys on Santa Monica a few hours ago, I do not know them.* But I say 'yeah,' like I'm in charge of something, right? Like, what, we all came out of the same book, right?" As he stretches out another, 'Yo-u-u know . . . ' The city Indians applaud loudly, getting the inside reference. Although there are still over five-hundred tribes represented in America, they are usually counted by a generic metric and just called *Indian*.

So, he says, 'The guns go off and these bullets are expensive kid, and they don't fall off their horses, either!' Shit, and I'm thinking their horses are moving, right? They can ride, bro! Ya see, most of these guys just got home from Vietnam, and they can fucking shoot, too! Wearing those weird-crooked wigs and felt buckskin outfits, beadwork lookin' kinda cockeyed, but the babes couldn't tell! So, they are all doing this fancy shooting and the cowboys are taking these burning ass rubber bullets for a change, and the director is pissed!"

The students, Indian and white, are really laughing now, as they get every innuendo. Charlie drops his voice into a lower register and cups his hand beside his mouth.

"'Sir,' I say to him, 'just tell them you'll give 'em an extra fifty dollars if they get hit and go down.' And he does this, right? Sets all the cameras back up and *bam*! Just one shot goes off and suddenly all fifteen Indians hit the ground at the same time. *Boom*! Like a pratfall! Dammit! He yells, *c-u-u-t*! And well, that means you got me three nights over at Linda's Lounge in Milwaukee this week, 'cause I didn't make it in Hollywood! Thank you for coming out! Honor the Earth!"

He leaves the stage to thunderous laughter and applause.

Dennis Banks is next on stage, and as he takes it, Herb spots his own brother Percy in the crowd. Percy is miffed because everyone keeps asking him where they can find Herb. *Hell, I'm the Oneida tribal chairman, why aren't they asking him where I am?* Percy thinks. He leaves the gathering early.

Herb makes his way to the edge of the stage. Dennis has been watching his every move and when they finally get a word together, Dennis speaks first. He doesn't tell Herb he's the reason they put Milwaukee on their caravan tour.

"Oh, you're the guy I was told to meet. You actually got a Washington DC insider to fund your alcohol program and they pressed Indian Health Services to pay five million dollars into it. Brother, that is miraculous!"

"A hundred and sixty-five thousand a year," Herb replies. "The government backs out of these things, too. Only been two years. Don't use that word, miracle. They love that one, like they did us some favor. Wasn't no big deal, the misery handed us is in perpetuity, so why not the pay they owe? Yup, owe. They only done what they should have done and a long time ago. Start looking at it another way." Herb was always modest about a personal accomplishment and never enjoyed standing out, or exaggeration.

Clyde joins in. "Is this the guy? I saw you at Thunderbird's."

"Yup. And I saw you. Surprised you could walk in here."

Clyde doesn't take this comment well. "What's the big deal about you anyhow, brother?" Always takes a bristly minute to get acquainted when with anyone new to AIM, no surprise there. Who else would sign on to such duty but the hardened? Not the average, and not the faint of heart. This didn't turn off a man like Herb, told him the Movement attracted the serious-minded. He liked that, in fact insisted on it. Even so, he quizzed everyone.

Dennis, quick to smooth things out, says, "He runs a program . . ."

"My wife does, mostly. It was her idea. Sister runs the school."

"A good idea!" Dennis adds. "It's for rehabilitation from alcohol, but not AA style, it's Indian-run and it works! Using our own methods. Indian counselors!"

Clyde is thinking he doesn't know how well it works, given that Herb was at the bar same as him. Herb reads his mind and responds, "Like I said, my wife, Dorothy, is in charge of that, and yeah, it's taking off. They told us we could have this money till it ran out and then we had to be on our feet in five years. I told them not as long as their feet are on our land, it won't go down that way."

"And they agreed!" Dennis says with pride. "Something worked. Damn, something big connected to Washington. In perpetuity!"

"Don't make it such a big deal; let's do it again, then it'll be a start."

"He calls a hundred and sixty-five thousand dollars in funding no big deal. Man, you are recruited!" Dennis says with a laugh.

"Last time I heard those words, I ended up in prison," Herb says.

But Herb feels appreciated, and after all the busting heads for the union, he feels relieved to sense a purpose among his own. Tribes of all Nations they are calling themselves in this hall, and he'd stood in many meetings and halls over the years, listening to more Red Power groups than he could recall, but none ever called his name before as strongly as this one. He's ready. They'd soon combine efforts and settle on one name, American Indian Movement, or AIM. He and Dorothy would be their third chapter in. Milwaukee AIM.

He pulls out his ID badge from his union local and knows that from that moment on he will be taking a new direction. He'd just organized twenty-five hundred men on union lines for an Italian boss, and that's the right background. It all began in the joint, where an Italian tough guy called him a wagon burner.

Mr. Antonio Valensteri himself had recruited Herb into the union, and not in the usual way—or maybe it was. After a bar fight where he nearly killed a man, Herb hadn't been in lockup an hour before he got into another scrap that landed him in solitary. He didn't speak a single word while there, and when he came back into the general prison population, an Italian celly told Herb he liked his style. Clearly, he'd learned the most important thing about doing time: Never have a conversation with the enemy. "That's a conversation you must not have," said Valensteri, wagging his forefinger, and impressive with his eloquent Italian accent. "But it takes discipline, no, more than that," the wise elder says, "it's in your soul, it's something one cannot cultivate. You remind me of us."

Herb didn't say much to him, either, until Valensteri finally asked, "Do you know who I am?"

"I know what you are, and if you think I am Italian, you're wrong."

"No, my friend. Don't you think I know my own? At first, I thought you were a wetback, but you're a wagon burner," Valensteri said with a triumphant smile.

Herb thought for a moment he was about to be in another fight. Then five rather large Italian cellies moved in close. He laughed and asked, "Did these guys get arrested just so they can protect you?"

"Do I look like I need protecting? I can always find my own in the joint. Nobody to help you, though. Unless you want my help?"

Herb knew who these guys were. Nobody ever touched them, not on the streets of Milwaukee and not here. He was suddenly curious about someone else's business.

"Why would you want to help me, or have anything to do with me?"

Valensteri spoke next in Italian, as he lifted a small shot glass full of anisette. Herb noticed he could eat and drink what he pleased in here, right under the nose of the guards.

"I don't know Italian. I don't know what you just asked me."

"I didn't ask you anything, my friend. I saluted you. After all, you are the original landlords of this country."

"That so? Then why aren't we collecting rent?"

"Ahh, that takes a warlord, not a landlord." Valensteri drained the little crystal glass and continued, "You preserve your language, it keeps you who you are and that protects your culture, naturally. Then, most importantly, have security to protect your family. Get your own funding to go with it, and you've got what we have."

Herb looked at the plate of spaghetti in front of Valensteri and said, "I think I like what you have." The important man wagged his finger to a guard to bring Herb a plate.

"Come to our family's restaurant when you leave here, I will sign you onto a Local. Iron likely, maybe United Auto Workers, no matter, job's the same."

"Which restaurant? Milwaukee has a dozen of those."

"Which one you think, hardhead? Nino's! There's no restaurant like Nino's, trust me." Herb didn't like trusting strangers, but he gently nodded anyway.

All the men nodded their approval. Herb had been invited. Nino's served more than great food; it served acceptance. Once you were in, you were in. Question was, would they also let you back out? Herb had no ambition to be anything but what he was, so he decided to make this clear from the start. But the old man spoke again, first, and Herb showed him respect and listened.

"I wouldn't want to mislead you, my new friend," said Valensteri, reading Herb's pause.

"Nor I you, my new friend," Herb replied. "You know what I have to do to be an Indian?" Valensteri stopped eating, taking this change in the conversation seriously, and waited for his answer. "I just have to wake up in the morning." The elder man digested this and respected Herb for it. Herb finished, "And it's all I'm ever gonna be in this life. We have our own ways. *Comprende?*"

"Yes, yes. I see. So, we will just have dinner. And then I'll assign you to a Local. It'll be good for both of us."

Herb was first placed in the UAW 75, United Auto Workers, then he was moved over to Iron Workers, all following a nice dinner at Nino's with his wife Dorothy beside him. For a while Dorothy worked hat check at Nino's, until she barged into the bar one night to drag an Indian out. She had just seen him achieve sobriety. "Dorothy, wait," he called out as she pulled him backward. "Don't embarrass me in front of my friends!" She gave her usual reply: "They're not your friends."

Early one morning soon after, Herb is standing amid concrete and steel in downtown Milwaukee—nothing holds the cold like concrete and steel—as he studies closely what he's there to spot. About twenty guys in a crew were building scaffolding up the side of a high-rise, and they are scabs, not union. He waits until it's gone up seven stories high before having a few trucks hitch up and pull the whole thing down. "What a fight that caused when that sucker ripped right off the side of that building," Herb later reminisced to Dorothy.

The Milwaukee police already had Herb on their radar, and they speed their patrol cars right up to the fight between the union organizers and the scabs just minutes after it ensues. "You grab the greaseballs, and I'll take the wagon burner," Herb hears a cop say. He is always out in front if there's a bad fight. Usually one he's instigated for the boss. He has a hard time cooling down once he gets started.

Dorothy doesn't have to bother with finding help to get him out of jail anymore. The union already has a lawyer before Herb arrives for processing. Usually, the cops stop for doughnuts on the way, the Italian cops anyway. Why waste time on all the paperwork, when Herb will just be walking straight out?

Dorothy has begun to be weary of something she has to deal with. Fresh out of jail and finished with work for the day, Herb has become a regular at the Thunderbird Tap on the edge of the red ghetto. What she doesn't know is that his most recent visit there will change the direction of their lives forever, and he will not be going back to a bar, not any bar. Union organizing has taught him skills the young American Indian Movement needs. It has also reminded him that he *is* a wagon burner. An exceptionally good one. The next time he's at the Milwaukee city jail, he'll be there to bail his wife out.

Dorothy began her days pretty much the same as most: she received the usual Indian in distress calls all AIM chapters got. On this day an urgent call came from a thirteen-year-old Oneida mother who said the authorities were coming to take her child. The girl was hysterical, and someone told her to call Dorothy Powless, who quickly got baby and mother to her house. She washed the baby up and combed her hair, after making a run to the local five-

and-dime store for some new toddler clothes. The baby was on her hip when the social worker arrived.

Accustomed to people who listened to her, the social worker realized to her surprise that she was losing her fight with this Indian woman. So she started reciting the state rules: if Dorothy kept the little girl, she would have to have her own room, separate from the other children in her house. Dorothy stopped her.

"It ain't gonna go down that way," she said. "She'll be in a family bed of kids, not alone in some other room—our way." And what room? There was no other room.

The social worker finally just up and announced that the baby could stay, but she was taking the mother with her. "She's underage, too, and under the rules of the state—" Dorothy interrupted her again. And again, her answer was no.

Dorothy was already deep into Red Power rights. She'd go to any length to win, especially regarding an Indian child. Herb Powless had walked into the middle of the scene. He hadn't said a word and didn't need to. Dorothy had just up and declared she was adopting them both. *Two more kids?* Herb thought. *Damn, Dorothy . . . where?* But when the social worker looked to Herb, he just added, "You heard her. Get out." The social worker had nothing to leave with but her rules. They were Milwaukee AIM and the word got around town fast if an Indian was in trouble. The thirteen-year-old mom was a product of white adoption. She explained that her parents loved her when she was little and cute, but when she got older and wanted to know about being Indian, they gave her a hard time. She became a runaway.

By nightfall, Dorothy left the supper table after an AIM meeting at the house to go find Herb at the War Memorial Center down at the lakefront. Something was coming down over an important protest called "Winter Dam." A rumor spread that John Birchers had gathered to help confront the Indians. It was all over a dam that had already destroyed important orchards, and Indians were angry, and AIM was present. Dorothy bundled up her son, little Geronimo Powless, onto a cradle board her mother-in-law had made her and volunteered to go find Herb. Once Dorothy was standing outside the large marble walls, something drew her in closer. A security guard was speaking rather harshly to a drum group, and he assumed she was with them.

He pointed to Dorothy and said, "You can't bring that thing in here!" Dorothy answered him back, "We don't bring our drum, we follow it." And then she did, right into the building. She stayed longer than she expected to.

Not having found Herb, she started home, with Geronimo sleeping sweetly on the board. Turning off of 45th and North Avenue she saw a cruiser's blue lights started to twirl behind her, and she found herself in a predicament. Herb had trained them all well for such an occurrence. "Most important rule," he said, "the only rule, and that's come from a position of strength. They can react like dogs, fear triggers a fight instinct, so, try hard not to show any emotion. If asked a question, don't follow it, lead it. It comes off better and surprises them; they ain't used to us speaking up."

"Lady, open your purse and show me what's in it." The flashlight in her eyes was blinding, and the officer young.

"You want to know what's in it, you open it." He was not amused.

He readily put Dorothy into his patrol car and, for the moment, let her hold the cradle board in the back seat. She kept her chin up. The baby stayed asleep. She reminded the man she had an infant with her, as his driving was erratic.

"Well, the state will decide if it's yours or not."

Once at the station house and booked, she noticed a man in a suit leaning nearby. He was a Hooverman, not a cop, meaning FBI. They handed her baby to the same social worker she'd seen that morning. Dorothy kept her demeanor. No call was allowed; instead she was told to fill out a piece of paper the desk chief handed her. "All the names of your relatives first, their addresses and phone numbers and places of business, then your neighbors, friends, and associates, and when the paper is filled out front and back, with no white left," the chief continued, "then you can go, so write fast and you'll get out of here." He said this while cooing at her baby and mocking the contraption he was in.

Four hours later, Herb Powless was waiting with their new AIM lawyer, Lew Gurwitz, who'd brought a local associate along with him; they'd been the reason for the dinner. Dorothy took the baby board from her husband and walked out. As she left, the arresting officer commented on her giving him the "hooey-hex" when he took that baby out of her arms, and he hoped never to run into that woman again. The station chief smirked, "Teach her right, not to be out here." When he retrieved the paper from back in her holding cell, he was stunned to see it was still completely white, on both sides, the pencil laid across it.

Once home she leaned over the open car trunk with her husband, who said, "Yes, anything, you pick one."

She did, as she pointed to a Magnum handgun.

"Well, any one but that one. What about something small, easy to hide? Something registered anyway, that one's new and very expensive."

"Why aren't they all registered?"

"Hard to do, I've done time, can't swing but what I buy off the street."

"Then I'll register them. I have a job, a license. Let's do things right." That was his Dorothy.

CHAPTER 9

Third Chapter In, Milwaukee, Wisconsin

"Add to our ranks nationally and be taken seriously." Those were smart words, even if they did come from an Indian who never left Milwaukee. Now Herb would leave and stand beside Dennis on a stage, but with an entirely different tack.

Dennis cut an imposing figure, his hair now shoulder length and held back in the traditional style of a Navajo wind band, cut from the cloth of a blue and white bandana and folded longways across his forehead and tied in the back. He looked fresh out of 1870 and could have been superimposed into a painting on a White House wall. When he spoke, he didn't hold back, and a local commented that "his medicine was in his voice."

Herb shook them up. He warned his listeners: "No lightweights need apply to our chapter."

Dennis speaks first. "Our AIM caravans aren't gonna be no 'Geronimo's Cadillac'—like back in the day, who was paraded around to show Americans the Indian wars had been won—rather the opposite, we ain't that horse with his head hung low and the warrior's lower!" Bill Means, a Lakota and a marine out of the wartime theater of Vietnam, said out loud, "I always hated that statue, I wanted to kick that guy's ass and say, 'look up, we're still here!'" Dennis brought out Leonard Crow Dog to show audiences that they weren't done yet. "Indian people have decided to save Indian people, and we are here!" A communal "hoh!" was heard all round. They were few in numbers at first, more like disciples, but the Movement was building, and fast, and to some ears it came more like a thunderclap.

Indian men and women approached Dennis after a speech. Some came from the rez, some were just out of prison, and some hailed from Harvard and from universities with Indian studies. Together, they knew a lot. Next, leadership traveled east to speak before the Boston Indian Council, introduced by attorney Lew Gurwitz, the dedicated lawyer who stayed with AIM for the full ride.

Wherever the caravan went, they always had to hit someone up for a place to stay. City hotels weren't safe or interested in housing them. There was never enough money, and what there was had to be saved for gas. In Boston, Lew had volunteered, saying, "My house! Well, my mom's anyway." Soon, a small, good-natured woman was meeting them at the door as if they were family just back from a long trip. After serving them a fine midnight snack of little potato pancakes and jam, she laid out soft pallets on the floor and let them know that her Jewish home is their home. Mrs. Gurwitz told them she hoped they'd take good care of her son. She added, "He doesn't get enough rest." Floyd Red Crow Westerman gave her his personal word he would do so, while the two were washing dishes together.

Another key player joined in that fateful night in Boston, a lovely and articulate young lady and her boyfriend, both from the Boston Indian Council. She told Dennis she'd just passed up a full scholarship to Brandeis University and wanted to join their caravan instead. A Mi'kmaq originally from Pictou Landing in Nova Scotia, her name was Anna Pictou. Her friends called her Anna Mae. She was bright, articulate, and her eyes sparkled even brighter when Dennis spoke. She wasn't the first this happened to.

Dennis also met Sam Sapiel on that Boston trip, a Penobscot from Indian Island in Maine. "There are old-school, commitment-minded folks among these Wamps nearby," Lew informed Dennis. "That's short for Wampanoags, and they'll lead to a wealth of support for what we are doing." The AIMers immediately decided to give a speech the following day at the very site where the first pilgrims landed. Russell Means, a tall and handsome Lakota, Bill Means's brother, was dressed for the occasion and presented all that was expected from a traditionally dressed Oglala Sioux, and that, accompanied with his booming range, lit up these "people of the first light." A reference to the local Wampanoags of Massachusetts. They sat around a fire and shared stories from out of the Hockomock Swamp, a sixteen-thousand-acre freshwater floodplain. "If tall boats had docked at Pilgrim's Point that night, our people might have torched them," one Penobscot in attendance announced. Tempers could run high if AIM was at the right place with the right speech. Dennis noticed that many who were not Indian also joined to support the struggle. One in particular was nicknamed "Hippie Jack." He came with Lew Gurwitz as his paralegal; this ponytailed Scots-Irishman came from firefighters in Boston, and also proved a good woodchopper for the sweat.

"The Indian fishermen here have as much injustice running with their land and nets as back home on your Leech Lake," Hippie Jack said, singling out Dennis. "Land prices got so high on their traditional land—including islands like their beautiful Nantucket and a place called Martha's Vineyard—that no Indian could pay. Not being federally recognized, they were just shoved off."

Dennis added, "All rich blue blood land now instead of red land . . . like it had been for centuries."

Lew pointed out that it'd be best not to complain about that too loudly, as the very support he hoped to raise for them, and any national attention to go with it, might come from some of those very rich and influential "blue bloods."

Dennis was not too interested in keeping his voice down, as it had just begun to rise up and he was not a respecter of persons. It was Indian land, and the people who had suffered on it were who he had respect for. But he used diplomacy. Lew was smart and dedicated and he'd heed his good counsel. For now, anyway.

Banks turned his attentions to the proposed press junket Anna Mae mentioned. She talked about how they could "break in." "Break in where?" he asked. "Into the American mindset, that's where! Until that's achieved, no one here listening can bring about sweeping change; we are just talking to ourselves."

"She is right," he said. He noted she was smart as well as beautiful.

Lew explained to the crowd that "treaties aren't just a good idea, they're law, the highest law of the land, formed by Congress, and they cannot be broken."

An Indian Harvard scholar spoke up: "Better get some congressmen on your side, then!" Anna Mae Pictou nodded, knowing he meant Congress could change it.

"Then how are they being broken?"

Dennis chimed in, "We're letting them! You can also stop letting them!"

Lew followed up, in his jocular New England style. "Hey, ya bastards, smarten up!" Everyone paused, quiet for a beat, then they all laughed, and Lew added, "Where I come from, that's an endearment."

Fists went in the air all around that night followed by a harmonic "Hoh!" piercing the air and reverberating.

When asked, "How can we best reach out to other potential Indian leaders?" Anna Mae spoke up: "That's easy enough, let's go get them." They decided to head out to the West Coast. But first to Milwaukee. Dennis planned to roust Herb Powless into doing something he likely hadn't planned to do— leave home. And Clyde Bellecourt had put his own brother, Vernon, also Ojibwe, into the "go get them" spotlight by giving Dennis his address in Colorado. Clyde knew Vernon could match all of them in leadership skill.

Dennis walked down First Street in Boulder, Colorado, and thought he was seeing things when he first spied a tall, handsome Indian man moving chairs around inside a beauty parlor. He looked at his matchbook and rechecked the address he'd written down. He was at the right place. Likely other passersby thought the man moving the chairs was the janitor. He was deliberate in restyling the place. Dennis opened the door a crack and said, "You open?"

"Sure. But that hair over your ears looks like you're growing it long, right?"

Dennis smiled and walked in. "I am growing it long. And it isn't cooperating as fast as I'd like. Got any grow-faster tonic in here?"

"Well, there is a shaggy stage ya have to live through. Comb it all back behind your ears for a while longer, it'll get there."

"They let you in here all by yourself?" Dennis said, putting on an act. He already knew who the big fellow was.

"Yes, they tend to let the proprietor do whatever he wants."

"You're the owner? You're a skin, right?"

"Yes, I am, and I am also Vernon Bellecourt," he said, extending his hand.

"Nice to meet you, Vernon," Dennis responded with a warm smile.

After they had talked for several hours, with the Closed sign up on the door, they went down the street to a Japanese restaurant Dennis frequented whenever he was in Boulder and talked into the night. And then the next day and the next. Soon Clyde joined them. They headed to Denver.

They met up with Russell Means, soon to be sporting braids. He had all the correctness that went with his stately appearance, sometimes moving people right into the street. He was in California when the Movement first found him, though, and he was teaching ballroom dancing, of all things. He came over to Denver and started AIM's second chapter with Vernon Bellecourt.

The AIM leaders in Denver would recruit Len Foster, an articulate Navajo who had recently tried out with the LA Dodgers. However, he had broken his arm and decided instead to attend an AIM meeting at the University of Colorado, his arm still in a cast. As the proverbial saying goes, "He walked in and never left." He gave a beautiful speech that night, with an important reminder to all.

"I didn't have the troubles most of you had. My father was good to us, and home, and I was good at sports and, well, it was all well enough, but still," he said, laying a hand gently across his heart. The handsome man continued, intermittently praying in his own language, a beautiful thing for all present. "I had a vacuum inside me, an emptiness. My father took me to my grandfather, and he said, 'time to build a sweat.'" He said sternly, "It changed everything."

Bill Means, Russell's brother, still sported his whitewall haircut. He said, "When I arrived home in South Dakota, I was asked to join the National Guard—well, not exactly asked. They'd soon be training our military guns on college students who had, in President Nixon's opinion, gotten too rowdy. Students, Nixon felt, were supposed to learn, not teach!" Bill went on to say, "that meant he'd next be asked to point a weapon at his own people . . . and students?" He refused, which got him a hitch in the stockade. He was freshly out of there when he attended the meeting in Denver, and from then on, he was AIM all the way. He liked meeting Herb Powless. A marine thing and a warrior thing.

Another AIMer walked over, Floyd Red Crow Westerman, as he had his own tour in the US Marine Corps. You'd be hard pressed to find an able-bodied Lakota who had not been in that branch. They would commonly ask the recruiters, "Who's the elite? Who sees the hardest fighting?" And the answer was always the same: "Join the marines."

Floyd would answer a different call that night, with his guitar in hand. Folkies had already heard of Floyd and his unique lyrics as a way of sharing his culture and they had begun to follow him everywhere, even into this hall. It gave the young lyricist a rare opportunity to address Indian issues another way. It was a segment of Americans who needed to understand their position and help them spread the word. From a stage, Floyd worked it with song.

With the key players gathered, the Movement was ready to move beyond their homes and ghettos and announce AIM's existence from a caravan traveling east to west and then back, uniting leadership, adding as many other dissenting Indian voices as they could. During recruiting sessions, they would set up a stage and hang a banner that read, The Red Giant Is on One Knee and About to Stand Up!

Leadership set a goal to gather eighty chapters, more if they could. Northwest AIM and several others didn't even wait till the caravan arrived. They were already formed before Dennis went west.

When they heard the drum in a community hall they just said, "Brother, move over! I gotta get there!" It was no matter if it was a Knights of Columbus hall, a Saint Vincent De Paul church, or the back of a mechanic's shop. A few progressive universities loaned AIM an empty classroom, and many Black churches offered their pews. The AIMers would fill them. Indian people, urban and rez alike, began pouring in from all over.

The drumbeats were from age-old drum songs and returned at this crucial moment in history to lift the Indians all up, together. AIM got their eighty chapters.

AIM leadership, along with other Red Power groups, began working with great minds, educated professors and writers like Vine Deloria, Jr. They were working to create a document to present to the White House. They'd all march together up to the Capitol, by invitation of course. This road trip to Washington would be named the Trail of Broken Treaties.

Herb had the most experience dealing with Capitol Hill and issued a warning. "They went to a lot of trouble and planning not to have this problem, and they won't welcome its return."

"What problem exactly?" Vernon Bellecourt asked.

"An Indian one," Dennis answered. "We don't have the numbers, politically, like the Civil Righters, so we gotta raise a bigger voice than we are. Good people will get behind us. I think it's out there."

"We'll show them what's inside our numbers," Russell Means added.

Dennis Banks recognized, while sitting at Dorothy's breakfast table, that the urban Indians were drawing the attention off the reservation road, and instead, for the first time in history, they'd be coming up a government road. By the time they reached Washington, 70 percent of their ranks would be rez Indians, dispelling the growing myth that they were merely urban upstarts and outsiders.

Dorothy objected to the use of the word *urban* to describe them—they were Indian. Herb's own mother, who was living with them, knew four languages—Ho-Chunk, Oneida of course, Menominee, and Potawatomi. She was very old school—"If not for the fact she still did her temple duty diligently at the Mormon temple!" Herb liked to throw in, as it irritated him greatly.

AIM was also bumping into a familiar old enemy—the government Indian. They looked Indian because they were, a well-heeled, often educated, and definitely more assimilated lot, and therefore more likely candidates to work within the system. Not a bad idea, except for the old recipe to pit one against the other. This strategy had been around a long time, because it worked—especially if the government sanctioning of one over the other went on in the shadows. That said, these alliances were starting to shift. More and more, educated Indians supported the Movement and presently helped to create the document to deliver to Washington. It was called "The Twenty Points." It addressed sovereign issues and the law.

Herb Powless decided to show his seriousness locally, much to his chairman brother's chagrin. Milwaukee AIM took over an old, abandoned Coast Guard station and boathouse in an area of Milwaukee called McKinley

Beach down on the waterfront, "And this time the land would be returned!" Herb swore it, before Nixon's aides got the idea. His Washington insider, Brad Patterson, a top aide and the Indian Policy Advisor under Leonard Garment, was all for President Nixon's self-determination policy for Indians, and it gave him the power to turn over the keys permanently, under treaty rights, rewarding an urban red power movement for the first and the last time. Herb scurried to find a tribe to officially accept the returned land. It was a peaceful resolution to an occupation and the *New York Times* wrote about it, and him, and when they did, they had no idea that Leonard Peltier would one year later be standing right beside him.

CHAPTER 10

Ceremony Is Coming!
Pine Ridge Reservation, South Dakota

Dorothy and Herb Powless spent every dime they had taking long road trips to South Dakota on weekends. Dorothy kept her graveyard shift at the brewery and Herb still ran the Local, so they could travel when they needed, and they'd pile the kids into the car and drive fourteen hours one way. They hit dirt roads getting through the flats before and after the Black Hills came into view.

The traditional Indians of Pine Ridge welcomed the AIM members, and an exchange of pride in culture went both ways. Since youth, Dorothy had rarely heard a good thing said about what she was, since her schoolteachers and church classes, which she had been forced to attend, hadn't said any. Dorothy watched her sisters spend most of their early adult life in a ladies' washroom trying to comb their hair and style themselves into passing for white. Dorothy recalled her daughter coming home from school one day and saying she'd been followed around by two girls calling out "Sapphire, Sapphire!" in an ugly tone. The reference was to a popular Black character on a TV show. Dorothy said, "Ignore them. They're ignorant, and don't know what you are!"

Dorothy wanted a redirection, a change, so she went to the source. She and Herb got out of the car with the kids at Victoria and Ellis Chips's property, which was unique in that it had been in the Chips family forever. It was airship land, that which was kept in the family for many generations at great personal sacrifice. All that was left was a square-mile tract, important as their ancestors were buried there. They were way out in reservation woods.

A Lakota Indian walked over to Dorothy and asked her, "What the heck is an Oneida?" Herb usually responded to this question by reminding other Indians they were called the *fierce people*. Instead she answered, "We were the ones getting our asses kicked in the east, so you could play with your buffalo another hundred years." Everyone laughed all around. A real Indian always carried a funny bone, and she was real, all right. Another asked if she could prove she was an Indian, to which she answered, "I'd like to see you prove I'm not." And that ended the conversation.

Herb told those listening that over twenty different tribal affiliates are in the city with them—Ojibwe, Lakota, Oneida, Potawatomi, one Penobscot, even, a few Mohawk, Chippewa Bad River, and Ho-Chunk—but mainly they're over in Chicago. People are coming together. "We aren't a club; everyone has their own voice." Dorothy added, "It takes a lot of people to move something; we're a *movement*."

Pride was fine with Dorothy Powless, but she wanted more. She wanted to do things right. These Lakota people were remote and left to survive any way they could. Oddly, the remoteness protected them; she was standing on ground where change wasn't gonna come. Prevalent culture did them a favor, by staying away. It had protected their ways. Oneida ways were different, but to her line of thinking any traditional way at this point was better than none. Here she was ready to learn whatever the old ones were willing to share.

Ole Man Chips, as he is called, is the Lakota medicine man who greets them. He and his slight, silver-haired wife, Vickie, welcome Dorothy and Herb along with others. His full name is Ellis Horn Chips, and his father had been a medicine man to Crazy Horse. For Dorothy, it is a beautiful time of awakening. Herb remains skeptical but respects these people of the Ridge.

"A late winter's night to hold a ceremony," Miss Vickie Chips explains. "Deep into the night all alive is asleep and quiet, the Creator can hear our prayers better, it is out of respect."

Herb's impressed with respect and the fact they make it hard to do, not easy. On that thought he climbs the hill to the sweat lodge and the fire circle. The elder notices that Dorothy Powless is staring fixedly at the goings-on up the hill—she seems to be counting every ember rising into the night sky from the rocks. Vickie Chips also notices that her new young friend has been cooking since she arrived. She's first tucked away some star quilts, the hardest quilt to sew, for the stitches must be finely sewn and well hidden. She's found time to do it all. She planned to give them as gifts when they leave the following morning. Indian way.

Dorothy listens as two young men are appointed fire keepers, then a door man, a cedar man, and others are asked to chop wood for those who will run the rocks. Rusty lawn chairs and torn leather car seats are set out in the snow around a hot barrel fire by an old trailer. It may be abject poverty, as she'd always heard about the Lakota, but to young Dorothy, it is a spiritual banquet. Herb surveys the scene differently, knowing this group had once been the greatest light horse calvary in the world, a true horse culture, and it was now a mere shadow of its former self. It angers him.

The drum songs can be heard echoing through the hills, and the snow begins clearing just in time for the meal. The flap door is opened on the sweat lodge, so the meal is coming soon. Dorothy, watching the fire again, doesn't notice that Miss Vickie Chips is watching her. The elder speaks directly.

"There is a rock for every rib in the buffalo. There is a moon drawn on the ground, like this . . ." Miss Vickie says. Leaning down and using a stick, she clears away the snow from the wet ground and draws what appears to be a half-moon.

"A *half*-moon?" Dorothy asks.

"No. It is full, just the other half can only be seen from the spirit world."

Dorothy is struck by something she has never felt before, and it makes her bold enough to ask, "Can we do it?"

Vickie Chips knows what Dorothy means, and responds quickly. They know what they can do and cannot do, and what they should do, so their answers tend to come with no uncertainty. All it took to speak up about anything, unpleasant or not, was the courage to say it. A Lakota had no small supply of that. Even after centuries of being beaten down and marginalized by hardship and poverty in a land that was ruled half the year by winter, they knew who they were, and the word "no" came easily. So did "yes."

"Sweat? Yes, we can do this. I'll ask. You aren't on your time?" Dorothy shakes her head. "Okay then. When the men are through with the rocks, it is permitted for us to ask to use them. When they are back up to the cabin, I will ask. This is permitted." She reassures Dorothy by speaking it twice and patting her arm.

Much later, Dorothy will learn that the question about her menstrual period was not intended as a caution of some kind—women had always been taught to believe "a period" was dirty and unmentionable—but this elder intended the very opposite. The lodge, the sweat, was a re-creation of a woman's womb. No man could sweat with women, for a female's power overcame all else. After all, women were the womb.

Oh, to sweat! Dorothy's heart thunders just at the thought. The flap in the small dome-shaped lodge is fully open now, and all the men are emerging on their hands and knees. They stand and stretch, steam rising off their hair and limbs. Then they walk slowly over to a clothesline that holds their clothes. Dorothy runs to the car and pulls a star quilt from the trunk. When she gets back to the trailer, she can hear Miss Vickie in what sounds like a heated exchange with her husband, Ellis.

They speak only in Lakota, but it is clear a debate is going on. Miss Vickie apparently wins the argument. She motions to Dorothy and three other women to come with her, and they start toward the hill. Miss Vickie stops first to point the men toward something to drink—water or pop from an old scratched cooler under a tree, and a large jar of tea sitting in the snow.

The men have started serving themselves, and a few kids are taking plates of steaming hot greens and bean and elk meat stew to the elders sitting on the trailer's wooden porch.

"Where are the women going?" one Lakota man asks in English.

"The women are gonna sweat."

Although Ellis Chips does not look pleased, the general opinion among the others seems to be, "Why not? Good for them!"

Vickie Chips goes into the trailer and comes back out with a large wooden box. Her daughter takes it from her and carries it up the hill toward the lodge. Dorothy follows.

Miss Vickie takes her time getting up the hill, but she takes charge once there and lifts a large eagle feather fan with colorful beadwork around its handle out of the wooden box. She speaks in Lakota a prayer that is long, and the sounds are beautiful to Dorothy's ears. At times she is fanning herself and then the others with smoke rising from a small flat bowl. Then she sprinkles something over the rocks, and they hiss loudly.

It is no matter to Dorothy that she doesn't know their language; its sound conveys more than words. She is in the presence. She feels love and welcome coming off the words as the elder puts all their hearts at ease. Dorothy knows that not everyone is pleased with their unexpected absence from the camp, but her mind is not there. It's up on the hill with the stars and the fire.

Dorothy had no authority to ask. She needed none. The world out here doesn't work that way. Every human being counts as important. Hard to believe there is anyplace people believe like that. The smoke and rocks lift away her doubt.

Miss Vickie speaks, and her words feel familiar and comforting. "We do not have to plan to do what is right to do. Something had a plan, and it isn't always a human being doing the planning. Standing around this fire means you have an open heart." She speaks next in Lakota and sprinkles something on the rocks. It smells like cedar, and it is healing to breathe in.

"You do not have to have an eagle fan, a pretty shawl, a certain dress, for the Creator is looking on the inside of you, not the outside. We don't pray for ourselves when we gather, we pray for others. Your heart is open just by walking up that hill. One day soon you will have learned the songs for the drum and will run the sweat yourselves. I won't always be here, and you won't always be, but the ways will be. This is the place where we've gathered." With those simple words, and some brief singing, they bend down and go into the lodge.

Two girls, one of them Vickie's granddaughter, arrive just as the speaking stops. Dorothy also notices that no one's feet moved when the drum stopped. The two granddaughters begin to run the rocks. Another girl inside is the door keeper. When not ferrying hot rocks to the door on a rusted shovel, the girls' hands rest gently on the outside of the lodge as they sing with their mother and grandmother inside. Rocks, heat, smoke, and song seem to mix in some glorious harmony in a naturally organized way.

Hours later, it is over. Hours that have passed like minutes for Dorothy, who crawls, steaming and feeling deeply refreshed, out of the buffalo-hide door into the night air. She notices as a young woman pulls her blanket off the clothesline and heads up behind the lodge with a giggle. Pulling her own star quilt around her shoulders, and lifting another she'd sat on, she quickly follows the woman.

Once over the crest of the hill and farther from any light, Dorothy notices the stars, thousands of them it seems, and so bright it takes her heart away and up to them. The girls, she notices, are lying out in their altogethers on their blankets, facing up to the night sky. *How daring!* Dorothy thinks, at first a shock to her eyes. Then she realizes that something about it seems natural and innocent, and she does the unthinkable, modest as she is, and joins them.

Miss Chips has headed back down the hill and it was Dorothy's first inclination to follow her, but something sent her after the girls instead. Watching them now and hearing their laughter, she thinks that they are youthful, but in fact some are around her age. She has not been young for a very long time, maybe never, but at this moment she feels so.

Reassuring herself that the men are all inside, smoking and still eating, she quietly spreads out the scratchy wool blanket she'd sat on in the sweat, catching a whiff of cedar smoke. She spreads her star quilt on top of the ratty wool, slips out of her meager clothing, and lies down on her back, arms straight beside her. She can see and hear her own breathing. The sensation takes over and a mysterious calm envelops her. She is still warm.

She lies naked beneath the grand sky of stars, facing up to their glorious abundance. She doesn't feel a hint of chill, as steam is still rising from her body. Her mind is clear, and she feels as never before, at one with both earth and sky. She knows as surely as the warm tears roll down the sides of her face that she is never leaving this moment. She'll carry it with her.

Home lies under these stars, finally home, and wherever she makes her family's life in the future, even if back in the city, a lodge is going to go with her. She squeezes her eyes tightly shut and with every breath draws in the love and assurance that the Creator has always wanted her to know.

She's been gone a little too long for Herb, and of course he comes looking for her, but by the time he arrives up the hill, all he sees is four women standing around a large fire with their backs to him, colorful quilts drawn around their shoulders, hanging down like floor-length shawls. Each reveals an abundance of flowing thick dark hair. Dorothy feels his presence and turns around.

He looks at her, startled at first, and then nods, a smile not quite reaching his lips. She waits a full minute before leaving the group to join him. They walk back down a rocky path, and once out of sight of both the cabin below and the girls above, Herb pulls Dorothy onto another path, one just wide enough for a coyote to walk.

"I got a pickup truck nearby, lady," he whispers. She instantly feels that familiar energy coming off him, and though accustomed to it, it still catches her by surprise. It could almost stop your breath, he is such a strong, self-assured male, and one who usually does not hear no for an answer.

"A truck bed? Well, I won't be on it. But then . . . I do have a blanket." He pauses, then gently uses his forearm to lift her sweet face up to his and stares for a moment as she waits. This is a custom of his, this stare, as if it were his way of giving himself over to her completely. She opens the soft quilt and lifts it above his head, and he reaches inside and pulls her small soft waist to him. He then lightly brushes her lips with his, moves his nose to her cheek and then up to her forehead, smelling her skin. He takes in the scent of soap and snow and pine mixed with her natural perfume. She can feel his warm breath as he does so.

Herb kisses her deeply, and she responds in kind. The bright stars come back to her, but this time from inside the blanket.

Driving back home in barely morning light, Dorothy shares her plan.

"You're gonna build *what*? Where?" Herb responds with his usual sarcasm. "Where do ya think you can do that, then? Right on our city block?" She doesn't respond with even the hint of a smile, and he notices.

He sees her sideways, without turning, as they've been married that long, and he takes his best shot, reminding her, "It's bad enough cops coming around when these guys drum in the attic, but a sweat lodge?" Silence falls between them.

"Dorothy," he says gently, "that's all gone, you can't turn it back. Ya can't reclaim it like a land title. We can do it when we come out here, but in Milwaukee? Oneidas probably would hate the idea the most; they barely do their own thing once a year in a longhouse, and a priest takes it over when they do. Or Mormon."

"Or maybe your brother Percy might mind, after all, he is the tribal chairman," Dorothy replies. She knows where the buttons are.

With a spark of frustration in his voice, Herb says, "Don't remind me and ruin the day. I met with him over something before leaving. What, I have to get a day pass to go visit Pine Ridge? He's a good man, but we sure see it all differently, always will. We ain't in Oneida anymore, so we can do as we like."

They're silent again until Herb asks, "How ya think you're gonna make Indians back in Milwaukee?"

"The same way they took it away from us, that's how," she says with real authority in her voice. He knows what she means . . . from within the lodge.

When she's determined, he knows there's no use talking to her. So they drive on through the snowy wilderness and don't speak again 'til the first light reveals the unnatural glow of the city. Herb muses at the name. *Milwau-kee*. It isn't an English word, and it isn't Italian, either. He thinks of the gift bestowed on him back at Pine Ridge, now lying in his trunk on some old newspapers to keep it dry. He'd taken his red beret with him, and a World War II veteran and Lakota elder had adorned it with two white eagle feathers. A precious memento, he'd originally thought, but now he feels it may have taken on a new meaning. Of course, it would be enough reason to take on such risks back home just because his wife was asking. But he realizes, right then, he wants it, too.

A year later, that same beret would be talked about in the *New York Times*, with Herb Powless standing beneath it. A lot was coming their way in the near future, and not just from his own backyard.

CHAPTER 11

Leonard Peltier, Cousin Razor, and Northwest AIM

L eonard was trusted with the driving as he and his Uncle Billy made their way back to the Seattle coast from Turtle Mountain. It took a year and a half to get back out on the road. The Montana mountain range would be near impassable even in spring, so they went for Wolf Creek Pass instead, over the Colorado Rockies. They'd miss steering off to the Crow agency to visit his Aunty Ida and Ben Stiff Arm, as they had when driving out. Peltier's aunt and uncle were teachers there.

The long trek home to North Dakota included ten-below temperatures and howling winds through Montana, but hell, no driving intimidated young Leonard. The trip back was easier, relatively speaking. Leonard was excited when they finally hit San Francisco, as he was promised they'd tour that city—that is, until they came to the first big hill downtown, "a mountain" Uncle Billy Robideau called it, with some kind of damn train tracks twisted along it. Uncle Billy yelled out, "Leonard, back the car up, go on son, back up this damn thing. Don't drive down it!"

Leonard knew that was not the right move, they'd gone too far, and he hoped he had the brakes left to go down. Maybe not. So he cut big swerves and snake danced all the way down, all the while wondering, *What kind of damn city is this?* He preferred the perils they'd faced out on real mountain land to those of this concrete jungle. They'd crawled up and back down treacherous icy roads, but these city roads were smooth as glass. Those winter slopes hadn't bothered Uncle a peep; in fact he slept through them. Cities had different perils, and just never agreed with him.

At the bottom of the hill, Uncle Billy jumped out, pulled Leonard from the driver's seat, and took the wheel. Leonard tried to hold down his laughter; it seemed he'd damn near scared his uncle to death. They drove straight out of town and didn't see a single sight. They drove through the night.

A few years later he worked his way into Seattle and pitched his tent in Uncle Billy Robideau's front yard. Then he found the Indian Community Center, and young Leonard became industrious. This did agree with him. His first home out west was in Portland, Oregon, with his cousins, then in Wenatchee, Washington, but he wanted better than picking apples all day. So he went to live with Uncle Billy. He wanted his own shop and did a lot of migrant work to get the start-up money. He went in with another Chippewa he met to create Howard and Leonard's Towing. A lot of their customers paid with plates of fry bread or Indian tacos at first. Leonard was glad to help them out.

He applied for a small business loan and was interviewed by a journalist from a Washington newspaper in November 1969. In the article, Leonard made an appeal for Indians to find work any way they could, mentioning that others might do the same. This notoriety, along with the local Indian Community Center's attention, brought in lots of work, and with savings all kept rolled in a coffee can, Leonard finally realized his dream of ownership. His signs and fliers announced that he could tow anything on wheels, just call the Indian Center, as they were yet to have their own phone. His "tow truck" was a heavy old pickup truck with large, rusted boat chains they got out of a dump. Always finding a way. Howard would steer, and sometimes Peltier would run behind the car being towed to keep it steady over the one bridge that stood between the thoroughfare and their shop. Leonard took a onetime job as a plumber to trade out for a hydraulic lift—a broken one, but he fixed it, and they were good to go.

Another thing came of owning a space—the locals asked to use it after hours for meetings. Not thinking politically as much as just helping out his own, Peltier always said yes. His dad Leo had taken him to meetings when Turtle Mountain was under termination, so it was an at-home feeling anyway. It seemed the Klamaths, already terminated, had a serious fishing rights struggle going on involving cut-up nets and harassment. Leonard got drawn in; after all, this was his new home and Indian was Indian. He began to attend the protests after work.

"They stole your land and you've settled for a fish out of it? And now they don't want to give you even that. A license? Those fish didn't follow the *Mayflower* over here! Commercial fishermen should need a license from us when on our traditional fishing grounds!" Locals began to take notice of Peltier's clever words.

Though becoming political locally, Leonard had just opted out of the recent Alcatraz takeover in 1969. The way he saw it, they already had plenty of support, and many took notice worldwide. Besides, he had a business to run and was in that mode. He didn't much care about a show. Not when local Indian fishermen were being beaten in their sleeping bags at night at their own fish camps. Torn-up nets were more important to him than a microphone. Others could do that. What was happening on one reservation was happening on all of them. But the moccasin telegraph mentioned Peltier's name around, and soon enough some Alcatraz Indians made their way to Seattle, including Dennis Banks, who asked to meet Leonard. It happened after he'd joined a group of local Seattle Indians who occupied an old abandoned fort, which put Peltier and his cousin Razor on the radar. Anyone showing skills in security or leadership got noticed. The Indians kept hold of the old fort and turned it into their Indian center. Movie stars came around it, just like at Alcatraz. *They can keep theirs,* Peltier thought, *I got a close-up look at Jane Fonda!* She helped their struggle by making that appearance. Leonard was aware that these city locations brought in a strange new resource to the Indian. A new day had dawned by 1970, as establishment types could and did occasionally weigh in—just not too close.

Two auto bays in what might have been a converted two-car garage have created his small mechanic's shop, and the neatly lettered sign overhead reads Howard and Leonard's Auto. There's oil on everything—the walls, his hands and face, all the paperwork. Leonard is content.

Maxwell House coffee cans hold a good collection of tools, and the driveway is crisscrossed with extension cords. When the lights flicker in the adjacent old shotgun house, the men stop work for a second, then go straight back to it, rain or shine, and in Seattle, there is a lot of rain.

An Indian grandmother is showing Leonard how her grandbaby's feet can get too close to the car's axle because of a rusted-out floorboard. Leonard doesn't say it, but the baby could also fall through a hole that big. Switching between English and her Klamath language, the grandmother is waving her hands and trying to show how the rocks spew in and hit them. Leonard nods, he can fix it, and waves to indicate that there'll be no charge. The young mechanic moves fast.

"Make time for paying customers sometime today, Peltier," Howard whispers. He's a big, tall man with a slumped and oafish gait. Leonard grabs his welding mask and looks up at the little granddaughter standing patiently waiting inside the cold damp house. He winks at her as the rain starts up for real.

Razor, Leonard's cousin, giggles when he notices that the mask is tied on one side by a short piece of rope. Razor is lean and wiry, true, but also razor sharp, always thinking and always talking. He misses nothing, even when you want him to, and he has been Leonard's shadow since arriving in Seattle a few years earlier.

His mom, Leonard's aunty Robideau, had been a wonderful influence during Leonard's young life out west. She is generous, loving, and a second mother to him when he sees her. Aside from his grandmother's home at Turtle Mountain, he is most at home with her. Leonard's mom, Alvina, is a good woman, too, but alcohol had grabbed her, and she is lost to him most of the time. Around Aunty, he feels real family life. He becomes prosperous as a few more years roll by.

Aunty Ida had mentioned the fish-ins often. "It was their land. Their nets cut up in the night. Without proper gear or money for boats, they're still the better fishermen." This permanently pissed off the commercial fisherman downstream by the mouth of the Columbia River as Indians got to the salmon first. Most women and grannies warned their menfolk to stay home at night where it's safe, but theirs sent them out to help.

On this bright summer morning in 1972, Cousin Razor has a plan for himself and his cousin Leonard. "Make time for paying customers," Razor says, always mimicking Howard. Being idle does not sit well with Razor. He is there to urge his cousin to drive with him down to Olympia. Leonard feels a certain obligation toward Razor, but the payback is starting to wear thin after two years.

"You always wanna go someplace, just to go," Leonard says.

"Man, I am wanted in Washington, I told you that. I am not going to just go, last place I should be. Fishing struggle happening. Damn game wardens are monitoring the banks, so Indians can't fish." Razor leans out to knock his cigarette ash far enough away from the equipment, as he stares at the light making prisms in the morning fog. "Goddamn, Leonard, let's go to California then, chase some sunshine."

"No. I'm gonna go help those fishermen like you just said. Not California. What do you mean, monitoring the banks?"

"Well, bro, Indians can't afford boats, ya know, just fishing off the banks, and these cops and rednecks are using wrist rockets to pick 'em off."

"Damn, that's mean as hell. Ball bearings in a slingshot? That can take an eye out, man." Leonard pauses to wipe some oil off his hands. "Well, I got lots of ball bearings myself. Let's go surprise them, we can hide on the banks, too, they'll be behind our people and we will be behind their ass."

"What about California?"

"I'll decide that when I decide that. You'd be gone forever if it was up to you. I better let Howard know I'm going off."

"Oh, he'll be glad, I'm telling ya. He will find another partner in no time and name him Leonard," Razor says, reading the withered news clipping with his cousin's name that is stuck up on the greasy wall. He traces the sentences, pointing to them with the end of a newly lit cigarette.

Leonard gives his cousin a disgusted look. "Hell, you're likely wanted in California. If I get a paying customer, it goes for your damn bail. Way ya go around showing off your ski mask? It's proof how dumb they are that they don't come here and pick you up whenever any filling station's robbed. They do that, ya know. Cops get to like you for things you didn't even do, you get popular enough. You just want to light any ole where, and that's easy for you, 'cause you got nothing to leave."

"I'd rather rob ya then beg ya," Razor says, coolly. He knows no jobs for his like, too much jail time on his record. Once was enough to ruin it. "Make ya fill out this long application and then last question is 'have ya done jail time?' Oughta ask it first. No job for you ever again, bud!"

They let their tempers cool a minute; this is a familiar argument. After a drag or two on his Marlboro, Leonard gives in. "What do they want us in California for anyway? I hear big numbers are flocking off the reservations since Alcatraz. They won't miss the two of us. I'm not a sheep."

"Oh yes they will; Dennis Banks asked for us personally."

"Us? Oh sure, us," Leonard scoffs. "Northwest AIMers, not us."

"That is us! Hey, bro, when the Movement calls, we go. You're the one always saying it, for the people, man."

"Well, I followed over to Arizona last year. Just beating those Navajo right on their own streets! I saw it, and I didn't just watch, either."

"Ha, you jumped in, and lucky you didn't land in jail."

"Those damn ranchers started beating me back." He laughs his hearty familiar laugh. "So, what, I didn't wait till I got home. I joined the Movement over there with the Navajo. Okay, dammit, pack for Olympia. Let's go drop some nets!"

"Pack what? Hell, I'm wearin' it. Let's just go!"

"Hell, Razor, you got a car; fuck, you just *go*! Likely it'll make it at least to the state line without me." Leonard pauses, then relents. "Okay, later tonight, but I'm not promising here and now about California." He pulls down his mask and sparks the welder intentionally close to Razor to make him jump back. Then he starts welding in the new floorboard.

Razor calls out, as he moves to the edge of the sparks flying. "Hey, bro, when you learn to weld?"

Howard supplies the answer, as he's just walked out, "Knew ever since I met him, plumbing, too."

Hours later Leonard goes home for dinner to a small brick house near the shop, where the first thing he does is kiss the baby sleeping in a dresser drawer. The young Indian woman in the kitchen is his latest girlfriend, who has no trouble noticing his mood is off and something is up. He explains that he's going to Olympia and wouldn't be back for a few, as he bites into his sandwich—leftover roast salmon from the night before with some crushed cherry concoction on toasted hand bread. The bread is more like corn pancakes. He eats it up, not mentioning LA.

When tears roll down her cheeks, he jumps up and announces, "We need some milk. I'll go get it!"

Razor picks him up outside and asks, "Did ya tell her?" The girl stands on the porch now, holding the baby next to a kerosene lamp, and peers mournfully their way. "She looks like you told her, but I'm betting you didn't."

"I told her what I always say, I'm going for some milk. I can stand a lot, but not their tears. Besides, I'll be back."

Razor laughs, "Uh, yeah, damn straight you will . . . there's a baby."

Leonard reminds Razor the girl was pregnant when he met her, but he loves children, and loves this little one, who is his baby, even if he isn't. Sure, he'll be back. Maybe he even loves this woman. He thinks of a son nearby that is his; he'll be back for him, too. He means it from the heart, even if circumstances dictate otherwise. It's the times he is in; choices made in minutes shift everything for a lifetime. That said, he still means it and waves a hearty goodbye.

Lately, Leonard can't get out of the way of something pulling at him. He likes to keep things orderly, as much as he can in this disordered world. He left his car keys in the dresser drawer—and he loves that Chevy Impala, which is top-notch clean. *It's a better gift to leave her than I am*, he thinks. And he put a wad of money near the baby in his drawer, just in case something happens to him. On a trip like this, something can always happen.

They swing by the shop for his tools, bumping up the driveway in Razor's rickety green Plymouth Road Runner. Leonard mentions, "It needs some new shocks, ya only had this car a few years." Leonard opens his passenger door and puts his boot out and for a moment it drags along the gravel, the car rolling to a stop. He takes a long wistful look up at the sign he'd painted himself, proud of every bit of it, all built by word of mouth and making a real living. *Oh well*, he thinks, *seems everything in life is just temporary, 'cause it always has been.*

Razor's afraid he might change his mind, but at a moment like this he knows it's better not to try to sell him. Leonard is funny that way.

"Why did Banks ask for us? Tell me the truth."

"Security bro, what else, some big recruiting meeting. It's LA, man."

Leonard hops out suddenly and goes into the shop bay and comes back with a big blanket roll. Razor doesn't need to ask what's inside. Hardware, of course. Leonard leans into the back seat and puts his toolbox beside the blanket roll to keep it from rolling around, then hops back in and says, "Let's go if we're goin."

Three months later, the name Leonard will be painted out, and the shop will become plain Howard's. Leonard will not return to Washington State for over three and half years, and when he does, he'll just be passing through, with a bullet wound in his shoulder and on the run for his life, trying to make the Canadian border.

CHAPTER 12

American Indian Movement Recruiting, Los Angeles, California
Summer 1972

Anna Mae Pictou noticed Herb Powless as he walked in with Dennis. She noted at a glance that he was Oneida and looked striking in his red beret with its dangling eagle feathers. His features were hard, his skin brown and weatherworn, and his eyes carried that stare she'd seen before. His rep was set after that takeover of his own last summer in Milwaukee. He had a few with him, but it was mostly a one-man show.

Anna Mae loved the Movement and anyone dedicated. She herself had survived the blueberry barrens of Maine, rough migrant work as a picker, and she'd had to deal with foremen, always white, who were beyond description. It was as if the barrens' owner looked for the dumbest white man roaming the earth and put him in charge over them. She'd moved on to auto factory work near Boston, joined the Boston Indian Council, and started a "Survival School," having survived boarding school herself, and a bout with alcohol. But this was the work she was born for. She was straight-up crazy over Dennis Banks. Well, who was not? After years of feeling hopeless, his words brought hope, making a real difference for their people of all ages.

Now she was with her own, like-minded and progressive Indians, and given that most tribes' belief systems were rooted in a matrilineal culture, the AIM guys were comfortable with a smart woman about the place. *As long as my smart suggestions can be co-opted,* she thought with a smile. *So what? Let them! Share and share alike!* LA was a fruitful area for raising travel funds, and that's how Anna Mae made herself even more valuable. She'd listen to speeches by night and by day get out on Sunset Boulevard, present folks with authentic beaded chokers and an ample amount of Movement philosophy, and that'd pay for gas for another hundred-mile trek. She made her way to radio stations, and some of the LA elite came her way, and she brought them to leadership.

Some appreciated her, and some did not. "Jealousy is not a word, it's an evil spirit," an elder once reminded her, telling her never to speak it. But it followed her everywhere, and she just learned to ignore it. She was a natural leader and was blessed with both smarts and good looks—luxurious black hair, a small, tight figure, and a pretty face with a smile that revealed joy for life. Some found that combination lethal, and some considered her a prize trophy. She remained aloof and in control, but she was not quite the tough girl she appeared to be. She knew great quantities of Indian history, and kept her truth close. She frequently called her sister and sent small packages to her two daughters back in Nova Scotia. She ached for them, but the Movement called, so she went.

Neither Herb Powless nor Dennis Banks suffered fools gladly, so they let others like Anna Pictou ride front car and take care of the fools for them. Lately, a new bodyguard named Doug Dunham was under her scrutiny. He just didn't seem like an Indian to her, nor an Indian enthusiast, either, or a bodyguard. She'd planned to crack this enigma wide open and make an enemy. It was another way she helped out the leadership, knowing who was who, and more importantly *what.*

The hall was already filling. When new folks walked in, Dennis would call out, "You made it here, bro, hey John T. (T was for Thomas), I sure got lucky!" John T. had called Dennis in to stop a grave desecration in Kentucky, for Pawnee people. John's own ancestors. They'd stopped it, too. Later he would elaborate, "We love being with our own, especially not in some Indian bar." Tonight's speeches would have a businesslike tone. Dennis was well into building a nationwide caravan.

Leonard Peltier had come in with his cousin Razor; they'd been introduced to Anna Mae as "security" for the hall. Peltier had vigilant eyes. She was aware of his dark good looks, but funny thing, he didn't seem aware of them. He wore nice slacks, as opposed to blue jeans, had a cigarette between his fingers, and carried an open bottle of Dr Pepper that he was too busy surveying the room to swig. A beautiful smile lit his face when a friend walked over, and Anna Mae thought he had hands like a piano player—soft, with clean, trimmed nails. Odd for a mechanic. It showed he cared. And it was clear that he liked people.

Razor, one of the Robideaus from a big, well-known family in Northwest AIM, was his shadow. It was a common name. Now in Seattle they were part of the Water People. *Many in that area, Anna Mae knew, came from a big tribe that was reduced to small bands so they could be pushed into Canada, their lakes taken from them. Their fish-ins made the papers; she'd helped with that.* Tonight, they were all together; many tribal reps and purpose permeated the room.

Herb Powless takes the stage first. Two women make fry bread on Bunsen burners at the back of the room. One stops to count heads, then pulls a sharp knife and cuts bread rounds into halves. Fried beef and onions go on them.

"I'm going to prison." Herb's voice rings out from the antiquated speakers. People are still entering the hall from the parking lot; their laughter stops with his words.

"What did he say?" Razor whispers to Leonard. "Hell, don't listen to him! I'm trying to stay out of there. Been, and sure as hell don't want to go back." Razor calls out, to Leonard's dismay: "Wrong destination, pal!"

"Shh. Listen, dammit."

"Yup, you heard correctly," Herb continues, his voice as serious as a heart attack. "Go with me and you'll need to have seen jail time or be willing to. You want to talk? Go talk, follow them other guys. I organized lines for the union in Milwaukee. Put on a chain gang, just home from Korea, went there at age fifteen. I know what it is to fight. You don't talk, and I don't want anyone with me that likes *talk*. You never have a conversation with an enemy."

"At least somebody is willing to do something, finally. So, shut up and listen for a change," Leonard says without taking his eyes off the stage or the man.

Minutes later, Razor calls out "Hey, brother" to Herb's back, as Herb leans to the stage's left and ignores him. That doesn't stop this Robideau. "What are you? Bad River? Chippewa? Greengrass? Where? Hell, if I'm gonna suffer, I might as well do it for my own. We got people from there, right, bro?" he says to Leonard. His cousin doesn't take the bait.

Dennis steps up next, as if Herb has been the warmup act. "What do ya think makes *him* so important?" Razor whispers to Leonard. "Look at the beauties in this room, all got their eyes on him. I have a theory about that, goes back to cavemen. The guy on the mic, or up on the rock as it were, doing all the talking? Well, he ate better. So, all the women want him."

Leonard exhales smoke, exasperated. "You never shut up a damn minute, and I don't notice us eatin' better." Leonard surveys the room, ever vigilant, as Dennis starts to speak. The crowd goes silent.

"Over eighty tribal affiliates have joined the Movement. We grew up listening to our elders talk about the termination of all Indian tribes. The Klamath Nation up there in Washington, and our Menominee neighbors in Wisconsin, have already been terminated, made a goddamn county out of a nation! Turtle Mountain, they tried it, Indians beat it, but they will try it again, for sure."

An Indian woman calls out from the audience, "They can't terminate us; we're standing right here! What do you mean?" Dennis had hoped for this question.

"It means making you live your life with your eyes cast down. When Navajo makes sixteen cents for every ton of coal, that's termination. When they sustain your poverty by lacing you up at border bars, that's termination! Great Menominee woodlands are converted to them! Gone! Terminated! An end to self-governing, and you're done! It means you will no longer exist as a distinct tribal people. And how can that be, when the very bones of our Red ancestors are buried in every corner of these United States?" He's met with thunderous applause.

An angry man who looks Chumash and catches Leonard's eyes says, "You are asking us to stand up against the most unforgiving power in the world!"

"Stand up? You just get up, and *we'll* stand up!" No one interrupts again.

While Dennis continues to speak, Herb heads down the hall to a door that leads to a back parking lot, ignoring Leonard's and Razor's attempts to engage him. They stay in their positions against the wall. A rowdy-looking guy runs up the stage steps, and Dennis extends an arm out to him. If he hadn't timed it right, Leonard might have pulled the guy backward by the shirt. Leonard sees he's obviously mixed blood and pauses to look him up and down. He's getting his first good look at the newcomer, Doug Dunham, who's been hanging on Dennis Banks all night like a bad scent.

Doug's self-dyed black hair is layered over light brown and tied back off his forehead by a leather strip with a few colorful plastic beads knotted into it. It looks like the headband you'd see on a Barbie doll Indian. He is muscle-cut like a military guy and maybe he is one, which would account for his strange manner.

Now that Peltier has seen Doug this evening, he recognizes the type. It's a West Coast thing. For one, he did nothing in the Indian way and didn't really intend to. *Riding on ego, this one. Where'd Dennis find this piece of work?* Leonard wonders, noting that no one knows him or speaks up for him except Dennis.

Doug Dunham is obviously used to being in charge. *And from where'd that be, I wonder?* Leonard thinks. *Better yet, why don't he go on back there? Likely he's been thrown out of his own community.*

As Leonard is thinking this, Dennis steps back in front of Doug and continues speaking to the crowd. Dennis's voice could still the LA traffic outside. He had that way.

Anna Mae walks over to Razor and Leonard and leans against the wall. "How's Frank's Landing lately?" she whispers to Razor.

She had to have asked around about us, Razor surmises, loving the attention.

"How you know where we're from, Miss Pretty?"

Leonard smirks, not so easily taken in, "It's a war zone, that's how it is." Everyone Indian knew about Frank's Landing; Peltier and Razor just came from there. They didn't seem to know it, but Anna Mae had, too. Several made appearances to help the Puyallup fishermen, including comedian Dick Gregory, so it made all the papers and made LA a fruitful area.

"And you took Fort Lawton back last year, far out."

"You shoulda seen bro, he says don't bring so much as even a match, it's a peaceful protest, and then the National Guard kept missing us, we can't get their attention for shit. Leonard lights this little fire, and we have a bonfire!

Got arrested and it wasn't pretty once they got us in the back. But yeah, we took it," Razor confirms.

"We?" says Leonard, eyeing his cousin. "Oh yeah, just us. No. United Tribes of All Nations done it."

"Okay, smart girl, you tell me, who's that?" Razor asks, nodding to Herb, who's still standing alone, leaning against a wall in the back hallway. Herb did not nod back.

"Part of the Iroquois Confederacy. Under the white roots of peace, white-hot Oneida. That's Herb Powless. He was the third chapter in."

"He sure don't look peaceful to me," Leonard says, eyeing him.

"Dennis gonna lead us all the way to Washington, DC," she says, her eyes sparkling at just the mention of his name. "And the Means . . ."

"Shit, that power town? He could get us all killed, too."

She turns back to Razor, a better target. "Ya heard of Mohawks?"

"Hell, everyone's heard of them."

"Well, Oneida are their brothers. They were in what upstate New York now is. Some removed to Wisconsin. Near the Menominee, who were terminated. As far as I'm concerned, we are Tribes of All Nations for good."

"Oh, it's up to you, is it?" Peltier smiles. "My dad's been talking about extermination of the rez since dubya-dubya two. Nothing new. So, what are we gonna do, sit around with a bunch and bitch? I got that back home." He's looking toward Herb as he says this. He knows one thing about the AIMer from Milwaukee: they both hate "just talking" equally. It's a start.

There is an awareness about Herb that catches Leonard's attention, and he wouldn't mind having a word or two with the man.

Razor catches his cousin staring, as Leonard does that rarely, and Razor repeats as if he knows something.

"That's Herb Powless, Milwaukee AIM." Leonard reaches out to grab the arm of a man who has just walked up undetected . . . another asshole who thinks he owns the place. It's a reporter carrying a camera, and Leonard pulls him back. "Don't get too close to the stage, bro, not when Dennis is talking. Wait 'til he comes off." The man seems unimpressed, so Leonard adds, "Don't make me ask you again. Our hall, our rules."

Herb overhears this and looks over at Leonard, then at Anna Mae and Razor. He gives a brief nod and exits toward the parking lot. He takes to the long hallway and doesn't seem to notice a sequence of posters saying *END THE VIETNAM WAR! VOTE FOR GEORGE McGOVERN!* McGovern is the Democratic candidate running against Nixon, from South Dakota. Huey Newton and Cesar Chavez are on the wall as well, in news clippings and other memorabilia.

Leonard makes a fateful choice, one most unlike him. He tells Razor, "Watch things," and follows Herb. Razor says to Anna Mae, "Watch things!" and follows Leonard.

A few Indian women—Pueblo, maybe a few Navajo—are sitting outside, colorful blankets over their heads like shawls. Dr Pepper bottles litter the ground, and some elders are sleeping inside old cars, their legs jutting outside. Cities are not their scene, yet they have come, and from long distances, too. Amazing, the array of different license plates—a few all the way from Oklahoma.

"Hey?" Leonard calls out to Herb and isn't amused when the man doesn't slow down one whit. "Hey ya, bro? Herb Powless!" A little pissed now, he decides to be just as blunt as the man ignoring him. "You truthful in there?"

Herb turns and stops at a mustard-colored Oldsmobile with Wisconsin plates and a sticker that reads Third Chapter In. He unlocks the passenger door and gently sets down the large leather tote he had on his shoulder. Leonard knows there's a weapon in it.

"You really plan to do something, for my people, man? They said Turtle Mountain in there. I'm Turtle Mountain. Chippewa," Leonard says as Herb Powless turns to face him, his fingers hooked into the belt loops over his hips. Then he just stands there, silent and ominous in his red beret. It is an odd standoff. Leonard is real, so he doesn't mind speaking first, unabashed, as he has nothing to hide. Then he says the damnedest thing his cousin Razor has ever heard come out of his mouth. "I'll go," Leonard says firmly, without hesitation or doubt.

Shit, he means it, is Razor's reaction, and he feels like everything has paused, the whole parking lot is one big still-life. It is as if fate froze with it and is waiting.

"I'll go, goddamn it," Leonard says again, softly, with no harshness to it. Just real.

Razor, as usual, speaks up next and out of turn.

119

"Go where? Fucking Milwaukee? Are you nuts, bro? I can't get you to go any fucking where and now you'll go? Shit, man." The pause continues and Razor is ignored. "Why does it always have to be somewhere cold?"

"I don't mind the cold," Leonard answers, looking only at Herb.

"I ain't gonna beg ya, brother," Leonard says, and Razor knows this will be his last word on the subject. Leonard is tough, but also vulnerable and easily offended.

Herb makes a small grin. "Then quit talking and get your shit."

Resolute and yet ready as always to be included, Razor opens his leather-fringed vest and says, "Shit, bro, I'm wearing it!"

Suddenly, three big cars, polished as glass, pull into the parking lot and stop side by side just a few feet from the building's back door. Herb shoulders his brown leather satchel again. Leonard and Razor are already out in front of him as four Black Panthers emerge from two of the long brown Cadillacs.

Herb walks over and steps in front of Leonard and Razor.

"What can I do for you gentlemen?"

"What are you doing here? This is our hall and our neighborhood," says a Panther wearing a black leather beret.

"Yeah, I noticed them posters inside," Herb says, eyeing the car's other occupants. Huey Newton, a prominent Panther, was on a news clipping. It was likely Cesar's people who secured the Indians the hall for the night. Cesar is a migrant farm leader who has a wicked fight on with the state governor, Ronald Reagan, a onetime Hollywood union organizer.

"Not tonight it's not," Herb says. "On loan. And turns out your neighborhood is sitting on Indian land. So, we borrowed both back for the night. Our meeting will be over soon, and it's invitation only, you see?" Two other Panthers step out of the cars. Leonard doesn't move but lets them know he sees them.

"What I see, brother, is you're wearing the wrong color for this side of town. Better take off that red beret."

"I'll wear what I like, where I like." The Black Panther pauses and looks the scene over, parking lot and all. His expression softens, and his voice shows respect.

"Travel out soon, brothers. It's Los Angeles, and not all of it is patrolled by us." He nods to an elder who has stood beside his car. "It'd be better to get on out before it's too dark. Especially with these families." He surveys the parking lot a last time.

"We are night travelers; we wait 'til it's dark. My car there, with the Wisconsin tags, will be the last car in the caravan."

"That so?" The Panther takes a good long look at the three Indian men and then says respectfully, "We'll follow you out, then, to the county line anyway. Good luck to ya." He raises his fist in the air and all three Indians return the salute. There's a new party in town, and it's no longer just a Panther party.

With this one act in Los Angeles, Leonard officially becomes part of Milwaukee AIM. In doing so, he changes his destiny forever, as well as that of many others.

CHAPTER 13

John Erlichman's Office, Capitol Hill, Washington, DC

Summer 1972

"What in the Sam Hill are they doing in Oklahoma? You said Kansas! Now I gotta call off men in Kansas and alert the Oklahoma office. Last minute like this, we look like fools!" exclaims the acting director of the FBI, Pat Gray. He is a man in a bad humor. He's in a tedious audition for a job nobody in Washington wants, especially this year. J. Edgar Hoover, although recently passed, is still in charge, even if not actually present. The sparsely decorated office is heavily fogged with cigarette smoke and an over-flowing ashtray with an untouched tray of sandwiches drying out on a side table.

Brad Patterson is listening, and he's not amused. A special adviser on domestic affairs, specifically Indians (his boss is Leonard Garment, special counsel to Nixon, and it's rumored they were old college buddies), Brad's a liberal in a room full of Republicans and definitely an outsider. Garment plays a mean jazz saxophone for relaxation, and his band includes a young Alan Greenspan, among other political rising stars. Buddies all around, but an odd mix. That was Nixon—all about buddies. Today they've gathered to interview a snitch. "Hoovermen" loved their snitch system, a cornerstone of the agency. They've recently decided to fight all subversives as "a group."

Meaning, if you were a member of the group, it was open season and membership alone made you criminal. It also made the rules relaxed.

The real outsider in the room is their thirtysomething informant known as Doug Dunham. He has been traveling with the AIMers for over a year now and gotten close to the leadership almost overnight. They have gathered today to hear his findings.

This is one of Doug's chances to be heard high up on the Hill, and he has planned to make an impression. He is wearing a hat that's more hippie than cowboy, farmer-style dungarees, and a brown cowhide coat with fringe. He has a strong jaw and a somewhat handsome face. Given Doug's getup, the Bureau men present wonder how he even got in their elevator without being jumped.

"You can't possibly know where they're going, when they don't."

It puts everyone off for this outsider to speak first.

Special Agent Donald Harmon is sitting right behind Doug—the snitch from Texas is his subordinate, though unofficially of course, given that everything about an informant is unofficial. The documents Harmon initials are very official. Agent Harmon is by the book all the way, and Doug Dunham is about to find that out. Those who watch over a snitch are as much a secret as the snitch himself. In such a system, everyone has to feel their way.

Dunham sees Harmon as a type, a clean marine, impeccable clothes, a mirror shine on his shoes, and as straight as a new suburban picket fence.

Just in his early thirties, Harmon keeps his weapons hidden and his manner gentlemanly. He speaks in a soft, clear voice, with just enough curtness to announce that he is used to being the sole decision maker. He has survived two tours in Vietnam and is not to be underestimated. He is of average height, and with prematurely balding reddish-blond hair. He boasts a very clean shave, even at night.

"It's a good strategy, really," Brad Patterson answers, and then he is irritated by that thought, which means the Indians will be impossible to preempt.

"Glad you're impressed with them, young man," says the interim FBI director, "because it seems it's our strategy as well! Who in here knows what the Indians are doing next?"

"It's my job to appear comfortable among them, sir," Dunham explains.

"They are put off by questioning. I wait and I listen. Next destination may be here."

"How'd you slip out for this?"

Doug sticks his thumb out to imply he hitched in.

Good lord, the acting director thinks. *What a strange man, someone on our payroll hitchhiking into Capitol Hill.*

"Don't get too comfortable, you aren't going to be around them long," Harmon says. "Why are we paying you if we've got to guess? We can do that on our own."

Harmon hates working with people from outside the agency and never passes up a chance to express it. He wanted crews he selects, trains, and trusts. This doesn't apply to Dunham, and he's hoping this meeting can present an opportunity to get rid of him. To Harmon's shock, Dunham looks the FBI director in the eye and speaks plainly. "There's no drugs this time, partner; alcohol maybe, but no more than is in this building. The drug war won't fly, sir." Harmon eyes him, incensed.

"They aren't Panthers with your made-up heroin plots. Hippies are attaching to them, sure, but they aren't running anything, and neither are the hang-around lawyers. I'll have to come up with something new if you're going to start raiding their houses, and likely you'll be breaking up a civil ceremony that is highly religious when you do. Good luck when that hits the six o'clock news! And it will." Dunham lets out an irritating laugh as Harmon, his boss, looks on helpless.

"And it will," Dunham repeats. "Some pretty important people already stand with them, and some on this very Hill. Some just feet from us now." Dunham seems to have the gall to threaten Brad Patterson to his face. Everyone present is aware that Brad is the adviser on all Indian affairs, reports directly to President Nixon, and has worked directly with several Indian programs of late, one in Milwaukee. They also deemed him "soft on Alcatraz," referring to that 1969 Island siege.

Patterson looks up from his cigarette. Everyone suspects a liberal of being soft when it came to anything, and Brad exhibits that very tendency when it comes time to deal with urban Indians. He has his reasons and isn't gonna be dressed down by a snitch. President Nixon himself had passed the message to Patterson's boss that he could assist as he liked, as long as nothing embarrassed him. A trip into Washington by an Indian caravan would do that very thing. He must stop it.

Brazenly, Dunham continues, "Let me do my job. Like I said, it's gonna take a minute." He goes to the side table for a sandwich like he's been invited to lunch on the Hill; the very action leaves him standing over them.

"What Special Agent in Charge Harmon is trying to suggest," Patterson says, not the least intimidated, "is that if you travel with them then why don't you steer them some, if they're just guessing anyway? Steer them far away from here."

"Oh no, they are not guessing. It's their system. They get there when they get there. They're on Indian time, and when someone in Oklahoma calls them over to put out a fire, they head toward it and turn away from their original destination, as it were. Kinda have a direction of their own, like a built-in navigator. A go with the flow kind of thing," Dunham explains as he crams what's left of the sandwich into his mouth and pushes his chair in as if to demonstrate he's all done with them.

Incensed again, still, Harmon thinks, *Does he dare think he can just up and leave when he feels like it, without being formally dismissed? This son of a bitch has already been around the Indians too long.*

"What took 'em to Oklahoma?"

"Comanche kid didn't want to cut his hair."

"Didn't wanna do what?" Harmon asks incredulously.

"In jail and they were about to shave him. He fought. Next morning, they found him with his hair woven through the bars, tight. They had to cut it to get him free."

"How'd that fix anything for him?"

"Well, they cut their hair when in mourning, sir. Kid was dead by morning, so I reckon he didn't mind after all."

"Substitute your plan for theirs," Director Gray says. He's thinking that no group like this one has ever come along before. You can charter as many wire-taps as you want, open files, and on review nothing is truly clear or planned out—just like the snitch is suggesting. A plan would sound concrete over the phone, but when it didn't come off as anticipated, nobody got angry or befuddled, not even family members back home. *Maybe they know they're being listened to?* thinks the director. *Nah. They aren't that sophisticated; it is just some strange system of complete trust. Like with well-trained SEALs in combat situations that have worked together so long everyone just falls in. Yet, most of these AIMers just met each other.* This uncertainty is getting to him.

Eventually, he speaks out loud in mid-thought. "It won't last, they're human." He knows to stop overthinking it. He also knows that by giving it too much attention he's beginning to admire them. "They're deadbeats, fringe off a rug, dust collectors. Not planners and not disciplined. They'll give out and give up. So they should be no match for us," he assures, hoping it isn't wishful thinking. Americans' natural liking for Indians could get tricky. It was easy to turn the public against the hippies—all the pot smoking, their appearing unpatriotic with flag burning, their cowardice with draft dodging. And when you took the church part out, people would always look the other way when it came to Civil Righters.

But the word "Indian" conjures up an old fear, something put to rest for a reason, and so there was a romance to it, which nibbled away at the very foundation of what being American stood for. Which came back to mean nobody knew what it goddamn meant, especially him. Snitch Dunham entered his train of thought.

"Boss, they're not like us, man. What's important to us isn't important to them," Dunham says, as if reading the director's mind. "Some of these Indians are eloquent speakers. They don't want a seat at any table, or on a bus, either."

Harmon interrupts. "What in hell does that mean?"

"Means they're dangerous," Director Gray responds. His agency knows Hoover's policies will always loom large. He'd created the Bureau. It is his house, regardless who sits at the head of the table. Recently his house had had a break-in, over in Philadelphia, and the tapes and records stolen by the hippie thieves had proven the existence of the Bureau's system of informants. It made for hazardous work now, and not just for the snitches.

They don't need another Alcatraz, or any other takeover for that matter. And no Indians are coming to Washington, at least not uninvited.

"If it's all a big guess, how can you help us . . . lieutenant, is it, or was it?" Patterson asks Dunham, ignoring the director's point and making his own.

"For one, I have their trust, for now, but it won't last forever. I was a marine corporal, sir. I am also a mixed-blood, but I'm not mixed up about that. I have a little ancestry, enough to pass, but that won't play nice forever."

You won't pass for a Panther, so when this gig is up, so are you, Harmon thinks. They've worked together before, and he knows his tone just seems to amuse Dunham, so he doesn't voice his opinion. Why give him the satisfaction? To Harmon's way of thinking, all cults, especially the armed ones, need to be dealt with by the book—crackpot Jesus-loving or land-loving, they're all the same to him, and this new group is among them. Going soft was not the answer.

"Okay, so we found another spot on the radar of malcontents," the director says, keeping his own counsel. He came to this meeting with just one objective, and that is to make it clear that there was an election year on. No time to be casual. They have enough fires. This is not a pacifist group, or a youth group, and regardless of how eloquent, it is nothing like the late Reverend King. One thing is needed to break this up.

"I want some weapon charges out of this. You've seen them armed, right? Harmon said you live with them now, get that on and we can end this quickly. Before it begins, whatever it is. We don't have to know. Go for what we do know. They're lawbreakers. Whether or not they were before, they are now."

Doug grabs another sandwich and speaks like he's running the meeting. "You'll get 'em, be patient. Most of the new recruits are anything but. Professors and law students, artists, and reservation Indians fresh off the farm, as it were. Maybe stole a pack of cigarettes once. They only have a few weapons kept in a trunk mostly, just to show some line of defense, families are with them. Only Indians get hurt. So far." He laughs, revealing the food in his mouth. This meeting is over, for him, anyway. He, too, has an objective, and he's made it clear to those present: they all need to be in for the long haul. He walks to the door.

Brad speaks up. His Nixon connection makes him the most influential voice in the room and the final say. Even Doug stops in his tracks. "Got a point. We waited it out with Alcatraz, and it worked, whatever you think. We cut off their electricity, moved the hippies out and the press out, and that meant the movie-star Indian-lovers got out. It worked, and over time they took the money we offered and left the island. These will, too."

Doug responds, not smiling. "Hey man, this isn't an island, remember that. It was easy to bottle up Alcatraz, close the docks and control the water and airways. These Indians are on the move everywhere, and not just to cities, either. And if ya ask me, that little Yankton Sioux John Trudell almost pulled it off. He was well-spoken over there at Alcatraz, and I hear he's booked half of the goddamn university tours for these Indians. They don't go away, they just reinvent. And wait 'til ya get a load of Dennis Banks on a mic." He smiles again. This is genuine praise for the Minneapolis Ojibwe, whom he has shadowed of late.

The FBI acting director speaks next, and plainly. "These radicals is what you mean. Stop calling them Indians. Who says they are? They aren't students, most of the leadership are in their thirties and have military tours behind them and were raised in cities. Perception is everything."

"Another reason not to delay this," Harmon says, contributing his first useful comment. He's thinking of the military backgrounds just mentioned.

"Who's admiring them now?" Doug asks, grinning. He is mind reading again, and not doing a bad job at it.

"Be careful with this. Even Nixon's own mother loves them; she says so in her letters to her son," Patterson says. He mimes a preacher exhorting his flock. "Don't hurt the poor Indians! Well . . . they are Quakers," he says with a grin.

"So was Herbert Hoover, didn't make him sentimental," Dunham says, laughing in his obnoxious way. "I think they make erratic choices 'cause they bore easily, as do I." He shakes the crumbs off his hands onto the carpet and starts out the door, the big floppy black hat in his hand dangling its bird feathers. "Like you said, Agent Harmon, I live with them." Reiterating that nothing here is going to end quickly or easily.

"Well, don't get too settled in, because this might disappoint you" is Harmon's parting jab.

Doug lifts his black cowboy hat to his head, waves a phony salute, and goes out. He can't feel more contempt for the men present and hasn't gotten ruffled by anything they've said. He's made his point, the one they least wanted to hear: the American Indian Movement would be around for a while.

Acting Director Gray waits for Doug Dunham to go down the hall, and then they all wait silently for the ping of the elevator before Gray unleashes his fury on Harmon. "Don't you ever bring trash like that into one of our offices again! You hear me?"

"Yes, sir. I apologize, sir. You asked to see the latest, sir. Well, he's the latest." Harmon knows his superior is right. Although he's worked for the agency for years, Dunham has no business in the executive offices of a senior statesman like John Ehrlichman. Harmon burns red-faced all the way through his thin hairline.

The only good thing is that Ehrlichman had not asked to join them, Harmon thinks. Even the executive branch is a bit concerned, or maybe intrigued, by the modern-day Indian problem. No one knows where it could lead. They use obsolete abstracts like the word *sovereignty*. Really? Where? On Manhattan Island? Certainly not on any federal reserved land for over a hundred years.

The notion is comical, Director Gray thought, or poetic depending on who is tossing it around; let the discussion stay in a college classroom, or around a campfire with old fogies, but not near the press corps. That might make it real. And nothing can make it real, or even appear real. That might unearth sensitive operations that exist in many of the country's barren regions across land lines that no one wants reviewed. Not by outsiders, not now, not ever.

Director Gray is ready to dismiss the room. "Let these hippies have their day with their urban Indian malcontents, but don't put out anything that might make it into the *New York Times* or cause someone on the Hill to take it seriously."

He dismisses everyone but Special Agent Harmon, who he singles out with a wagging finger to stay behind, and Patterson, who he can't dismiss. Agent Harmon now considers his own career and the fact that this so-called Indian problem is helping him up the ladder. "Next time, until you know what a snitch is going to say, better to have it discussed first on a park bench over by the Potomac."

"Yes, sir," Harmon replies to his director.

"Who in hell is this character anyway?" Patterson asks, examining the file in front of him. "He knew a few things."

"Where'd we get him?" Director Gray looks at Harmon.

"We didn't get him, sir, he was already here. He's one of ours, well, he has worked for us before. He's out of Texas."

Patterson interrupts as he thumbs through the large file. "His snitch grade is high." Meaning he never turns in misinformation. "From money, it looks like, over in Dallas. Yup, marine, didn't have to tell me that one, a former police officer that got into some trouble. Oh yeah . . . I didn't recognize him with that dirty getup, Douglas Dunham. He spends money like he's from Dallas, and he's spending ours, not Daddy's. God knows, he looks like one of them, doesn't he? And he may be playing us, more than working, I know the type. Doesn't take long before they forget which side they're batting for. It's why they blend in so goddamn well."

"I know a few names here, out of Wisconsin," Harmon says, looking at the file himself.

"I imagine you do, Harmon," Patterson says. "It's why we called you in on this one, Milwaukee's your town. Some real leadership might take hold of this thing and then it's gonna get really expensive and aggravating. It's already aggravating. And for the record, yeah, I like Indians, too, the ones that know their place."

Telling them what they already know, Brad Patterson taps a file photo. "I helped push a grant for one of these guys, this Milwaukee man right here. Impressive as hell, this guy, on the mic and off, and a pretty decent fellow, articulate. Insisted we pay for the alcohol problem we, America, created, he says. He had his facts down and his numbers, and sure, we fast-tracked their grant."

"And you gave him the damn place," Director Gray says, as he lifts his eyes to Patterson. "Might have been going too far." He is referring to an abandoned old Coast Guard station sitting out on Lake Michigan that local AIM decided to reclaim last summer. Officially recognizing the Urban Indians of Milwaukee, and the *New York Times* did get ahold of it.

"It was an experiment," Patterson answers without looking up. "It was all done peacefully. I would like to preserve that." Something in the file catches his eye. "What in the hell was he doing way over in South Carolina on a chain gang? That doesn't sound right."

Agent Harmon checks the file. "Marine training base is over there, sir. Also decorated, Korean theater, sir. Just home, it looks like."

"I can see that. Shit," the director says, yanking the file closer to himself. "He ran a local, a real union guy; and to do that he's a little connected, I'd say."

Harmon knows "connected" means Italians. They're under investigation, too, indefinitely.

Speaking to Harmon but looking at Patterson, the director says, "Close this file for me, sir, and before November? You got RICO now—use it. Less rules with the judges. It's clearly evident they are breaking laws as a group, so you can bust any one of them." The director turns to Harmon, who says casually enough but firmly, "Yes, sir." Everyone walks quietly and quickly out of the office. When agent Harmon finds he is alone, he opens a new file and labels it MILWAUKEE AIM. A photo of Herb Powless in the *New York Times* is stapled inside the file folder, along with pictures of his family and Dennis Banks.

That one directive moved the problem of the American Indian Movement over into the budget for the Counterintelligence Program, COINTELPRO, which meant an open checkbook. The highest ranks had come to a decision, and the smart thing was to say no more about it.

Donald Harmon knew there had been no way to end that meeting on a happy note. Things didn't end because they ended happily. The responsibility sat on him heavily, as heavy as the big dome outside in the distance. He'd leave Washington, DC, with his wife and kids and head to Wisconsin. He loved Wisconsin, and he could visit his mother.

*Big Mountain Lady
(Illustration by Leonard Peltier,
courtesy of International Leonard Peltier
Defense Committee [ILPDC])*

Ghost Dancer (Illustration by Leonard Peltier, courtesy of ILPDC)

*Child In Ceremonial Clothes
(Illustration by Leonard Peltier,
courtesy of ILPDC)*

*One of the 38 (Illustration by Leonard
Peltier, courtesy of ILPDC)*

*Indian Still Life (Illustration by Leonard
Peltier, courtesy of ILPDC)*

Geronimo (Illustration by Leonard Peltier, courtesy of Blue Skies Foundation)

Protector of the Woods (Illustration by Leonard Peltier, courtesy of ILPDC)

Playing a Lover's Song (Illustration by Leonard Peltier, courtesy of ILPDC)

Daydreamer (Illustration by Leonard Peltier, courtesy of ILPDC)

Solitary (Illustration by Leonard Peltier, courtesy of ILPDC)

Spanish Mustang (Illustration by Leonard Peltier, courtesy of ILPDC)

Man with Robe (Illustration by Leonard Peltier, courtesy of ILPDC)

I Was Young Once and Had Many Horses (Illustration by Leonard Peltier, courtesy of ILPDC)

I Was a Young Warrior Once Too (Illustration by Leonard Peltier, courtesy of ILPDC)

Diné Elder (Illustration by Leonard Peltier, courtesy of ILPDC)

Down but Not Out (Illustration by Leonard Peltier, courtesy of ILPDC)

Nalani on Star Quilt (Illustration by Leonard Peltier, courtesy of Blue Skies Foundation)

Snow Maiden (Illustration by Leonard Peltier, courtesy of ILPDC)

Home of the Brave (Illustration by Leonard Peltier, courtesy of ILPDC)

Blue Warrior (Illustration by Leonard Peltier, courtesy of ILPDC)

Micmac Madonna (Illustration by Leonard Peltier, courtesy of ILPDC)

I Shoulda Won That Dance; A Study (Illustration by Leonard Peltier, courtesy of ILPDC)

AIM group shot. Back row, circled (l–r): Vernon Bellecourt, Floyd Red Crow Westerman, Russell Means, Bill Means, Dennis Banks, Clyde Bellecourt, Herb Powless. Front row (l): Dorothy Ninham-Powless (*Courtesy of Photographer, Dick Bancroft*)

Leonard Peltier and sister Betty Ann (*Courtesy of Leonard Peltier*)

Mark Noble Powless on left and on right relative unknown, a brother of Mark Noble Powless (*Courtesy of Cheryl Powless*)

Powless children in Milwaukee; top (l–r): Tony and Vincent "Buddy" Powless, bottom (l–r): Gina, Cheryl, Georgia, and Geronimo Powless (*Courtesy of the Powless Family*)

Peter Grant and Leonard Peltier at Oakalla Prison, British Columbia, Canada (*Courtesy of Attorney Peter Grant*)

Leonard Peltier extradicted from Canada (*Getty Images*)

Dorothy Ninham (l) with elders at AIM gathering
(*Courtesy of Photographer, Dick Bancroft*)

Circled (l–r): Russell Means and Herb Powless at Winter Dam Protest, Wisconsin
(*Courtesy of Photographer, Dick Bancroft*)

Dennis Banks (r) at BIA Building Occupation, Washington, DC
(*Courtesy of Photographer, Dick Bancroft*)

AIM Attorney, Lew Gurwitz, from
Cambridge, MA (*Courtesy of Photographer, Dick Bancroft*)

Sacheen Littlefeather, of the Apache Nation, at the 1973
Academy Awards in Los Angeles, holding Marlon Brando's letter
(*Getty Images*)

Dennis Banks at Winter Dam Protest, Wisconsin *(Courtesy of Photographer, Dick Bancroft)*

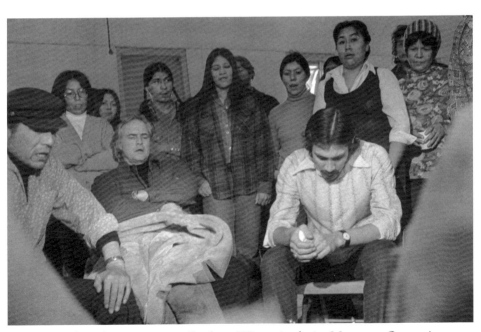

Marlon Brando with Menominee at Gresham, Wisconsin, during Monastery Occupation, January, 1975 *(Getty Images)*

Leonard Peltier, at USP Marion *(Courtesy of Photographer, Dick Bancroft)*

Herb Powless on mic, founder of Milwaukee AIM *(Courtesy of Photographer, Dick Bancroft)*

Three Lakota elders in children's school desks at AIM gathering
(*Courtesy of Photographer, Dick Bancroft*)

AIM gathered, spreading awareness and speaking for the rights of Native Nations in America
(*Courtesy of Photographer, Dick Bancroft*)

Dorothy Ninham-Powless and her husband, Herb Powless (*Courtesy of Dorothy Ninham Family Archives*)

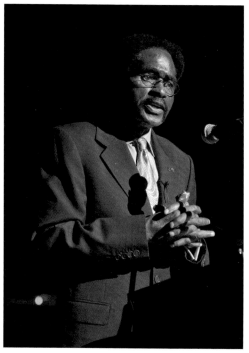

"2012 Bring Leonard Peltier Home" concert, spokesman Rubin "Hurricane" Carter. Concert at the Beacon Theatre, New York City, produced by John Scher for Dorothy Ninham and her Wind Chases The Sun Foundation (*Ebet Roberts/Getty Images*)

Leonard Peltier support rally with Peltier on sign (*Courtesy of Photographer, Dick Bancroft*)

CHAPTER 14

The Powless Home on Third Street, Milwaukee, Wisconsin

Summer 1972

Inside an old Chevy van, not his own, Herb Powless is at the wheel and Leonard Peltier rides shotgun, quite literally. Razor sits behind Herb and next to him is Stanley Moore, a Bad River Chippewa. Another group is tailing them in Razor's Roadrunner. There'd been few stops before reaching the Colorado border. Daylight might chisel away some of the ice from the higher elevations but not by much. Before breakfast, if there is any, the AIMers will be pushing a car or two over the Rockies—a place of summer on the ground and winter at the sky. Horned sheep carry icicles on their whiskers at the tiptop; later this same day it will be a hundred degrees down below.

Leonard doesn't even brace for how the frozen asphalt will feel underneath his back. As sure as where he sits, he'll be under a car before this trip is at an end. He has his tools with him, always: fuel pump, starter, battery charger, muffler. As long as it isn't a transmission issue, they'll all get there. If a problem is sizable enough, they'll be dumping a car or negotiating with a wiseass gas station mechanic for a trade-out for parts. Either way, what comes, they'll get there.

Even as he thinks this, Leonard notices that Herb is pulling over toward a Gulf station, and right behind him, so do about four others in their caravan.

No one is in a hurry to jump out. Every car needs a fill-up, but there is little to no money to spare. Razor opens the back door, saying, "I got this!" A waft of freezing early morning air comes into the car as he exits.

No one else makes a move since Dennis hasn't emerged from his car, not even to make use of a bathroom. Razor comes back smiling, and Dennis's car moves up to the pump first. Everyone hops out, headed for a bathroom or the woods behind the station, or a wall. Cigarettes are purchased and lights passed all around. Razor finally makes his way back to Herb's car holding two steaming black coffees. "They went for it!" he exults in a low, hoarse whisper. "Went for what?" Herb asks, leaving the word "jackass" hanging. Herb doesn't like anybody exiting a car too quickly, makes him suspicious.

"Old trick I used many times, my friend; especially out here, I thought it would work. I told the man inside, with a town sheriff leaning nearby"— having his morning's first doughnut and coffee—"that we were looking for a campsite nearby for about twenty more cars. We wanted to make it another hundred miles, I say, but we were getting too low on gas and needed to go ahead and pull over sooner than expected. Likely we'd just go on into town, camp a few weeks."

Everyone in the car smiles, except Leonard, who says, "You know they hate ya when they'll part with their money to get rid of ya."

Hours later they are in the beautiful Colorado Rockies. Razor has his floppy black hat pulled down over his ears and face. Leonard leans out the window and pushes the ice off the windshield without Herb backing off the accelerator one bit. After a minute or two, he asks Herb, "A chain gang, huh? That's pretty wicked, man. I seen a few things, but nothing heavy like that."

"Well, stick around and you will." Herb puffs on his cigarette like a question had not been implied. "I ain't apologizing, and I ain't interested in talking to anyone who's looking for one."

Leonard smiles, self-assured, and says, "It ain't like that, nobody has to apologize to me for a damn thing, ever. Just making conversation, brother."

"Got drunk and fell through a glass window of a dry cleaners. Old couple were out back, lived there, so called it 'home invasion.' South Carolina, so they marked me as Black and sent me up the river. Pretty usual, nothing heavy about it. They didn't know what I was."

"Still don't," Leonard says. Herb likes his answer, although he doesn't let on that he does. Leonard can just tell.

By the end of the day, they are crossing the plains—farmers, horses, cows, and hay transports. The caravan line is rarely unbroken until finally, another stop is made and AIMers line up to make phone calls back home, and Leonard notices that Doug Dunham has actually talked a convenience store clerk into letting him use her store phone.

A day later they are in Milwaukee. Twilight fades as Leonard notices the familiar purple haze of another city skyline, and the blue hue behind it indicates a big body of water nearby. Then he sees a scratched mailbox marked Powless.

Dorothy Powless is busy moving her children into one back bedroom while she readies for the arriving guests. She has no idea how many, and she hasn't asked. They'll make room for all. The children are used to this, and so is she. Georgia, her oldest daughter, just twelve, peeks out of the kitchen, asking, "Scrambled or fried? Mom, there might be enough eggs if we scramble them?"

The cars start to pull up onto the lawn and parallel park up and down the street. Floyd Red Crow Westerman steps out first, holding the guitar he's carried across his lap for two thousand miles. He dings it a bit on the front stoop. From Westerman's swagger, Dorothy can tell he is drunk.

"Don't worry about it," she answers Georgia, "from the looks of things they won't all be eating. Fry a few and use a lot of grease." Dorothy moves to the front window and is watching the drive when her little baby girl Gina pops up under her arm. "That's a lot of people, Mamma."

"Takes a lot of people to move something."

Dorothy spots something outside the window as her tone changes. "Go and stay in your bedroom with the others tonight, no matter what you hear. Go, go." Dorothy quickly retightens her ponytail and starts to the kitchen, but then something stops her, and her eyes turn back to the window.

She notices that the last passenger to emerge from the car is dressed differently from the others; he is in slacks and a plain black leather vest. He moves differently, too—confident, strong, and sure-footed. He seems to survey the place, looks up at her at the window, and though he doesn't smile, he doesn't lower his gaze, either.

Huh. It's like he's never seen a woman before, Dorothy thinks, having no idea she's getting her very first look at Leonard Peltier. Then Dennis Banks walks in the back kitchen door, and on hearing his familiar, warm hello, she dashes downstairs.

An hour later she shoves a plate of steaming eggs and fried sausage links under Floyd's nose. As expected, he runs toward the bathroom. She follows and lifts his black hat just before he bends over, taking care to flip its dangling eagle feathers inside the bowl of the hat for safe keeping, then she sets it gently outside in the hallway. When Floyd is finished throwing up, she hands him a cool wet washcloth.

He nods a thank you, wipes his face, and says, "I ain't used to anyone looking after me."

"What are ya used to?"

"Well, mainly I take the stage at night, sing a little, raise awareness for the people. Then later, I throw up."

You can't lead Native people without a sober mind, she thinks. When he starts to heave again, she steps back and almost trips over little Gina, who has stationed herself by the black hat and has pried a square of folded brown paper out of its liner. Dorothy takes it from her just as a pair of hands come around Gina's waist and turn her away from the bathroom scene, lifting the hat away from her as he does so, making sure the eagle feathers are still safe inside it.

It's Peltier, and Dorothy is clearly glowering at his intrusion. He hands Floyd a can of tomato juice over her shoulder. "This will help ya out, brother, drink it down fast." He'd put a dash of tabasco sauce inside it, from her kitchen.

"Is it a remedy you use?" Dorothy asks.

"Nope. Never need to."

"You don't drink, then?" she asks, eyeing him.

"Now, we both know that," he answers. Put off with being questioned, he goes back down the hallway. Gina follows him. "What's in that little can?"

"Poison," Peltier answers her.

Floyd drinks it down quickly, never leaving his spot between toilet and tub.

Dorothy opens the square, twice folded, and begins reading the list of names scribbled in longhand across the inside. She stops and flips it over and makes out letters stamped in red and black: Super. The brown paper was cut from a bag from Sioux Nation Supermarket. She then reads the Lakota names: *Debbie Swift Bird, Grady and Hilda Good Buffalo, Samson Spotted Elk, Edna Spotted Elk, Kenny Eagle Hawk, Eleanor Eagle Deer.* "What happened to these people?" she asks Floyd, her eyes deadly serious.

"You don't wanna know."

Gina rounds a corner, miffed she can't spot Peltier. He leaned out from the kitchen, a full plate of steaming sausage and eggs in hand, and yanks her hair. At that moment Floyd can be heard heaving again. Gina looks up at Peltier.

Doug Dunham, leaning against the hall wall, says, "Here comes that poison." Leonard eyes him suspiciously. He stands where he can hear everyone.

Dorothy heads for the kitchen, where she encounters two young women who ask, "How can we help?" The look on sweet-faced Nilak Butler is eager, as she is particularly fond of Dorothy, and the feeling is mutual.

Uncharacteristically, Dorothy responds coldly, "I know who you are, Nilak." She turns to Anna Mae, saying, "And I know who you're not," then goes to the sink as if they'd never spoken. She's seen Anna Mae close on Dennis's arm earlier.

Anna Mae moves out to the hall, bumping into Dunham.

"Who am I not?"

"Betty. Dennis's wife," Dunham offers. He's enjoying her displeasure. She leaves out the door, Nilak with her.

Nilak whispers into her ear, "Dorothy is all about loyalty." And yes, this is cited as a great disloyalty, but they're acting like young girls, because they are. Dorothy Powless, like Herb, knows the pressure cooker they're heading into. It is no place for girls.

Before they left Milwaukee, Dennis asked Herb if he'd change his mind and go with them when they headed to Washington. He gave his usual response: "If it gets heavy, call me. If you're just there to make speeches, leave me out."

CHAPTER 15

The Map Room, Department of the Interior, Washington, DC
October 31, 1972

Dennis Banks's car is near the head of the caravan, and even the DC police are staggered by the number of cars following. Usually, Doug Dunham never leaves Dennis's shadow, but today he's in the next-to-last car. No one has noticed or cared; there's far too much else going on. Kola, a Lakota, is crammed in with Dunham in a yellow Volkswagen. "Damn, almost everything is closed, shop after shop," Kola comments. "I thought they weren't expecting us?"

"That ain't why they're closed, friend, this is just an old, fat, southern town; they just call it a city. Don't plan on doing any lifting while you're here, they roll up at dark." Dunham laughs. Kola is not amused and looks forward to being back with his own as soon as they've parked. This guy has a haughty spirit, and nobody needs that today. *Besides,* Kola thinks, *how does he know so much about it?*

"A funeral for a dignitary has fewer cars!" says a watching DC cop. "Locked bumpers and still coming." It's obvious from the big crowd welcoming the caravan that somebody has planned all this, just no city official.

141

"Where in hell does that old codger think he's walking to?" the same cop asks, noticing a tall, silver-haired Indian man dressed in buckskin and heading toward a freeway embankment. "He can't climb over that!"

"Anywhere he wants to, I guess! Maybe looks like it's Arlington Cemetery?" Answering his partner, while leaning over from the driver's seat of the patrol car to get a better look.

That's exactly where Lakota Ray Two Elk is headed. He'd promised a neighbor back home that he'd visit his son, recently lost in the A Shau Valley in Vietnam. They'd up and buried him there, with honors, since his parents, being in a remote part of Pine Ridge, had been too hard to find. They weren't notified of his death until after burial. Two Elk could be relied on to give him a good visit and a decent Lakota send-off.

DC has been caught off guard. The police, all fifty patrol cars full, finally get the notice they've been waiting for. Chain of command sounds the alarm up past the desk of the Commissioner of Indian Affairs, to the desk of the United States Deputy Secretary of State, and then back to the Department of Interior. Of course, the Department of Justice gets wind of things first off and scrambles like jets.

"Who in the hell do they think they are?" is a common query from DC cops.

"Well, sir, Indians," is the common answer.

"What Indians, and from where?"

"Plates say Idaho, Massachusetts, Wisconsin, New York, and Texas even." From everywhere, it seems.

"What Indian is there left in Texas?" Turns out there are tons of Indians in Texas. Who knew? A North Carolina plate then passes by them, as well as one from Arkansas, then Illinois, then Illinois again. "Hell, fifty cars strong and counting!"

Nothing the caravan does is by the book: no real permits and no clearances of any kind. No parking permits, either, as those weren't readily available. Worse, no housing, because no one has given anyone in authority in Washington a straight answer about that yet.

Over in John Ehrlichman's office, commands are buzzing.

"Where in hell is Dunham? I'm gonna wring his neck with my own hands!" fumes the acting FBI chief.

"Sir," Harmon says, "he was relieved of duty an hour ago." Harmon had just spotted Dunham in the crowd and it looks to him like he is hiding. Harmon had pulled his index finger across his throat when Dunham catches his eye. He just leaned out of a rusted yellow Volkswagen and hooted for a minute before giving his boss the middle finger. Harmon liked to think he would get lucky and see that snitch arrested before the day was out. Unfortunately, the system gave his kind more protection in the great wide open than it gave someone else under protective custody. Maybe Harmon would get lucky and catch him in a face-off during a riot. *Likely we'll see one little riot out of all this.*

Through the window he spots a tall man in full regalia walking with a staff. "Christ," he says through gritted teeth, "how's it gonna look on the news tromping over the likes of that figure on our city's street?"

"Don't go near him, young man, unless it's to salute. I passed him walking in. He brought his medals on him—European theater, Battle of the Bulge, just for one."

Harmon looks to his new recruit, a young, handsome, very tan Californian named Ronald, nicknamed "Ronnie" early on. Agent Ronnie is literally running to Harmon's side when the director's voice stops him cold.

"Did you just notify me, Harmon, that you finally spotted our illustrious snitch? Our Texas man, you know the one?"

"Sir?"

"Yeah, I thought that's what you'd say."

Director Gray turns and addresses the newly arrived Commissioner of Indian Affairs, Louis R. Bruce. "And what do you have to say about all this, Mr. Bruce? You told me not to take this seriously. How did you, dammit man, miss a hundred cars on a freeway! Sir?"

"I didn't believe they'd show. They never talked like it was real."

"When *did* you start to believe it? Believe it now?" says the bewildered director. He directs his attention to one of his own.

"Harmon, we have a few giving us intel on them, and they are gathering over on New Jersey Avenue next," the director says staring at the ashtray. He looks up and fully vents. "Do not let one car get close to Jersey Avenue! Not one goddamn Indian car. Stall them, tell them we are going to help them out, find places for them. Shit. Do it now! A church let them sleep on the floor and pews night before. Hope they'd turn around and head back out. What do they think they're gonna do on *Jersey Avenue* anyway?"

"Hold a press conference, sir, I saw it on this flier."

Harmon holds out the flier and the director unceremoniously rips it from his hand. There's a hawk in flight above the heading, and though the words mostly end in exclamation marks, it is otherwise professionally done.

"For godsakes, Indians with a copy machine. I bet press have already been alerted. Am I the only one in this office that knows there is a president being reelected this week!? This . . . goddamn . . . week! Only grace we got going in this deal at the moment is the fact he is soon out of town campaigning. So, move them right back out of the city by tomorrow, the next day at the very latest, and I don't goddamn care how! I better hear it's happened, or I am going over to Jersey Avenue myself! Now you can run along, agents!" he says, not noticing the forlorn expression on special agent Ronnie's clean-scrubbed face.

As Harmon and his new recruit take the big boss's order and begin to exit, the main door opens toward them. The air fills with tension. As United States Attorney General Richard Kleindienst walks in, they almost expect him to say *boo*. "Good God," is Harmon's reaction as he backs back into the room, pulling Ronnie with him.

The AG looks quiet, official, and if he snapped his fingers, they would have all scurried out like mice—all except the FBI director, who likely called the AG in. They file quietly out of the main room. Surely, they all have work to do on the street. Harmon remains there with young Ronnie.

"When is this ours, sir?" asks the head of the DOJ unceremoniously.

"I imagine it will be turned over as soon as our president hears about it, sir," the interim FBI director replies. "I'm hoping that buys us all a little time, for everyone's sake. It's a lot of civilians, sir, and we have a long night ahead of us, and the press will eat this up with a spoon. You get my meaning?"

"Yes, sir, I do. But we don't have time and my people will handle any fallout you don't deal with, starting now. While they are still on the street, I guess we're running a tap on every phone they might use. Keep me in every conversation going forward. Special Agent Harmon, good to see you here, sir."

"Yes sir, see this, sir," Harmon says, handing him the press release. The attorney general reads the title out loud, "*The Trail of Broken Treaties*. Well, good God, what in hell does that portend, ya reckon? My guess is they are here to send a message, not just to sing songs and picnic in November. It's just a matter of how and where. I'll send in a woman I trust and get back to you." With those words, spoken softly through clenched teeth, he kicks out a chair, sits down, and dials on the rotary phone. The conversation is muffled. The others in the room try to look busy. Someone mutes the TV that is blaring Nixon's expected welcome to Chicago in three days.

As the DC officials continued to discuss the big mess down on the street, it was growing cold outside and the issue of housing loomed large. Trail of Broken Treaties organizers, of which there were many, were just hearing the Bureau of Indian Affairs had nixed their plans, contrary to what they'd been promised. Dennis Banks was livid when he heard about a memo out of the Department of Interior signed by its director telling people not to help them. Hank Adams, a distinguished Fish War leader from Northwest AIM, warned Dennis it would be best if he negotiated; without Herb available it was a good idea. Hank impressed the government reps, white and Indian. Though Hank was a talented negotiator, he knew it was true that others were being asked to rescind all help to the caravanners, even if it'd been promised, churches, all government Indian organizations, even their own National Congress.

How were they going to feed the several hundred people already in DC and the many more still coming in? Dennis thought. Likely a thousand by morning, maybe two all told.

Banks and the Bellecourt brothers scrambled and did some pretty fine talking, and soon Commissioner Bruce started making big promises, the first being that they could stay in the Department of Interior building, at least to get out of the cold. Dennis did mention to him that Marlon Brando was threatening to come in and take over the microphone. He'd actually shown up in Milwaukee—until he realized the Federal Marshal's bullets weren't going to be Hollywood issue if they started flying. Likely he'd sit this one out. *But the BIA Director doesn't know that*, thought Dennis. He was desperate.

At this point, the local Black community were the only ones chipping in anything to help, but they could only provide so much. A kind and efficient Black minister, Reverend Greenly, formed a soup line, and the women Indian elders pulled out their Bunsen burners and were soon flipping some fry bread back and forth to go with hot soup. "They brought their own flour," the Reverend said in relief.

Leonard missed Dorothy's cooking; he missed her, too. She joked that they'd have to take diet pills with them to DC, since the women weren't doing the planning. Herb had recently put her in charge of a skeleton crew at the Coast Guard station house; Peltier was part of that crew. Milwaukee was a good practice run for Leonard for this DC trip. He'd recently stepped in front of Dorothy during a protest in Milwaukee that turned into a riot. She kindly reminded Peltier she could take care of herself, to which he replied, "It's me I'm looking out for, lady, for if they hurt you, I'm gonna be all over this street!" She let him stay. On those words she locked arms with Leonard. Stanley Moore, on her other side, said, "Limp, Dorothy, and they won't hurt you, they'll just go ahead and arrest you," to which she answered, "I can't be arrested, I'm working third shift tonight!"

Dennis knows a drastic move is needed in Washington and sends Leonard over to the Department of Interior to check out what Commissioner Bruce has offered for lodging. A young Potawatomi from Missouri Band, Henry Wahwassuck, flanks Leonard, as does Razor. Peltier knew Henry from the Wahpeton boarding school. Henry's silver-haired mother, Josetts, tries to join them. Instead, she's pulled aside by a *Washington Post* journalist. Her words make more papers than the Twenty Points. She mentions that more than two hundred and fifty tribes are represented as she spells her nation's name for him, twice. She also spells out their troubles.

Leonard eyes Razor with an expression that says, *Move it pal, let's go!*

Razor grumbles back, "Go? Where is this Department of *Interiors*? Get a street map, Leonard. This ain't my town."

Leonard shoves Razor's shoulder, saying, "There, there's my direction.

Move! The town ain't that goddamn big—hustle, man, ask somebody, people are cold!"

Leonard is glad to have Henry along. He was tough and stand-up all the way—the man to have in a brick-throwing contest, and likely they'd see one before this was over. As big a pain in the ass as Razor can be, he is also dependable if times turn tough. He is also glad the Bellecourts are here. They'll all lock arms before this day is out.

Dennis and Anna are busy holding a short press conference at which Dennis describes the "Twenty Points" document they plan to deliver to the White House, as Anna Mae and others hand out fliers. People on the street hand them food and money. Chief Billy Tayac, a hereditary chief of the Piscataway Indians from along the Chesapeake Bay, was closest by and waiting for AIM's arrival, as he is AIM and often opens his land to visiting tribal people, but no one expected such a huge turnout.

Over at DOI, Razor spots the giant buffalo on the agency's shield and says, "Well, here's the place, bro!" They go to the door, Leonard first, as always, but it doesn't open. Leonard tries it again; the door is jammed tight.

Leonard sees movement inside and yells, "Hey! Hey you! I see you!"

No one has told the staff inside that they are hosting a group of Indians for the night. Seeing the three men outside, they lock the door and are hiding, except for one secretary who moves the curtain aside to take a look. Anita Harjo, now forty-one years old, matronly with short permed black hair going silver at the temples, takes a peek. Her shift has just ended when the call comes in from her immediate boss telling them not to implement Commissioner Bruce's directive to "welcome the Indians." He is across town, so Anita's boss makes the decision to bolt the doors and wait until he returns. The three urbans outside the doors, looks to her to be two Chippewa and a Potawatomi, they just look rough to his boss's city eyes. His tone implies there might be trouble. *Beautiful trouble*, Anita thinks.

Anita lets them decide, even though she doesn't agree, but she's learned that she has no power. Given her after-hours drinking problem, she has little power anywhere these days, and she's learned to just obey and go with the flow. *Still*, she thinks as she steals another peek, *all Indian people have heard about AIM.*

Leonard Peltier and the others leave the vicinity of the DOI about as fast as they got there. Leonard doesn't have any patience with disrespect, and he's heading toward New Jersey Avenue, where Anna Mae and Dennis are supposed to be waiting, following the press conference. But they've already headed over to C Street, where Bruce has promised use of the famous Map Room for the night. Located in the basement of the DOI, it used to be a game room for presidents' families, with pool tables and bowling alleys and couches. And a TV. Dennis has seen a reporter or two at the press conference and is eager to see if there's nightly news coverage. Reporters will have a lot of dead time with the president headed out of town, which could work in AIM's favor. Russell Means runs into him and joins.

In the middle of C Street, Dennis almost collides with Leonard, who is running toward him with Henry Wahwassuck on his heels and Razor just a little behind.

"It was all a trick, Dennis, they locked the door against us!"

Dennis is not buying it. "They said we had the room for the night. These people are cold, Leonard. The man was serious!"

"I'm just telling you what I know; I didn't get to debate it with anyone. They wouldn't come out. We knocked. We called. Nothing. And the curtain moved, so they knew. It was all a trick." Leonard scans the streets around them, not knowing what might be brewing. Russell's head turns with his.

Dennis is well aware that hundreds of Indians have followed them from the press conference, and he leads them all straight to the Department of Interior, home of the BIA. Kola suddenly comes running up along with Doug Dunham, who steps in front of Dennis and whispers that he has gotten a surprise offer. Dennis smiles, but those who know him are aware that it's not his good smile.

"They have us a place!" Dennis says. "The man came up to Doug here and made an offer. Nice big place, too, will fit all of us. Hot showers are waiting, and food for all, and cots and blankets. They want us out of the city for the night, and we need to head on over to the stadium."

Russell Means's voice rises. "Redskins Stadium? Fuck no to that offer!"

Doug waits, on edge. Then Razor hands Dennis a piece of paper, a memo. At the top of the letterhead is the Buffalo insignia from the DOI. The director is its author. It is asking all churches and Indian-affiliated groups to rescind help to the Trail of Broken Treaties caravanners, if they have offered sleeping accommodations. Dennis is fuming, and now he's holding proof.

Leonard says his usual: "Tell us what to do, Dennis, and we'll do it."

Dennis scans the tall building and says, "They don't get it. They just don't want to. We didn't even plan to visit here. What's here for us? Not Indians."

Doug takes his shot and says, with a hint of desperation in his usually cool and calculated voice, "Dennis, man, don't think it!"

Simultaneously, Dennis says, "Let's go in this building."

Just as he speaks, the commissioner opens the doors as if they were expected. He leads the large group down into the Map Room, into the big basement. No one but the commissioner knows a riot squad is forming next door on the roof.

Once all the AIMers are in the Map Room, the doors are unexpectedly locked, trapping them inside. Then they do precisely what Dennis knew was likely an inevitability just an hour before, and the Indian AIMers take the building.

CHAPTER 16

Sleeping Accommodations in Washington, DC
Early That Same Evening

In the next minutes, they have broken windows and are no longer only in the Map Room, they are all over the whole building. Then the commissioner himself unbars the main entrance doors. They open easily and two hundred Indians, for starters, just walk in. Now that Clyde Bellecourt and Russell Means are in the building, Dennis gathers them up for a talk with Commissioner Bruce, whose first words are, "We can't accommodate all of you! We don't have room! These are offices, not a hotel! And a president is getting elected this week! Don't you people own a calendar?"

"We own yours now, pal," Clyde says, turning the man's small desk calendar around. After licking the lead end of a pencil, he scribbles something on it.

"I'm sorry, there's just no room or sleeping accommodation here."

"Well, you're leaving, it'll make room for one more," Dennis says. "We just took care of the sleeping accommodations ourselves. The ones that you promised me would be no problem, when I first called you. Send out for some food real quick, too, as we are your guests. Indian hospitality, if you recall what that is."

"You think you're staying the whole night, all of you?"

"No, the whole week." Clearly, this bureaucrat still isn't getting the picture. "We don't have the means for this."

Almost on cue, Russell Means steps in with his brother, Ted. Dennis smiles for real this time. "Oh, we brought our own Means. Go!"

As the commissioner stands up, Anita Harjo comes in with three boxes of files. She eyes Dennis speculatively. He doesn't recognize the middle-aged woman with dark circles under her eyes as he moves to relieve her of the files. She hesitates to give Dennis the one on the bottom and is reaching to take it back when the commissioner speaks up officiously. "People have been waiting months on what is in those files so they can get their lease checks. I'll have to take them." Anita pulls back on the box.

"You're not taking a goddamn thing but your ass out of here" is Russell's reply.

Dennis glares at Russell. "I'll protect those and leave them right here, or better yet, we will get them to the proper persons. Go, we are letting employees leave."

Dennis takes all three boxes, knowing somehow the matronly Indian woman wanted him to, or she would not have made a point of coming into the room with them. He doesn't notice at the time, but on the bottom is a separate file stamped Termination Policies and another labeled National Sacrifice Areas. Anita Harjo leaves the building, purse in hand, carrying another file containing many of the lease checks destined for the waiting Indians, but was not able to get all. Indians were at the mercy of the BIA to collect lease money for their lands; rarely did much of the money collected trickle down to its Indian owner. That said, those waiting for these checks were usually desperate to get them. Reservation land was leased at BIA discretion, often with ninety-nine-year automatic renewal policies attached, then the BIA "managed" the money.

At Bruce's desk, Dennis makes his first phone call. "Long distance, please, Milwaukee," he tells the operator. When Herb Powless answers, he says into the phone, "It just got heavy. Ya coming?"

Herb replies, "Yup." A man of few words, so they count.

Dennis Banks had dialed the Powless home from the desk of the Commissioner of Indian Affairs, Louis R. Bruce. When it rings, Dorothy and Herb both spring out of bed and head for it in a dead run. As usual with middle-of-the-night calls, all their children cluster around, Georgia holding the baby. Herb picks up with his typical late-night greeting, "Yeah?" Next Dorothy hears him say, "Yep, uh-huh. Okay then," before he hangs up.

"It got heavy" is all the explanation he gives before a quick kiss on Dorothy's forehead. He heads toward the door to her black '69 Charger.

Dorothy starts toward the bedroom to pack a duffel for him, but doubles back to the phone, all six kids in her wake. "I'm gonna line up a lawyer," she calls out to Herb. Georgia repeats this, as Herb can't hear her with his head inside the car's open trunk. She means she's going to call Lew in Cambridge and try to coax him onto a jet. They'd made a habit of talking under the trunk lid, as they guessed their home was bugged by the white van that was a constant presence on their street.

"Go lawyer shopping; gonna need a senator!" Herb responds.

Again, minutes later, in the backyard, Herb pulls his pretty wife's face toward him softly and in the old familiar way.

"Don't let anything in that town scratch my Charger," she says.

"Ain't you worried about something scratching me?"

"No. You don't scratch as easily." Dorothy kisses him back, but quickly.

Herb booked it past the old Coast Guard station boathouse and then out toward the state line, gunning the Charger's engine and loving the sound of speed. He'd spend most of the trip reminiscing about how he and Dorothy first entered the decaying old Coast Guard station on the edge of Lake Michigan, still buzzing over this recent takeover. They'd held on to it for over a year now and had recently been granted its official land title. Third Chapter of the American Indian Movement had land returned, and the city mayor, governor, and White House had all complied. Treaty land! Urban Indians were recognized by Washington.

Herb had just peeled back the rotting wood panel covering a door in the station when Dorothy's scream brought him running toward the big kitchen.

She'd simply walked in the back door, no key, and just discovered that the stove worked, after all these years. "God, woman!" was his exasperated reaction. *Well, she had over a dozen Occupiers to feed.*

The Powless children started bringing in the groceries. They hadn't been there an hour before federal marshals showed up. Herb literally shooed them away like flies while informing them that the American Indian Movement was now the building's legal resident by order of the Third Chapter In, of Milwaukee. He then handed them the relevant treaty language in a letter addressed to the city's mayor. Later, it became real—the land was returned on Washington, DC's orders. All Herb had done was simply refuse to leave and then successfully negotiated all the way to the top levels. Earning the respect of the top Nixon aide hadn't hurt. They'd proved themselves to Brad Patterson with the alcohol program, and Dorothy knew immediately that the station house would make the perfect halfway house for the Indians in recovery. Peltier loved the place at first sight and had recently put in a game room, and Herb's own sister, Marge Powless, moved her Indian school over from her flat and added a language room. Leonard loved teaching the kids and families how to sport a tipi out back, and he coached softball, and one day he walked in and said, "Look at this!" It was a punching bag a Panther had donated. "Our Indian boys will love it!" Leonard scoffed at the people from AA when they came in. "Hey, we got our own counselors, medicine people; besides, why be anonymous, ya lay drunk out in the street and everybody knows your name! Now ya wanna hide it? Damn mister, be glad they know ya now! We'll do it our way!"

AIM used the center and sobered up first, and a zero-tolerance policy was laid down. And while Russell Means was not crazy about the idea, they all voted for it and obeyed it. If not for sobriety, likely there would never have been an AIM.

"Dorothy was right about that, ya can't lead Native people without sober minds, and it all started in Milwaukee," Leonard loved to say with real satisfaction as he hurried to open an Indian Employment Agency out of the AIM Office. Some good had indeed come from the Herb-Brad-Nixon connection. Little did Peltier know, it had also made all of them in Third Chapter an especially hot target.

Herb's destination is 1849 C Street, Northwest, in downtown Washington, DC, home of the Bureau of Indian Affairs. To most all Indian people in the United States, it is unlovingly referred to as the BIA.

The minute he crosses into town, he finds a phone booth and calls his Washington contact. He's put right through to Brad Patterson.

"Come on over and let's talk, have a powwow, as you like to call it," Herb said, hating the expression. It reduces a rather large, complicated event into a few minutes' coffee-break expression.

"Herb, that just isn't possible, can you get away and come here?"

"No." Herb has no intention of leaving the occupied building once he gets over there and gets inside.

"What can I do from here, then? In exchange for you leaving and taking every single goddamn Indian out of this town with ya?"

"First off, we want to give our Twenty Points directly to you, and from you to President Nixon. No go-betweens on this one."

"I don't know that I can promise that. If you hadn't taken that building, maybe, but I might not get over the Berlin Wall myself, if you get my meaning."

Herb gets it. "Berlin Wall" is an inside joke between them referring to the German surnames of John Ehrlichman and H. R. Haldeman, who guard access to the president. Months earlier, a government building break-in had only tightened the security on who reached the president and with what. Even adviser Brad finds the door locked against him of late.

Brad ends the call, "You know me, Herb, I'll do my best."

Herb takes his last shot. "And you know me, sir. Ask the president to turn back termination on the Menominee and just read the points. That's the deal."

"Menominee? In Wisconsin? Oh, sure, sure. I'll try it. Be safe over there and exit town soon, Herb. That will impress us more than words. You're good for that."

Dennis honestly hoped it would be a welcoming affair and they'd all sit down on Capitol Hill together. Herb knew enough about Washington dealings to feel sure that was unlikely. He hoped their speeches would go well and they'd get press. But most of them were naïve about Nixon's liking for Indians and underestimated his policies, which had as many layers and tunnels to them as their town.

Another little matter was the recent Watergate break-in. Nixon's hair was already on fire. And now Indians were on their own. A bunch of upstart urbans with hundreds of reservation Indians in tow wouldn't get a welcome mat, far from it. Nixon turned it all over to the DOJ.

Herb parks Dorothy's Charger in a lot at a Black church and leaves the keys with the minister's wife, where he knows it'll be safe.

Then he flags down a Yellow Cab driven by a Jamaican working the grave-yard shift, his hair wrapped a mile high in dreads and his cab full of pot smoke. There is great reggae music blaring from rigged speakers. When they turn up C Street and stop at the Department of the Interior, the driver peers at the scene in disbelief. Up on the roof is a big colorful tipi. Fire is coming out of a barrel next to it. "Ahhh," he says. "Beautiful, man. That is remarkable ...beautiful!"

"This is the place," Herb says, tossing three dollars into the front seat and getting out. "Hang loose, my friend!" the cabbie says and sputters off. Herb finds the building's main entrance strangely quiet and raps his knuckles on the front door. Leonard sticks his head out and then pulls his Third Chapter leader inside.

"Shit, Herb, you just walked right up here?" Leonard says, looking left and right. Leonard had Stanley Moore at his side; Herb knew him of course, the Bad River Chippewa from Milwaukee. They had both been appointed security detail by Dennis.

"I shouldn't have been able to," is Herb's terse reply. "Well, you took a building, now let's see how long you can keep it."

They wouldn't want to keep this one, Leonard thinks. Half the vintage maps in the Map Room have *War Department* stamped on the back of them. From the rooftop they've watched the riot squad gathering forces since the take-over the day before.

"Where in hell did you get that tipi up on the roof?"

"Oh, uh, Razor and Kola liberated it from a display."

"Well, get those guys to lie down up there. Snipers on the roof next door."

Leonard heads for the back stairs, with Stanley on his heels. Herb goes to find Dennis, likely in the commissioner's office.

From the roof, Leonard can see that the riot squad is on the move up the street. He grabs Henry and Razor and orders the others to go downstairs and create a bigger barricade at the building's front door. He tells Kola to find Crow Dog and Dennis and get them back to the Map Room and stay with them. "Tell them trouble is coming pronto! Stanley, tell everyone else out into the street." He meets Herb on the way back down the stairs, and they run together, Herb voicing what Leonard already knows. "Take the fight as far from here as you can. Protect this building; now we're in it. So are a lot of families."

Leonard gives Henry and several others their instructions: "Get right up into their faces. Look them in the eyes, too, don't take your eyes off theirs." None of them have ever faced a riot squad in gear before. They listen to him carefully. "Keep your cool now, just run them off."

"Why get so close to them, Leonard? Maybe they'll see us and back off?"

"No. They ain't marching down here to back off! Up close they can't get a good swing in and hit ya with those clubs they got. Protect your head and your nuts." Henry Wahwassuck makes an up and down gesture like a windup toy that makes everyone laugh. Then they stop laughing, lock arms, and move out as a unit. Leonard notices Henry is wearing a blue wool Seventh Cavalry cap. "What? I took it out of a display case."

Herb has joined them and he calls out, "You got fists, so use 'em. You ain't hippies. Protect the men and women inside this building!" Then he joins on the opposite end of the line.

The Indians do as they've been told, moving right up to the riot squad and staring them down hard. Half of the squad look like kids under those heavy plastic masks. Pasty-faced, well-fed city boys not used to having anyone fight back. They are facing seasoned rez and city Indian men, hardy from city work or bronco busting and ranching and walking a hundred miles a week. *Herb's right*, Leonard thinks. *We aren't hippies.*

The DC squad is facing something new: people with a cause they are determined to defend. In a matter of minutes, they literally chase the police back up C Street, and the AIMers aren't even armed. They hit a few in a hard fight, fast, which gets the message across. Lew Gurwitz about loses his breakfast when he hears it on the AM station in Boston. His phone is already ringing—it's Dorothy Powless. Lew assures her he is on his way.

After facing their first riot squad, Leonard, Razor, and Henry sit down on a stoop out of breath. Leonard notices Henry's face has blood on it. Almost motherly, he quickly cups his head and looks for the source of the bleeding. Then he pushes his head back and says simply, "Go wash that off." It isn't Henry's blood.

Dennis is busy going through files and has picked many of them up off the floor.

Herb is busy knocking occupiers' heads somewhere inside the building, as someone had thought it smart to bust up the toilets. He is a little put out with Vernon Bellecourt and says, "Damn, half of them in here are whiter than you, Vernon! Are you letting any wayward fuck just walk in here?"

Dennis speaks up for the defense. "They've been joining us since the streets. And a lot of employees were already in here, they stayed, and we couldn't tell who was who. We needed to lead the workers out or they were going to charge us with kidnapping. Hell, half of them stayed. The commissioner stayed!"

Vernon is not backing down from Herb. "Some good people in here, man. It's not our way to say go. Shit, Herb."

"Our way just changed with that riot squad up the road, notice that?" Herb addresses Kola and others who are standing by. "Listen to me now. Line everyone up, and anyone we don't know is leaving. Or separate them out to another side of the building and put a security line of who we do know between them."

"How can we tell?" Kola shrugs, as there are hundreds inside.

Herb grabs a young guy by the back of his T-shirt and asks, "You are what?" The boy answers, "Navajo." Herb says, "Say something in Navajo." He answers, "Yat-ta-hey."

"You'll do. Figure it out, man." He let go of the boy's T-shirt. "Take him with ya!" Then he stops another man, wearing a necktie. "What about you?"

"I brought my students by to see the new Native Embassy, they just mentioned it on TV. I just happened to be in town with them. I'm Kiowa, dad's side, mom is Comanche."

"Ya ever been in a fight before?"

"No sir, not one, this will be my first. I'm a civics professor at U Denver."

"Hell," Herb says, grinning, "I'm locking arms with this man!"

"Where's Crow Dog?"

Dennis points to the stairs that lead to the Map Room, where Leonard Crow Dog is busy planning a naming ceremony. Herb heads straight to the roof instead.

Hours later, Lew Gurwitz arrives at the front door, and Doug Dunham tries to shove him back outside until Peltier catches him. "Hey brother, back up! I know him! Lew, good to see ya, man, Dorothy got you here quick. Come with me." Clutching his briefcase, Lew stays close behind Leonard as Doug Dunham, unnoticed, leaves the BIA building and heads up C Street to 935 Pennsylvania Avenue—FBI headquarters.

CHAPTER 17

Snake Dancing Across the Potomac
November 7, 1972

"Where did you say?" FBI Director Gray asks Doug Dunham as he hangs up on his phone call to Brad Patterson. "Why in hell would they go there? There's nothing to take over, just one big graveyard!" He is referring to the only feature of note he can think of at Pine Ridge Reservation, a massacre grave site at little Wounded Knee village. *Surely they wouldn't aim for Mount Rushmore or Custer State Park?* Gray cringes at the thought.

Having just gotten this information himself, Brad Patterson has a notion that this is going to be the start of one big string of takeovers nationwide. "Still going on guesses, goddammit!" he says out loud, ready for someone else to take on this headache. He knows now he is out of his depth. He accepts the FBI director just hung up on him, that is fine with him. He's out. Let the DOJ sort it.

"Well, this tanks it," Gray says. "We are gonna get them out of town with sixty-six thousand in traveling money, and that's some hefty change. Now it will stay the Justice Department's problem, period, full stop! We are sending fifty federal marshals up ahead of them to Pine Ridge, and if we're lucky, we will beat them there." Doug is surprised that the FBI director is sharing this information with him, then he notices Special Agent in Charge Donald Harmon has just walked into the room.

161

"I am happy to thank you, right here, for your service, Dunham, as we certainly won't be needing you further. I won't be guessing at a policy in Pine Ridge, it's our federal area, and besides, we have the whole of the tribal council there who is already cooperating." Without knowing the details, President Nixon has just helped outfit a goon squad, and Pine Ridge is already feeling its heat. "Goon" is a label that stuck the minute the tribal chairman there, Dick Wilson, referred to his men as guardians of the Oglala nation. And it's as good a name as any for a vigilante police force made up of mixed-bloods and white ranchers. In fact, they've been in place for some time, but now they'll be sanctioned. One can only imagine the confidence Chairman Wilson felt now with a government power giving him an open checkbook.

"I'll need to leave a different way, sir, or they will notice, and that won't bode well. You don't think I can just announce it to them?"

"Oh, after this week, I'd say a few secrets are out of the bag, Doug. Besides, let them get started on feeling paranoid. *Ahhh*, a real strategy for a change!"

"I'm not leaving them this way. I didn't agree to that." Dunham's eyes are hard.

"Like I need you to agree," Harmon says, smiling. Then he sucks in his breath and stops.

"Your call, Special Agent," the director says, "and take this downstairs. Let Doug oversee the delivery of the money. His last official act. We have a treasury problem, so we are calling in a favor from a bank or two. Seems this Mr. Bellecourt will only accept cash, and the weekend sat down on us. How much trouble can one damn thing be, after another? Well, go get cash!"

"Bellecourt and a few other six-foot-five Lakota men in his company are meeting you at a bank, so you can't miss 'em. Soon as I find one." The director is on his last nerve, not at all a man used to having terms dictated to him.

"Not meeting me," Doug says. "Harmon says I'm out."

Harmon is smiling and clearly enjoying Doug's discomfort. "Yes, he's leaving us, sir. I'll go drop it."

"Okay, then let it end on the street, where this belongs," the director says to Harmon. "See the Indians get their money, and then let us know from a phone booth."

"And Doug, lose our phone number." Harmon emphasizes this by handing him an envelope. It is stamped in red: Final Remittance. They are done.

162

Harmon turns to walk Doug out. On the way, the snitch has his say. "Oh, don't think I don't know why you hate me. Your worst fear is that some big dark man is gonna rise up in this town!" He uses his hands like claws and springs, scratching hawklike, into the air. He is suddenly raving like a demented preacher, and his Texan accent grows prominent. "Gonna rise up to take all your chilluns! Some new form of the Black man is here, and he is a commie-lovin' red giant with Jew money and government support puffin' him up! And now these fools," he says, pointing back to Harmon as he winds up like a madman right through the FBI lobby, "watch him now, how dare they let 'em in to *touch all your stuff!*" He laughs as he finishes.

Harmon keeps his calm resolve through all of it. He is the far more dangerous man between them, as his allegiances are clear. He stares Doug down with a gaze that communicates clearly that he can see to any situation that arises and says, "Doug, don't come back to this building or this town, son."

"Oh, oh, sir, I'll go to any damn town I want. I'm the freest man you know, and you helped with that!" With this, he passes the elevators. Harmon now knows for certain something he'd guessed, but too late. Dunham is seriously disturbed. Men like him join the force, and then they leave just as mysteriously. His military record had been stamped "passive aggressive," and Harmon realizes the passive part is about all eaten up, leaving this man capable of anything.

"So long, comrade!" Dunham calls out as loudly as he can. Cackling, he walks beneath the big portrait of J. Edgar himself in its oval frame, as he runs down the last escalator of the building, not waiting to ride it. He points back up at Hoover's portrait, saying, "Boogeyman is coming and you, hey, your super cock," he says, pointing now to Harmon, "is right there ready to meet him!"

He then starts singing dramatically just as he bursts out the main front doors. "*All we are saying, is give peace a chance!*"

Harmon makes sure Dunham clears the outer doors and, hearing the security locks click back into place, he exhales. "Good riddance, dirtbag!"

As Dunham walks down the sunny sidewalk, he's thinking that he'll for damn sure go anywhere he wants to go. If he wants to get back in their favor, he will, as they are going to need him, and he'll see to it. Or join the opposition if he's of a mind to. His choices are wide open. That's the beauty of the

163

snitch system, he is owned by no one. A real free agent, and for life. The look on their faces when they spot him in the Indian camp, what could the FBI do about it? "Not shit, that's what," he says out loud. Then he makes a wild dance down the street heading back to the BIA building.

The previous night, Herb and Dennis had sat together on top of the building, the last of the night's fire burning down in the old barrel near the wrapped tipi poles. Herb's face was tense, Dennis's eyes vigilant. Another riot squad was likely to surprise them before morning, and each wave had been more intense. Herb laughed at Dennis's homemade tomahawk—a leg off an expensive piece of mahogany furniture with a heavy glass ashtray from Commissioner Bruce's desk roped to it.

"What do ya think you're gonna do with that?"

"Protect the medicine."

"Where is Crow Dog?"

"In the basement."

"Best go ahead down there yourself. Follow the medicine. We will take care of what comes out here. Leonard is out front; if you hear it get close, then you and Crow Dog go on out a window from downstairs . . . Dennis?"

"Yeah?"

"Where's Hank?"

"Still over there. He's sweating getting it all in writing like you forced him to. He's afraid a new request might make them forget their other promises."

"Should've gotten it all in writing to begin with. Just need him to get three words and they can forget everything else. *Will not prosecute.* That's all they need to write out and sign." Dennis seemed to have his mind on something else; he looked the tired leader after seven long days and an end to his first takeover.

"Bro, you know where this leads now? And where it doesn't?"

"Where doesn't it lead?"

"Back," Herb said. Dennis got his meaning.

Crow Dog had announced at the naming ceremony the previous night, "These people like *paradise lost*; come see paradise still." He was welcoming everyone to his Rosebud Reservation with that call, and so that's where they are heading as they caravan out of Washington, DC.

By morning light, the AIMers head over the Potomac. Police cars' flashing blue lights move pedestrians off the sidewalks ahead of the undulating caravan snake-dancing its way out of the city together—destination west, Pine Ridge. For the leadership, they will first stop in Milwaukee for R and R at the Powless home. Many would stay at the Coast Guard station and boathouse; Leonard Peltier would be proud to show them to their new Indian accommodations.

Razor is insisting that they need to stop at the first gas station after the bridge.

"Why not get on out of town and as far from here as we can?" Leonard asks.

"Where ya think I got all that gas for the cocktails we ended up not needing this week?"

Razor leans forward from the back seat and says to Leonard, "I'm starting to feel good, man, maybe for the first time in my life. Ya know?" Leonard does know, for sure, though he does not answer back. He feels just the same.

Some Defenders, a DC version of the Black Panthers, have gathered to see them off, and Anna Mae leaps to a car window to return the friendly fists in the air salute.

When Razor hears about the travel money, he says to his cousin Leonard, "Sixty-six thousand dollars! I could run a whole country on that!" To which Leonard replies, "Please tell me when you're running the country, so I can leave."

There were major victories, even if not yet fully realized. A van loaded with documents is headed to North Carolina and will rendezvous with

AIMers later. How fitting that the docs recovered by the Trail of Broken Treaties are traveling southward across the old escape route from the Trail of Tears into North Carolina.

A day later Rufus, Crow Dog's cousin, is waiting in the yard with Dorothy Powless and many others to welcome AIM to Milwaukee. Rufus has been teaching some urbans how to erect a proper tipi. A charred one sits nearby. Herb looks at Rufus, who shrugs and says, always positive, "It will happen." Herb's young son Tony fell asleep during his door-watch.

Another trouble nearby is little Gina, who is scurrying off with two white puppies tucked under her arms and another under her chin. Rufus has just shared with her the meaning of dog soup. Dorothy rescues the puppy under her chin and the minute her back is turned, Leonard hands it back to the child from behind his back. She is determined to relocate every dog within a mile's radius.

"There goes your dog soup," Leonard observes to Rufus.

"It can happen," he replies.

Dorothy goes over to check the rental car she'd contributed a week's pay for and puts her finger into a bullet hole in the trunk. "How am I supposed to explain that to the insurance?" Razor had borrowed the car for a midnight run on gas and picked the wrong Virginian to mess with.

Leonard gently pulls Dorothy's finger back out of the hole, fearing it might stick, but keeps hold of it. Gently, she pulls it from his hand as Leonard remarks, "Herb is actually happy for a change, feeling ten feet tall."

"Yes, well, if he needs to be any taller, he can stand on my shoulders any time he wants ta."

Dorothy sees Herb has noticed their exchange and she walks off, saying, "I'll bring you out some pie. Cheryl will be disappointed if you don't try her blueberry pie."

"Well, you look in one piece. That's good," Dorothy says to Floyd Red Crow Westerman on reaching the long food table. She hands him a bowl of chili. "Be careful, it's hot." It brings her peace to see Floyd eating like he is starved; she knows what that means.

Leonard walks over, accepts a bowl of chili, and says, "Not hot enough for me." He reaches over to pull Gina's hair and she hugs him around the legs. *It is great to be home*, he thinks. It feels like home.

Dennis comes around the corner and says, "Dorothy, I see ya have three little cooks, with the girls, but ya gotta have a few doormen." Catching sight of Buddy Powless, he says, "Ah, there's a good cedar man."

Buddy exchanges a look with Leonard Crow Dog, whom he'd been watching mix tobacco with Rufus. He is taking a special interest in all this, and it hasn't escaped his mother's or Crow Dog's, either.

For her part, Anna Mae turns up her nose at blueberry anything, including the pie. She's had enough of those back in Maine. Her eyes follow Dennis. She plans to sneak him off somehow, maybe to the van near where he's walking. She'd just pull him in. *He can't work forever*, she thinks, appreciating his beautiful face.

Dorothy walks over to Herb, who misses nothing, even if he pretends to. "Who you off talking to, woman? Looking for my replacement, are ya?"

"Hah," she responds playfully. His very presence works on her instantly, not to mention his touch, and that being the case, she never passes up a chance to rib him. "If I was, Herb, he wouldn't come out of your crew. That's for sure."

Herb takes the idea seriously. "Where would he come from?"

"It'd be someone who told *you* what to do," she says with a smile, teasing him.

"Oh good, thank you, lady. For a minute there I was worried." He knows no man exists who can tell him a goddamn thing. Especially after Washington. He also knows all their heads have gotten big. They were just on the cover of the *New York Times*. This is both good and bad for business. He knows that, too. On that thought, he looks his wife in the eyes as he says, "If I ever stepped out, would you forgive me?" Dorothy's smile faded as she answers him.

"You'd never know if I'd forgiven you or not." On that she walked away.

Milwaukee's streets have been lined all the way to Dorothy's neighborhood with Black Panthers and hippies surrounding the red ghetto, and hundreds of urban Indians, supporters from all over town with their fists in the air to give them a heroes' welcome home. Herb notices that many from the Auto Workers also turned out. Sheets of lasagna have been brought in from

Nino's to add to their noonday feast. There are cases of rich, dark Chianti, which Dorothy unceremoniously hands straight back. Cops standing idly, one or two waving here and there, take those off her hands.

Tonight is to be relaxing, safe, and festive. Then all will give thanks in ceremony, where one prays for others, not for one's self—three rows deep in the tipi tonight.

Floyd pulls out his guitar and begins to strum as Dorothy and some helpers lift a long table over closer and start filling it with food that is still coming in. Other family members gather quilts and pallets to make beds for those who want to rest. Leonard goes to help some men splitting wood for the sweat. It'll be hauled to another location out in some nearby woods. There will be another meal later as well, more of a breakfast. This includes fresh eggs sunny-side up and Herb's favorite, shaved potato hash with wild mushrooms and pearl onions, plus stewed apples. An ice-cold bucket of fresh water with a metal dipper is passed and spirit food of corn meat and berries. Soon they'll all head out. Leonard calls out, "Hey, Floyd, did ya hear Buffy Sainte-Marie is coming, to play for the Station House Indian School? Yeah, for real man, and she'll sleep there!"

"Whatever ya do, don't wash those sheets, Dorothy." Floyd says. Buffy Sainte-Marie is a popular Indian headliner; everyone finds pride with her songs, especially the AIMers. She is raising money for their Milwaukee Indian School.

As they start to pull out the next morning, their hair still smelling of cedar smoke, Leonard reminds Dorothy he will be straight back, only working security 'til they get there. He loves the alcohol program, and a lot else in Milwaukee. He fits.

"Okay. Hope I see ya again," she says casually.

"I hope ya see me again," Leonard says, and jumps into the green hatchback.

Floyd hands Dorothy a folded square of brown paper and says "souvenir" as he climbs in beside Leonard. Anna Mae is paying close attention, as she was the one who'd passed it to Floyd. Dorothy opens it after they'd all driven down the street. It contains a single name: *Raymond Yellow Thunder.*

PART TWO

"AND THEN THINGS
GOT HEAVY"

CHAPTER 18

Crow Dog's Paradise, Rosebud Reservation, South Dakota
A Few Days Later

Something had changed between them. Leonard wasn't sure what it was exactly, but the lightheartedness they'd all felt back in Milwaukee and some of the camaraderie had dissipated. For the most part, almost all of them rode silently up to South Dakota. Well, they were a bit exhausted and almost all of them were still nursing a few wounds after the encounters with the riot squads. Even their unstoppable youthful energy had evaporated. Nature would do that to you when things got heavy, slow you down on purpose, make you think. Leonard didn't sleep regularly these days. Either he conked out into a deep, sober sleep, or got by on just a fifteen-minute nap, but he always jumped up ready to go.

Leonard was grateful that Floyd Red Crow Westerman was in his van because he pulled his guitar out and sang for a lot of the drive, or just strummed. Even his warmups were welcomed and soothing. When wavy yellow grass started to pull up underneath them, they knew they were finally passing out of the Nebraska sand hills and heading ever closer to the Ridge. Leonard had heard of this place all of his life; his folks talked about it, everyone Indian did. He was finally going to see it for himself. Herb was asleep in the back seat. Leonard woke him when he popped the glove box open looking for some matches. He pulled out an envelope stamped Final Remittance in red. It was a fresh blue-gray envelope, not a good sign. Herb reached for it. They were driving Doug Dunham's van. Herb had had a fight with him before they left and made him stay back with the women.

Rosebud Reservation, their destination, was a bit north of Pine Ridge. They'd slept overnight in the hills to be sure to pass into Crow Dog's place well before nightfall. They hadn't planned on the roadblocks that cut off every road. They had to go around, way around, and make a road a few times. Family members who were out looking for them emerged from byways to help them find a back route. Cars followed horses for miles.

This development worried Leonard and others who were security-minded because they wondered who'd escort the elders' families back home in the dark. Goons were about, and it made night traveling especially dangerous. "Goon"—what a name to pin on a tribal chairman's posse. Leonard knew all he needed to know about it; they were not guarding their people. Maybe they would all just camp the night and smoke together, Leonard hoped.

It's a majestic lot that comes to welcome AIM, the royalty of the Ridge. Matthew King is there, and Charlie Red Cloud, and Old Man Ellis Chips (short for Horn Chips), a descendant of Crazy Horse's medicine man, with his wife Victoria, and Grandma Cecilia Jumping Bull. Her husband Harry is a descendant of Sitting Bull; she came from the Black Elks. Grandma Loud Hawk and her sons, and Henry Crow Dog, also known as "the old man." Chief Frank Fools Crow is present with his wife. The real thing, all these men and women. The elders of Pine Ridge, the descendants of the Seven Fires.

Dennis says of Henry Crow Dog, "They say his medicine was so strong he could touch you with an eagle feather and you went down, all the way down to the ground, passed out cold at a Sun Dance." Leonard and Razor both hang on the stories and listen to their first pure Lakota since Leonard Crow Dog gave the naming ceremony in the BIA Map Room. They learned things, but weren't taught them in some pretentious way, just picked them up, as they felt part of it.

Suddenly Grandma Jumping Bull points and yells out something. Grandma Loud Hawk sheds tears over whatever the elder woman is saying in her language. Her eyes light up in wonder as the moon casts a faint glow across the blue veins and wrinkles of her tiny hands that now cover her mouth like a small fan.

She points at Leonard, who asks, "What's she saying, man?"

"Oh, she's happy," Anna Mae says, shedding her own tears of joy. "Chief Fools Crow says she made her boys bring her. They didn't want to in the dark with Goons about, but she said she'd walk if they didn't. She wanted to see the longhairs for herself."

"What? She's pointing at my hair?"

Charlie Red Cloud says to his elder, Frank Fools Crow, in his perfect Lakota, "These city Indians want to be Indian more than we do."

Frank nods in approval and says, "They haven't had to be yet."

Kenny Loud Hawk, just returned from Vietnam, says, "She excites easily," referring to Grandma Loud Hawk. "Last year she had a heart attack watching the war news 'cause she saw helos shooting down at people. She thought they were shooting at me and my brother, Russ," says the usually shy, young, hard-eyed Oglala. "When a helo flies over, she runs out and shakes her cane up at it!"

Leonard offers a Camel to young Kenny. While he exchanges a look with Dennis. They are both thinking, *Helos, out here, why?* They digest this information with solemn expressions. Razor whispers to Kenny, "If they ain't protecting ya none, what are the helos for?"

Charlie Red Cloud knows that out here, isolated, and far from TV cameras, the challenge will be altogether different for AIM. And after DC it will be easier for some to look the other way if something happens to them.

"We are together now," Fools Crow says. "We have always eaten from a common bowl, and our hearts are in common, too."

"That's why they call us communists all the time," the old man laughs. Charlie Red Cloud and Chief Fools Crow both know they don't need anyone from anywhere else telling them what their troubles are, they lived them. That said, they can sure use help from these younger Indians, and they welcome them.

Selo Black Crow invited AIM to the Ridge a year ago and wastes no time outlining the problem, beginning with when Raymond Yellow Thunder's sisters first come to him for help. He was their brother, and he was missing. Black Crow first met Dennis Banks on that day. It was a common affair, Indians missing, Indians arrested over trifles, and of late, murdered and left in trunks of old abandoned cars, or on the side of the road to freeze to death. What was not common was the new attorney general, and his looking into it.

AIM had become an intermediary for the marginalized people of the Ridge. Ranchers didn't like the outside influence or the nosy newspaper reporters that came with them, prying into the leasing arrangements on Indian land. So, they held a private meeting to discuss how to best eject AIM from the reservation by any means necessary. They met secretly in the BIA Building Offices, which housed the jail down below. The state attorney general, called Wild Bill by the locals, spoke and assured the ranchers listening, agitated over this Yellow Thunder business that he could take care of the problem, Selo knew otherwise. Dennis raised a crowd of four hundred AIMers who stood in the street, quietly waiting for them all to come out of the meeting. As Wild Bill himself stood there dumbfounded, Dennis spoke clearly, not even having to raise his voice. He demanded justice for their slain brother. Selo shared the story with the newcomers.

"Raymond worked rodeo on Nebraska border, a good bronco man and a rancher, hired out. His sisters say he is never away long. But last they saw him was a week ago. Then they come to me, and we found out what happened to him."

Raymond had come home from work on his payday, and as always had honored the payday tradition of letting one of his girls pick an item from his brown bag. The smallest of his nieces stood on her tiptoes in her nappy, reached in, and pulled out a can of tomato soup like it was a treasure. They'd all clapped their approval.

Raymond's sister retrieved it and leaned close to him, hoping she wouldn't smell hops on his breath. He knew what she was doing. She was hoping that if she got dinner on fast, she could keep him at home, but there was no chance of that. His Auntie Jane took the brown paper bag, fetched her scissors, and began to cut it into squares, as paper was scarce. The scissors drawer already had a small stack of such squares. Two pieces carried the name of someone dead, missing, or murdered on it. She was going to take them with her to her blanket circle later, a place where the women kept up with the goings-on. It was all they could do for now, just keep a count of what they heard. Raymond Yellow Thunder's name would be on a paper square by the end of the week. He'd be number twenty-two.

When Black Crow finishes talking, Dennis asks, "Did you go to the authorities?"

"Yes, all of them. FBI, BIA, state, and tribal. Hell, it's those tribal Goons killing us. The state lets it happen. And the federals not caring if they do, they pass the trouble around. We are left to save ourselves."

Anna Mae takes a special interest in this story. She is determined to contact a newspaper about it, in Minneapolis. Cities are familiar with uninvestigated missing and murdered when it involved dark-skinned citizens. Somewhere off the Ridge was more likely to publish the story. Leonard Peltier promises that when he gets back to Milwaukee, he'll go to the press, too. Dorothy and Herb know a radio station that would air it. Besides, Herb doesn't want the Coast Guard station to be without one of them for too long, so he'll likely be heading back by morning.

While Leonard was still on the road back to Wisconsin, there was a parallel incident up at the Ridge and at Dorothy's place. The Powless home received its first firebomb, but Dorothy and the kids put out the fire. Then, a few hours after leaving Crow Dog's, Frank Fools Crow's cabin also burned down to the ground. It was clearly arson. No one knew who'd done it, but they knew what prompted it—they were all being sent a message. The message was to AIM, and it meant for them to *stop*.

Frank Fools Crow wasn't home a minute before his cabin caught fire; it was timed so he'd have to watch it. Some rare artifacts were burning inside while the elderly Fools Crow couple stood together wrapped in a blanket, watching the flames. Dennis Banks later recalled the commemoration poster he'd seen on their wall by their cabin front door. It depicted a young Lakota man whose hair is pulled up tight, wearing a traditional porcupine headpiece referred to as a roach, and his muscled chest is covered with Sun Dancing scars. It read Commemoration Pow Wow, 1934. A line beneath its photo of the Indian said, *Frank Fools Crow.*

Likely the arson was punishment for attending the meeting over at Rosebud. That was Frank's assessment when his grandson came running up with a bucket of water from the well way down the hill. Chief Fools Crow reached out and grabbed his elbow to stop him. It was already too late. The flames cracked the window nearest the door and then consumed the poster. Herb and Leonard had gone home to Milwaukee and had just missed both fires.

Over the next few months, Herb would begin to go back and forth to Pine Ridge, as events demanded. The year turned over to 1973 and things continued to fire up at Pine Ridge, at a pace that was unimaginable. Leonard wanted desperately to go back and work security for those people. Not long after watching Herb drive back out to South Dakota, Leonard feels a little left out. He'd be here in Milwaukee missing it all that came next, but it wouldn't be at the Powless house, or the Coast Guard station. He'd be sitting in jail.

It starts on November 22, 1972, when he strays off with a few men Herb considers loafers, men Herb has kicked out of the Coast Guard station. They are all at a diner called Texas when Leonard is confronted by an off-duty Milwaukee cop. It doesn't occur to him at the time that it might be a setup, and he is disgruntled anyway at not being on his way back to Pine Ridge with the others, he knows he is needed there.

After the usual long wait for a waitress to take their order, Leonard raises his voice, at which time men in a nearby booth turn to stare him down. Leonard does his usual in such a situation: he returns an even more menacing stare. This usually wards off a problem and prevents a fight rather than start one, but not always.

"Hey asshole, what are you staring at?" the off-duty cop says.

"Not much," answers Leonard.

Though an unlikely place to lose it, they both dive at each other, and the fight continues all the way to the outside parking lot, until a Beretta drops out of Peltier's inside jacket pocket. It is not clear it has a broken firing pin, as it sits on the ground, but the cop chooses that moment to identify himself and accuse Leonard of trying to shoot him. Then, conveniently, cops are suddenly everywhere. Leonard is handcuffed and stuffed into a patrol car.

Dorothy, upon hearing the news, goes straight to the jail with Lew beside her. Three months go by before Lew can get Dorothy in for a visit. He confirms the worst news: there is no way Peltier is facing a fair trial in Milwaukee, especially not after the recent event at Wounded Knee. Leonard has already heard a caravan of AIMers have taken over there, the occupation is all over the news, the Indians in jail talk of nothing else. She has to be clever in what she says. Lew has stopped over, as his only hope of getting anywhere near Wounded Knee is to ride in with them. Others depend on the same; a small crew with a camera were recently turned around at the roadblocks. Orders are to keep all press out. Herb organized a two-day overland trek in some rather harsh conditions to take them around.

"I'm heading east again," Dorothy says, knowing Leonard will know she means west, and that that means Wounded Knee. Likely on a supply run for Herb.

"That's the problem with you Indians, you don't know your east from your west." They smile together and he leans down to light a cigarette between his cuffed hands. "I hear what you're saying. Guess I'm in here? The one time I can't go, you finally go somewhere."

"Well, it's a special occasion, ya know."

"Don't make it too special, watch yourself." Dorothy plans to ride all the way to the Knee on the metal bed of a pickup truck hidden under a tarp. In winter, it'll be special all right.

"Lew is gonna get your bail, before we go."

"Make bail? For this? How in hell? Lew says ain't no way I'll get a fair trial."

"I got my ways. I work, I can do things. He's got his ways, too."

"Maybe I'll go east too then, yet. Farther east first though." She knows he means California or Arizona, maybe he means New Mexico. "I'll circle back."

"I thought you might." She pauses and then looks him right in the eyes.

"Well, I hope I see ya again."

He looks up with his warmest smile and returns their customary farewell.

"I hope ya see me again."

Leonard is not used to sitting in jail. It has been over three months now, and soon, three turns into four. He plans everything out in his head, even saves things to think about later so he can stretch out the time even further. Jail is loud and filled with the sounds of desperation. He knows Herb Powless is likely missing him, as he was now in a war zone. AIM had made the commitment to stay the line of defense whatever came. One cannot imagine it unless living it. The beginning to the end began with the latest murder, that of a young Lakota named Wesley Bad Heart Bull. His funeral was the problem, when his mother, Sarah Bad Heart Bull, wanted her son's body for the funeral and was beaten on the courthouse steps over it. AIM was there, in a town called, of all names, Custer. Weeks later, on February 28, 1973, AIM occupied Wounded Knee, in a caravan led by Indian mothers and grandmothers. *Why not,* Leonard thought, *it had been their idea.* Thoughts of Dorothy and the recent experiences at the Coast Guard station house have helped calm his mind. Floating above everything and watching life play out over things you've done, changing out actions and circumstances, and the results as well. Then he plans his leaving. Wherever it might be, it'll be where Herb Powless isn't.

He remembers back to his recent falling-out with Herb. Herb ran everything in Third Chapter when he was in Wisconsin and he was as bad an enemy to have as Dorothy was a good friend. They relied on her to patch things up between members when fights occurred, and she was dependable for that. She had a special place in his heart. It wasn't his style to have designs on a brother's wife, and besides Herb had a wicked long memory, unlike Dorothy, who was an open door. Of late she had drawn a lot of strange bedfellows, not just him.

One day a G-man in a suit came to her back door with a stack of yellow slips, which meant gun registrations. He asked if she was a gun enthusiast or what. She responded, while calling Lew on the kitchen phone, "You FBIs live on my street year-round now and know everything we say and do. So you tell me what I've been doing. You'd be the ones to know!"

When he threatened to arrest her and take her downtown, she replied matter-of-factly, "I can't tonight, I'm working third shift at the brewery." Even cops were charmed by her. Whatever she was up to, she was a good, decent, hardworking woman and mother, so that was the end to that conversation.

The G-man went on to recommend that she become an arms dealer, get a legit license, and legally buy whatever she wanted, no questions asked. And how many wouldn't matter anymore. She had, after all, registered everything properly. He knew before coming out to the house that he had nothing on her other than that she was Herb Powless's wife, which was always grounds if they felt like it. Problem was, they didn't feel like it. She was clever and strong-minded and could usually make authority feel foolish while they got nowhere. Questioning Dorothy was fruitless. She knew to shoo him away, and this very night some important doings were brewing, in her very own alley, where Leonard and Herb were about to have a falling-out. It happened right before the diner incident and Peltier's arrest. Likely it contributed to it.

Milwaukee AIM had decided to move all their available weapons to South Dakota, as AIM had made a desperate call for supplies. Herb planned to drive them up and he had neighborhood children dragging hardware through the alley insulated by doubled pillowcases. Leonard was sensitive when it came to kids, and he spoke up to say he didn't like them being involved. Herb had no patience with being directed, especially now. It was a sensitive time, he was in a hurry, it was a life-and-death-type risk on both ends, and timing was critical. Furthermore, he didn't like it his damn self, but had few alternative decoys. Desperation in his getting out of town and desperation waiting for him on the other end. His chances for success were limited by every minute, and Herb's temper was short. He didn't react well to being questioned in his backyard.

He knew the FBIs were just on the other side of the alley perimeter watching their whole goddamn street. He leaned over to smell Peltier's breath, and that was his first mistake. Dorothy seeing it happen was another. Leonard pushed Herb back, not gently, saying, "Stay out of my face, old man."

Herb grabbed the collar on his leather coat and before they could get into it, the Beretta fell out of Leonard's pocket for the first time that day. Leonard picked it up. Not for real, for Leonard knew it was broken. Herb stood as close to it as he could get and said, "Go on. Point it, but then can you shoot it?" There was a long pause that even Dorothy knew not to mess with. She nudged the children away from the scene. She could feel this coming, it was just a matter of time, but did it have to be right now?

Herb didn't flinch when nothing happened, he just reached over and wrenched the gun out of Leonard's hand and laughed when he saw it was broken. "Peltier, you're just holding a stick. Stay away from me. Stay back with the children, you like it so much. Dorothy can take care of you; she has a real gun."

At those words, Dorothy reminded him the heat was coming; their daughter had let her know they were already on the front stoop. She offered to drive off and lead them away from Herb and the follow car. Herb nodded yes.

Leonard took her elbow roughly, saying, "Let me do it. It's dangerous. Besides, how do you know they'll even follow you?"

She looked Leonard in the eye and assured him, "Oh, they'll follow me," and then she jetted off toward her black Charger.

Feeling left out and still angry with Herb, Leonard headed off in the other direction—eventually toward downtown, to a diner with his friend Stanley. Nearby the Coast Guard station, where off-duty cops were warned to be on the lookout for AIMers.

So, Leonard Peltier sits in jail while all in the world that mattered to him is headed to Wounded Knee, South Dakota. By the time he heads out there, Wounded Knee will have ended. He will not see his friend and enemy Herb Powless again for two years. Peltier will return to Wisconsin, under the threat of that outstanding warrant, to help take over an abandoned monastery in Gresham, Wisconsin, to stand with the Menominee. On New Year's Eve, when it's about to turn 1975.

CHAPTER 19

Special Agent in Charge, Donald Harmon,
Rapid City, South Dakota
April 1975, Three Years Later

If you walked up behind Donald Harmon in his Rapid City office, he didn't turn around straight away. Anyone who got that far had already been checked out by about twenty men. So, no unexpected guests. Harmon had spent little or no time with his men when he was in the marines, but in his satellite FBI office he fraternized with them almost exclusively. Rapid, for short, was what was left of an old gold mining town. No more gold worth noting, no longer a boomtown, it had seen little change in the twentieth century.

Drilling was going on farther west, but that was a highly protected operation, and since it was classified, few spoke of it. Harmon never did. Tourism to Mount Rushmore mostly brought outsiders to the Black Hills, and that was about it except for a biker contingent on its way to Sturgis every year. Lately, they all turned back after hitting the park, as this government-maintained reservation had gotten a rep. If you wanted to see an Indian dance, best to do it at the foot of stone presidents these days, and then go over to the Custer battlefield in Montana with your picnic basket. Or to Hot Springs; now that was a real frontier town and worth a Sunday drive.

That it was not at present safe to drive across reservation land was of great embarrassment to Harmon. This was his charge when he originally came to

185

Pine Ridge, and it had only grown more dangerous. A proper cleaning up needed to be done, and as far as Harmon could tell, it wasn't about to be. That soured him, as he had never fully recovered from the same damn situation in 'Nam, where his generation of marines had been the first to stop a war rather than win it. This too must "stop" soon, but when?

The FBI and the South Dakota governor's office had been sufficiently humiliated and headed for trials that came off like shows. The upcoming trial of Dennis Banks, now that would be the granddaddy of them all. Snitches liked to collect their paychecks by simply spreading rumors that AIM was planning another takeover. Not likely. There couldn't be another fallout to match the Wounded Knee aggression that had ended a brief two years before. *"A seventy-one-day siege,"* the press likes to repeat every breath. *Indians like to call it that, too. Some siege,* Harmon thought, looking at the press clippings on his mostly empty board. *More Indians died daily here than in that whole operation put together, so what was the fuss all about?* Harmon had become accustomed to feeling humiliated. He just had to attend a meeting to be reminded, any meeting.

There were the reservation Indians, considered assimilated, that were for Dick Wilson, the tribal chairman, and therefore against the AIM presence. AIM supported the traditional people who were under attack for not conforming. To conform meant to sign over the land to be leased away. The traditionals held strong. AIM was called in to get their back. To become the face of what "no" looked like. All three groups disliked the FBI presence, as it was the one thing they all three, goon, AIM, and traditional, had in common. Who could be proud of being chairman in charge of such a rising murder rate, and the highest per capita on any reservation in the country? Who wanted to be chairman of so many thousands of starving people? Who would want to get reelected to that? Well, chairman Dick Wilson did, and on his reelection, AIMers deemed it rigged, and that started the whole kit and caboodle. And once the siege ended, AIM was out of the spotlight. Agents like him got the damage control.

Harmon's bulletin board contained photos of all the AIM leadership and tribal people of interest, snitches' contributions, newspaper clippings, mostly local, that covered the supposed siege. There was also coverage of a string of riots, one named for the town of Custer. It happened because a white man had been tried and the Indian mother objected to the fact that her son's murderer was only being given the same sentence another had been given for killing a calf. These only made the newspaper because riots were sparked by AIM. Also, the murdered boy's mother wanted his body for burial, and when told "no" she charged toward the sheriff, who belted her in the face. The look in Russell Means's eyes when Sarah Bad Heart Bull was clubbed on those steps, well, all hell broke loose then. A trial followed that, as they tried the mother for starting a riot. *Started it by her bleeding face, I guess*, thought Harmon. So, another riot ensued. Herb Powless was at both, so he didn't get home for a while.

Harmon felt that local law didn't know how to run a proper investigation or roadblock, but the AIMers did know how to run a proper riot. Then the beloved Pedro Bissonette was murdered. He was head of the Indians' Civil Rights Commission and had also been a talented boxer in his day, Harmon noted. His body was stolen by AIMers and put into a tipi where a wake was held. The press got hold of a picture of him showing that he'd been shot in the chest at close range. It made for one ugly picture. No one knew the names of the AIMers who stole his body for burial. *They could have been charged with desecration of a corpse*, Harmon thought.

It ultimately all fueled the siege, which Harmon refused to justify with a name. A whole hodgepodge of escapes and weapon charges followed, including busting a pilot that helped fly Dennis and his young new wife, Darlene Nichols, up to Canada. Wasn't hard to catch up with the idiot who eventually had to come back to his airfield. He'd flown low over the frozen trees to avoid radar but couldn't avoid a landing strip. Harmon went personally to handcuff the scruffy pilot until he caught a side look at a familiar face. Goddamn if it wasn't Doug Dunham. Harmon's first words were "Son of a bitch!"

Doug laughed his jaunty familiar laugh as if they were old college roommates reuniting. As Harmon walked off the airfield, silent and fuming, Doug followed his ex-boss and started up with his usual nonsensical chatter.

"Dennis's new wife is sure a looker. Name's Darlene, and he calls her a young Indian Joan of Arc. She's a young everything if you ask me."

Harmon wasn't asking him a goddamn thing and was disgusted. He already knew about her; she was pregnant with child number two.

"I made note of the fact her middle name is Japanese, yep, ya heard right, *Kamook*. Catchy, ain't it? Her daddy named her after some Japanese fella, uh-huh, visited here once from Japan. Good ole Dennis, he can sure pick 'em."

"You are damn sure not taking notes for us, so shut up, will ya? Get out of here, Dunham. If you know what's good for you get back on that Cessna and file a flight plan back to Texas, California, wherever you got the plane. We have enough trouble, and you don't want any of it. Trust me."

"My own plane, well, Dad's. I have a speaking engagement and I plan to do just that after a coffee."

"Who in hell would have you speak to anyone about any goddamn thing?"

"Over in Wisconsin, your home state, sir, the John Birch Society asked me."

On those last and final shocking words, the two parted company forever. Herb Powless awaited Doug Dunham in Wisconsin, and not to welcome him.

The siege had ended, but the surprises kept coming. Now Harmon had to deal with the aftermath. Indians would rightfully call what came next a reign of terror.

CHAPTER 20

The Good Boys and a Buffalo Hunt

Like most servicemen, Donald Harmon is adept at protecting his personal life, behaving one way at work and another at home. Gail, his dear wife, travels with him to all his assignments. He shares even classified information with her. Only Vietnam had ever separated them. She wrote him every day there and he saved every letter. When he got home to Wisconsin, they ceremonially burned them in their backyard and vowed never to be separated again. She signed on at his Rapid City office as a stenographer, and when the FBI ordered Title III wiretapping investigations, she set them up. A light assignment, as few Indians have phones. He doesn't ask her to record his recent airport exchange with Dunham, as he is a former employee and the exchange entirely accidental.

She keeps busy typing up 302 documents, required paperwork when investigations were made, arrests, snitch meetings, or other surveillance called for. She orders their office supplies and is a great pal to the other wives. A real team player. Donald is very proud of her.

Gail Harmon is from a little town outside Saint Paul, Minnesota. Her Norwegian heritage shows in her blonde bob and bright blue eyes. Her skin tans easily in the South Dakota sun. Constantly on her feet, she plays golf every Tuesday, and though small in stature, is always the boss. The kids dread having her as their substitute teacher, because you do your assignments if she is at the head desk. She carpools to the grocery store or church with other wives from the local air force base ten miles from Rapid. Their husbands are frequently gone on long stretches when duty calls and just as suddenly home

191

and underfoot. Their life is a good one, and their husbands' work details remain a mystery.

Not so for Gail, as she is by Harmon's side and has been since he first spotted her on campus at Michigan State. She easily could have qualified to be in the Bureau, if in another time, or another place, or another's wife. Her Donald was high-maintenance, and one to a household was enough.

She still wears his fraternity pin, and around her neck, under her fashionable collegiate blouses, hangs a small cross with an opal at its center, a gift from her father, a rear admiral, given to her on her baptism day. Honest to a fault and a strict disciplinarian, she seems to smile only when Donald walks into the room. Unlike most husbands in the Bureau, he can do that daily. Not today, though—he must babysit three elected state bigwigs during a buffalo hunt—all of them connected in interest to the upcoming AIM trial.

The state attorney general, who planned the hunt, is known to his constituents as "Wild Bill." He loves votes, whiskey sours, and buffalo. He loves Indians, too, or so he says, but he means it in a kind of paternalistic way, like they are his cross to bear. After the international embarrassment of the Wounded Knee aggression, he has kept a tight hold on the whole situation. He works closely with the Sioux tribal government and insists that Harmon do the same. This troubles Harmon and does not feel natural at all. To his way of thinking, it is the reason why nothing has moved forward. In fact, it has escalated, with no sign of resolve.

The AG announces his arrival by bellowing his hellos all the way from the back entrance of the complex. *Does this man ever quiet down?* Harmon thinks. Today's event is intended to get him and Harmon on the same page. *What the hell page is that?* Harmon wonders. *They've blown half their budget on arsenal, for what? To hunt buffalo. Or for show, as it keeps everyone paranoid.*

Harmon thinks it would have been better to spend it on more men and tighten the noose slowly, but the governor wanted to make a show of force. *Let's just hope the guy can stage a decent hunt* is Donald's final thought before his entourage files in behind him in camouflage.

Soon they'll pile into trucks, and a larger truck will follow, pulling some jeeps on a long flatbed. Harmon wonders what this is costing the state. Also along for the ride is a woman dressed like a Hollywood starlet in a too-small halter top. She hangs on the attorney general's arm much of the time, and Harmon can only be grateful that they are riding in the jeep behind his. A few of his men have been carefully selected to go along as a buffer of sorts, as Donald can lose his temper in a discussion. This hunting event is an assignment, or he'd spend the day playing golf with Gail.

At the hunt site, the buffalo are already bothered, due to being pushed up against the edge of a small basin, maybe thirty of them. "My God, what beautiful scenery," Harmon says, while pouring his favorite subordinate, Special Agent Ronnie, a cup of coffee from a thermos. "But why, oh why can't these guys run things better?" he says, as Ronnie listens on patiently. "We can only hope the governor hasn't had his coffee laced by the attorney general."

"Yes sir, hope is all we can do." Ronnie answers. "His voice is growing louder. I didn't think that was possible, sir." Ronnie is wearing fashionable Levi's jeans and a golfing cap. His dark wavy hair reaches a little beyond its rim, and SAC Harmon notices.

"Well, for God's sake don't let him back behind the wheel," he says just as "Wild Bill" speeds over in a Land Rover and tells Harmon to jump in, patting the leather seat beside him. Harmon obeys, thinking this might call for more bravery than anything required of him since he came to Rapid.

The AG is red-faced, loudmouthed, and well-lubricated. *How does he expect to have any serious conversation under these circumstances?* Harmon wonders, and he's mad enough to reach behind him into the cooler for a cold beer of his own. He can hold whatever he drinks. *Let's see what information I can get out of this undisciplined man. Might make the day interesting, yet.*

Agent Ronnie watches them drive off, thinking, *At least we're out of the office, and for the moment, it's quiet. Serene, even.* On this warm day there are no reminders that the big ordeal at Wounded Knee was ever here. Hard to imagine that troops and tanks rolled by and actually exchanged gunfire with Indians. Unreal! Although there are few visible signs left, it is not in the past to the local Indians nor to Special Agent Ronnie.

There's not even a dent left in the yellow grass-lined roads to show they ever came through. Even the burned-out entryway to the old Custer courthouse has been repaired, and if the old men didn't sit around and talk about those two old Indian ladies who threw Molotov cocktails into it, no one would likely even remember it. If not for the AIM presence that had stayed behind, this whole place would just seem docile as the buffalo. AIMers are acting as bored as the FBI lately, with leadership scarce in their camp, until the trial starts.

Hours later, the hunting party pulls up to a gathering of trees that shade a few stadium chairs, and Harmon notices a local senator is among their group, occupying one of them. They look dressed more for the beach than for hunting, but they're all elated at having already bagged two buffalo.

The governor is a gentleman who does not enjoy crude talk, but he is willing to acknowledge that the young attorney general, who talks in third person, referring to himself as Wild Bill, sure lives up to his nickname.

"You getcha a charge about way-long and you load this beauty," the AG is saying, holding out a pinky finger and referring to the .257 Roberts rifle leaning on the tree behind him. Harmon is well aware that the .257 couldn't kill a buffalo and hasn't been used to do so. But the senator and the would-be starlet both seem impressed. Harmon imagines the AG took that fine rifle out of his own personal arsenal. Goons actually go around town bragging about all of their unregistered weapons, and some came from the governor during and after the siege.

During Wounded Knee, Bureau men ran out of armor, and the AG just took them over to his home and tossed them hardware from an overstocked gun cabinet like Christmas gifts from a Santa bag.

He continues his story, saying, "You wait now, patience is part of a hunt, ya see. Let 'em all gather in a group, then *pow!* Take one down right in the middle. The rest will gather around the one that's hurt. They smell the blood, ya see. Then . . . act fast and take 'em all if you want to."

Displeased, Harmon retreats to his jeep. Noticing the key still in it, he pulls out the hunting map provided and drives off. He'd rather spend his time with the buffalo than this crew. They have about equal entertainment value, a buffalo being about the dumbest creature he ever hunted.

He speeds through the backland and hops a small hilltop before realizing that he's angry and better not flip a government jeep. He pauses to smell the fresh air and heavy grass scent. The horizon is so clear he can see Montana. He'll be glad when he and Gail are back in Denver, likely his next post, and the sooner the better. He plans to take Agent Ronnie with him up the ladder.

Ronnie is an excellent subordinate and will train into a fine G-man one day. Got him out of Cal Poly Institute, and he would have made a fine engineer if the Bureau hadn't had a watch on him and intercepted.

Ronnie's partner Jack is already a dad with two young sons back home, and all he wants is a decent convenience store and to get home to those boys and the wife he adored. He enjoyed working Watts when he was a cop and is used to leading with a handgun. He would always be more of a cop—a good arrest cop and a good man—but to Harmon's thinking Ronnie's the one who will follow him all the way up the line. Harmon was ignoring the fact that agent Jack was more like him, the one who excelled at everything Bureau. Jack was also a passionate do-gooder. For Harmon, Ronnie was a lighter spirit, positive to a fault, and Harmon needed that demeanor around, for he, too, like Jack, was Bureau all the way. A price for that excellence might be becoming a little too jaded before his time. A laid-back California boy around might help balance things out. Especially if assignments like this one kept coming.

This show isn't likely to hold much longer, as trials are the beginning. Jail time is not going to be pretty for some of these urban Indians. The remnants left in the camps sit around and wait for Banks to show up and soon there'll be enough weapon charges to clear out the whole goddamn place, move this back to the city projects where it belongs.

On that thought, he starts up the jeep and heads up the hill to an old wagon road. At the top, he can see and smell smoke. Way out here? Must be a large campsite for that much smoke. Sure enough, he sees about ten long tables draped in canvas, and a giant turn of barbecue spits. The smokers look brand new. How in hell did they get this menagerie way out here? There are waiters! Then he spots his worst nightmare and drives the jeep close enough to bump him.

Tribal Chairman Dick Wilson just smiles an inebriated smile. Harmon offers his usual salutation: "Son of a bitch, who invited you out here?" Red-faced and in a bad humor, the chairman raises his beer can in a gesture of a toast to Harmon, saying, "So, the buffalo didn't toss you out of here like I'm going to?"

"You mean the two we got over that hill in a bag? Nope. Didn't throw nothing."

"Well, get a little closer next time. They don't let you walk up to them like that because they're afraid of you. You'll find that out the hard way one day. I corralled about thirty for ya and thought you might hit at least one. They seem tame, until they're not. Hope ya hunt out here long enough to experience their true nature. Take some bar food back to Wisconsin with ya, something worth remembering from your days with us."

"Why is it I don't understand a goddamn thing you say? Riddles. I'm not a kid. Speak English, will ya, buddy, just once?"

"Oh, it's not what you don't understand that's bothering you, Agent, it's what you do. I learned my English at Holy Cross Boarding School. I got slapped upside the head, and all I could think to do was keep asking the goddamn *Wasichu* [Lakota for "White"] what I was doing wrong. What was wrong was answering her in the only language I knew. I finally put praying hands together, and she put a plate of food in front of me. First plate I got after two days. I was six. English is my only language, I know it real well, so listen up."

Harmon looks the chairman in the eye at those words, for the bastard actually sounds serious for once.

"Get your men into some fatigues and out of their golf clothes for a minute; get 'em to a target range, for practice. And don't come in too close, not this week."

More goddamn riddles, Harmon thinks and turns to leave, offering his usual farewell, "See ya around, sumbitch." He can hear Wilson laughing behind his back in his usual obnoxious way. The golf course and Gail sound just about right to him. So, to hell with old Dick Wilson and his whole fake tribal council. He just doesn't like the looks of him—never did, never would. This hunt is over.

At the end of the day, the whole crew saunters into the only decent club bar in Rapid if one wants a scotch. The talk continues about court dates, and Harmon knows that means roadblocks. "Jewish lawyers and Jewish press. Neither a good thing," he overhears the governor say. "Not facing a pile of soft judges this time, but more like a frontier judge." This talk triggers a recent memory for Harmon. Ole Dickie's roadblocks were letting too many through, so in a heat of frustration, he'd run down below his tribal roadblock and set up a Bureau one. For a comical minute it was like musical chairs, as Dickie sent some men below him, cursing loud enough for all to hear, "That government bastard thinks he can block my block!" Then comes a Subaru station wagon driving particularly fast on dirt and with eastern plates. Attorney Lew Gurwitz steps out in boat shoes onto snow, no socks. "A damn hippie reporter," Harmon guessed, and he approached him, his reflection mirrored from expensive sunglasses.

"Not today, partner, just turn around and try to make the Nebraska border before it gets dark and aim for the one gas station in a hundred miles before it closes." He looks down at his watch and adds, "Oops, too late for that." Closer up Harmon now recognizes the Boston lawyer.

"I'm coming in to talk to clients."

"Not today you're not, and they aren't your clients yet. Got to meet them first, don't ya?" Letting Lew know, he knows who he is and where he is going.

"Who are you to tell me where I can go, other than an unelected official?"

Harmon knows to make note, this one would be harder to curb, if at all. He still doesn't let him through. "Oh, you'll thank me, 'cause those gentlemen down below me, they can tell you to git. You saw to that, defending their rights and all, huh, Mr. Gurwitz?"

Even the rules Lew knew for certain he could depend on were disappearing before his eyes, as fast as the South Dakota snow. The reason for blocking roads. Lew pulls out his bar card and then the agent has to let him through. At the time he was headed to the WKLDOC Office (Wounded Knee Legal Defense-Offense Committee).

Back in Rapid, Harmon sips a scotch and water as Dick Wilson passes him. He then backs up and sits one stool over, using the stool between them for his M-16.

"It rates its own chair, does it?" Harmon asks, without looking up. He has regained his composure after an earlier interlude with his wife.

"It's earned a chair, better than you."

"Really? You might remember occasionally, Dickie, that you don't really know a thing about me. We see your dossier, but you don't see ours. Yours is pretty simple. You took a whole lot of money out of Washington, and you can't give it back. You can only kiss their ass to get more. 'More' is the usual budget item out here, right? Look closer at me and we can make this even simpler. I am Washington, see. There's just one field, and one checkbook, for that matter."

"Ahhh, partner. I hurt your feelings, I'm sorry. I don't need to see a damn thing. We've been doing this longer than you. We all went military out here and came back, too. Didn't have to be drafted—volunteered, and likely saved your ass, and your daddy's and your granddaddy's. My people have been the first to serve, all wars. If we don't have someone else to fight, we will just fight each other, 'cause we like it and we're good at it. Got a few combat veterans walking around, and some just got home when Saigon began to fall a few weeks ago. Their expressions tell even me not to fuck with them. They brought their guns home, too. I could make a coat out of the medals one family got. They could make Rapid fall fast as Saigon." Harmon recalls recently seeing a C-130 transport plane at the airfield, unloading many flag-draped coffins, carrying mostly Indian names. He is somber-faced at the memory as Chairman Dick continues.

"Now, the college boys you advance to officers based on their school grades may not be so safe. Wanna keep ya safe, it's one of my many jobs. That's all your suits say to me. Safe. I don't need to see no dossier. Governor has asked me personally to do this job. You'll learn, out here in the frontier they pick your enemies, and your friends, too."

"Got anything else to say to me, Chairman, sir? As I stand in your buffalo shit that might as well be under some banana trees to hear you talk. Just talk."

Seething, Harmon tosses down the last of his watered drink and gets up. "Maybe you didn't notice my badge." Harmon slides it into his palm to make the point. "I don't take orders from a state governor and never on a cold day in hell from the likes of you. This is federal land, partner, government property. End of story."

Dick jumps to his feet, lightly for a big man who's a bit soused, and says, before Donald can walk away, "Watch what you go thinking is government property out here, friendo. It'll all be long over before you know what hit."

Wild Bill comes over and stands at the seat of the M-16. He presses Harmon's shoulder gently, then removes his hand and speaks plainly for once. Chairman Dick lifts his weapon and walks off, sweaty brow and all.

"I need you boys to get along, goddammit. Now what is that gonna take, Special Agent Harmon? Some sensitive things are cooking. We need a united front. That tribal chairman is no TV sergeant, even if he looks like one. He's a good man, and don't underestimate him. He's also a damn good shot and is just as likely to pull a Crazy Horse out here as any of the rest of them. Technically, they're all kin."

Harmon puts some bills on the bar and walks out.

CHAPTER 21

One Hundred and
Fifty-Two . . . and Counting

Anna Mae is damned weary of seeing names on the bulletin board from the jumble of small squares of paper, each neatly cut from brown paper bags, each with a name and a number. None of these cases have been investigated and Anna Mae is determined that they not be forgotten. She has just added the names of two Indian children, next to "Edith Eagle Hawk and children." Edith's car was rammed by a known goon, and all occupants perished.

All the names are a heartbreak to their family . . . but *children*! Of late, all the ceremonies they attend seem to be funerals. She adds a number in the lower right corner of a brown paper square. Sometimes family members come into Calico Hall and pull a name down and hold it closely, then sometimes they pray over it and then put it back up. As if it is all they have left of their son or daughter or father or brother. Even this Indian community gathering spot could be dangerous because of the goon-watch that went on anywhere near a traditional spot or place AIMers guarded. Even the sweats were not safe from drive-by shootings.

At least Dennis is coming to the gathering tonight, she thinks. The fact that he is going on trial soon scares her most of all, because it means AIM leadership is soon to be doing all their leading from behind bars. Unthinkable.

She so wants to go home to see her own daughters, and she knows that is soon. She'll stay by Dennis's side and keep his spirits up until trial, also a good place to speak out about their wrongful incarcerations and about the murders. Then she'll make her way back to Canada and home. Maybe Leonard would travel with her. There are strict instructions that no AIMer is to travel alone.

Too much was going on, and an odd climate of fear had settled in even among the AIMers themselves lately. Infighting had reached a whole new level. Special Agent Harmon had recently picked her up after ceremony. She'd made the mistake of walking to the grocery store; they were out of everything, the old ones were hungry, and her sister had sent her a prized ten-dollar bill. She had covered barely a mile of the seven-mile walk when he slowed his car beside her.

"Get in, Anna Mae."

"And if I don't?"

"Well, I could chase you through the woods, but it's really hot outside."

"And you'd never catch me."

"Oh, I'd catch you. Tell ya what, I'll follow you to the grocery store and then give you a ride back and pull up in front of all your friends and wave when you get out. Or . . . you can get in my car on this isolated road, and no one sees us, and I can run you over to the store and then take you back."

The threat having been made clear, she climbed in the back seat and lay down. She knew there was a smirk on the triumphant bastard's face. Lately she had come under suspicion due to this very thing.

Some pretended to question her, saying it was to prove to everyone present that she was not hanging around any Rapid City cops. However, this damaged things further. If she knew they were just grandstanding to bring the truth out in the open, doing it for her, they still were pointing fingers at their own. Naturally, she resented the hell out of it. Leonard handed her a smoke after their questioning her and announced to all, "I tole ya, assholes, she's innocent, now shut up about it!" Kola had spoken up and reminded him, "She's your friend, after all." The rumors started with Doug Dunham because she accused him first. He'd recently confessed before the Church

Committee. Well, she sent her own findings to the Church Committee. They were a select government committee put in place to investigate FBI wrong-doing, among other things.

Confessed snitches and so up close, made them all second-guess! she thought. The only feeling of trust and friendship she knew she could count on was from her AIM women friends. And, of course, from Dennis. Always Dennis.

Just when the ceremonies made you feel bigger than life, something happened to remind you that everyone was just a human being and capable of the same notions and fears that all humans feel when in danger. Impossible to concentrate under. Dorothy Powless had long ago said, "They put the blood on our hands to keep it off their own. Then it's harder to know who the enemy is."

As Harmon's FBI sedan arrives in Rapid, they climb out and go up the back steps of the BIA offices. Anna Mae knows the destination won't be no grocery store and she can feel her neck crawl and prays no one that matters will see her going in there. AIM's spies are everywhere, too. That had been her own idea. A recent Goon had joined AIM, by staying in the Goons.

Once inside the interrogation room, Harmon passes her a cigarette. She opens the thin white paper, disconnects it from the filter, and holds the tobacco in her hand. It somehow makes her calmer. Then she lays her head down. He speaks to the back of her neck.

"Look, Ann Aquash, that's right, you changed your name at Wounded Knee. No longer little Annie Pictou. You should have stayed in Boston. Look, no one can run around lawless and at the tip of a gun decide what they're gonna do. Not happening in this country."

"No one can but you, ya mean," she says. It sounds like her voice is coming from under a blanket. "Why is it Americans get so upset about the law except when they're the ones breaking it? Well, guess the Church Committee can decide that. They've answered they are coming, ya know. Yep. You know."

She's smart, he thinks, smiling. He knows that will hang her eventually; it would draw her out. It had something to do with why he keeps arresting her and not charging her. She makes it a little too enjoyable.

"Okay, so you are a special case. Brown University, but no, you turned that down. Or was it Dartmouth? I get those opportunities confused, you shoulda taken it." She suspects if he knows that much, he knows it was Brandeis; he is baiting her.

"A smart cookie. Well, dumb enough to fall for Dennis. Yeah, we heard that. Your father's name is Levi. Last name. Don't see that every day out here. So, with the crack-up of all this coming soon, as Banks goes off in handcuffs, where will that leave you? Why not help us really help these people? I know you care about that . . . I think. It's hard to tell what an AIM Indian really cares about, if goddamn anything. But maybe you do. Like I said, you're a special case."

"Can you run through this rap a little faster? I have dinner to make and I need a grocery store—one I don't get shot in."

"What for? You out of brown paper?"

She can say it with the best of them: "Fuck you, pig. We're done when you're done."

"I can tell you this sincerely, miss, I am absolutely ready to be done. You miss your family in Nova Scotia, and I miss mine."

"Yours is with you." This time she is smiling because she doubts he knows how she could know that. Two can plant doubts. She's playing with fire.

"Why'd ya inflate the numbers? Press people get ya to do that? Yes, I know you run over to Minneapolis ever' chance ya get. Sixty maybe? But a hundred and sixty? No way, lady." He just laughs in his disrespectful way.

"I'm including the miscarriages happening near those uranium drills, the yellowcake poisoned the water supply out there, or so our expert is willing to testify."

"Oh sure, expert. Lotta things could have caused that."

"You'd only know if you investigate it, Agent Harmon. Tell me, how many does the number have to reach for you guys to investigate a murder?"

"I know the temperament of your men. Seen this before," he replies, undaunted. "You are already under suspicion, and it'll only get worse. Call me. If you can reach a phone by the time you wake up. Call."

He slips a piece of paper under her elbow. Lifting her eyes, she sees that the bastard has written his phone number on a torn piece of brown paper.

"When that phone never rings pal, remember, that was me calling."

CHAPTER 22

Rapid Diner with Special Agent Ronnie
June 25, 1975, Early Morning

The Rapid City diner that Special Agent Ronnie frequents for breakfast looks like any typical Western eatery in or out of the Dakotas, whether down into Texas or all the way back to his home state of California.

He surely is homesick, and the closest thing he can find to his momma's breakfast is in this diner. A small beige pottery cup with a thin blue line around its rim holds his creamed coffee, and a matching plate sits beside it. He always lifts the top off the dish of orange marmalade first thing, as it smells a little like the orange trees in his mother's Santa Barbara yard, smells like childhood.

His father was a sweet man, and persuaded his son not to join the armed services and as he was a little softhearted for active duty, he did join the Bureau. It had more of a family orientation, and Ronnie was a sentimental sort. They instantly became a second family. He was lured into the FBI out of Cal Poly by the idealism that he'd be helping people. And for the most part, he felt he did.

Being an Eagle Scout had prepared him more for this duty on the rez than his training. He knows there's no plan here and there won't ever be one. It bothers him that the murder rate is climbing—one report said the highest per capita for any reservation in the United States. It is the accepted norm that it is Indian on Indian, and an unofficial policy to look the other way. The remote region makes this a challenge, and the fact that the locals do not trust law enforcement makes it an even bigger one. Who could know, when dead drunk, what had hurt 'em? Maybe the arresting officer did it, as that was the first face they saw sober. The problem was bigger and needed a bigger solution. On this bright, beautiful sunny morning, Ronnie decides to turn his mind toward optimism, as it is his nature, especially when he spots Ann Richards sitting in the diner. What luck! He goes straight to her booth.

She works part-time in their Rapid City BIA office as a radio dispatch. He'd recently run into her when taking a message over to Gail Harmon, his superior's wife, who also works in that office. He'd come in from the field after investigating a drive-by shooting. Some dumb drunk, likely, had just fired into a car and killed an Indian girl who was just sitting inside it doing her homework. Another wasted life, and not an uncommon call. Someone dead in a trunk. Someone dead in a shack that burned down. Mindless killing and common, and often suspected as being the work of the Goons. They were supposedly "guardians" of Oglala, but what guarded folks from them? Not the Bureau. Not him.

He shakes off the negative thoughts and plops into the booth across from Ann. Pretty, sweet, and smart, he wouldn't be surprised if the Bureau is watching her for recruitment; she has all the qualifications and is neither Goon family nor AIM. High time to start recruiting women anyway. It'd get them out of poverty, bring them into the fold, get them to work with us, he thought, instead of against us. When he'd first seen her at the dispatch desk, a call came in and he saw her change from a sweet-voiced girl to someone as officious as any grown man. All no-nonsense concentration on work. She is just his type, and in California she would have passed as a local Italian girl, as Catholic as he is. She is, however, full-blood Lakota Sioux.

Though he has no inkling of it, Ronnie is far more starved for company than he realizes, and that can make for some strong, if not accidental, attachments. Strange that would be so, as the girls in the office congregated to get a look at agent Ronnie, whenever he was near. He dated several, but wouldn't even call it dates. He was looking for something else, something serious-minded. Ann was a good bet. When Ronnie sits down uninvited, Ann doesn't look up from the paper she is scribbling on. Glimpsing it, Ron says, "Damn, girl! That's calculus?" then immediately apologizes for cussing.

She still does not look up and tries not to grin. "Calculus two."

"Whoa. Been a while. A long while."

"Well, if you let it go too long, Ron, you'll forget all of it. It's like a language."

Boy, his name sounded sweet when she said it. He immediately pulls over her papers to get a better look, takes her pencil, and begins to scribble in the answer.

"Stop that!" she laughs, reclaiming the paper. "Not bad for a cop. Where'd you go to school?"

"Cal Poly," he says with pride. "I'm an agent, not a cop." He knows she knows.

"I'd be only too glad just to get into Haskell. It's in Kansas. I'm at Oglala Lakota College now, but they don't have what I need to get my degree. And I don't have the money to go to Haskell without a scholarship, so please let me get back to it."

The waitress comes over, looking a little disapproving. She waits every morning for Ronnie to come in, and this morning she'd not gotten so much as a greeting. Seeing the two sitting together, she half wonders if he's not an Indian himself, given his dark hair curly toward his ears and his complexion.

She takes his order but doesn't ask Ann if she wants anything. Ron asks her if she wants any more coffee, but under the gaze of the white waitress Ann just gently shakes her head no. She doesn't want anyone, not even a person getting paid to do it, to give her anything they didn't want to. "No thanks," she says to Ron.

When Ronnie's cup is filled, Ann helps herself to a sip from it.

"Hey, just make yourself at home, girl!" he laughs.

Ann's smile fades as she says quietly, "Your boss is here."

Into the silence that falls between them Ronnie says, "You know, he cares about the Indians out here, really. He does."

"No, he doesn't." She pauses. "It's okay, he is just doing a job. I get that. He thinks the end justifies the means. I know the type. I work in law enforcement, too, ya know."

"Well, tribal cops are a little different from us."

"Ya think?" she responds, laughing but respectful.

Soon they are having a real conversation, and Ron likes feeling he's made a real friend. He hasn't made many friends from among the chronically discontented agents—family men, older and not used to his friendly, rather effervescent ways. He isn't a hunter or a golfer, so he spends a lot of his time reading and waiting and arresting people who need a hospital for their alcoholism more than handcuffs. Or pulling dead bodies from burned-out cars.

Mainly, he is along for the ride, and his partner, Jack, is the arresting officer. Coming out of the Los Angeles Police Department, Jack felt right at home with a set of handcuffs. Easy for him to mistake the AIMers for Crips and Bloods, but Ronnie doesn't see it that way at all. On occasion, maybe, but rarely. Former vets in the Bureau will reference their recent duty in Vietnam and quote the adage, "Kill them all and let God sort it out," and they can't always tell an AIM member from a Goon or a local, especially if long hair is involved.

Ronnie's role is usually to help people put on their coats or shawls and then take the children to a relative somewhere. Pretty heartbreaking most of the time, and a strange duty for daily consumption. He, like Jack, longs for a new post. Jack is always reminiscing about Chicago and what it had been like to fight Black Panthers. Nothing, not even the AIMers they arrested, could match the violence in that city. Some of the AIM came from cities, and Ron for one is grateful the local Oglala have them in sweat lodges every spare minute. God help this place otherwise. The city Indians know their way around a weapon, and the tribal chairman gets his entertainment by scaring the hell out of everyone about that, frequently planting false information and making it worse.

Deep into a debate now, Ronnie and Ann speak in low voices as Bureau men file into the diner. They are in no hurry to get to their posts for the day.

Referring to the Bureau, she says, "I wish they'd raid White Clay . . . um, in Nebraska?"

"Oh, I'm quite familiar with the borders. We have no jurisdiction in White Clay, but I agree with you entirely. They sell enough booze to these folks they could drink down half the state. Makes me sad."

"Sad? No, mad! It's the whole problem. Poverty equals alcohol equals violence. Add it up. And government doesn't accomplish anything in the way of curbing any of the three. We need a bigger hospital, not a jail." She pauses. "Sorry, Ron."

"I'm not. You said Ron instead of Ronnie. I'm stoked!" Just two young people with priorities more personal than working out problems that have no immediate answer. "I'll see ya at radio dispatch office later?"

"Sure. Where else will I be? Class at night, the days I spend getting down every word you guys say!"

"Ha ha. I'm going over to Porcupine area before it gets too hot."

Ann doesn't show it, but her eyes change as she grows concerned. "What ya got way over there?" She's also thinking *that area's always hot.*

"Not much. Another Title III," Ron says, catching SAC Harmon's eyes. He lifts his coffee cup in salute, then stands and walks over to join his boss's table.

"That gal is Lakota, isn't she?" Harmon asks immediately.

"Sure, sure. Originally near Kyle. Well, nothing's near anything out here, but yeah, she works for Indian police, Dale Richards. It's where we spotted her."

"I know where you spotted her, Ronnie, my man." Ron just sips his cold coffee, ignoring the implication. "Yep," Harmon goes on, "Got another crumb I have to keep an eye on. Saw the complaint last night, well, you know, you brought it over. Not today though. Hop on with Jack, but you guys be careful with that Jimmy Eagle stuff and that grub farm, remember what today is." The grub farm is his nickname for the AIM camp at Jumping Bull ranch, and the day is special because it's the anniversary of Battle of Little Bighorn. Dick Wilson had given the FBI maps and the layout of hidden bunkers over there, and they'd need to check them out eventually. The Jimmy Eagle situation is just a good excuse to knock on some doors.

Ron looks at the map with the bunkers drawn in and smirks, saying, "Sir, you're not buying into this, are you?"

"Ahhh, it's possible. But I don't see them constructing a rabbit hole, much less something this sophisticated. I'll get over there soon enough. National Guard is coming in for maneuvers soon, and now somebody tells me bags are stacked up at the Indian hospital. Some nurse saw them and freaked. I'm thinking procurement just over ordered, or probably left over from Wounded Knee. We should've knocked the whole hill out while we had them all in one place. Well, like most else out here, not my call."

"So it's real, or it isn't." Ron said, keeping his eyes down on the map.

"Most likely more bunk—most of these threats turn out to be Chairman Dickie's wet dreams. He's bored and useless and dancing for government dollars . . . gotta get 'em some way. Sent him all those guns so now he thinks he's gotta shoot something.

"How'd you get passed that Jimmy Eagle paperwork again?" His boss Harmon was unwrapping a piece of Juicy Fruit gum from its wrapper, making his suspicion all the more innocuous. Ronnie had answered this clearly, just last night.

"Indian Sheriff was afraid to go look for him, nervous."

"How again? It's his jurisdiction."

"Yes sir, but it was a bloody affair, more assault than theft."

"Still a misdemeanor at best."

"Yes sir, sure, sure, but he was afraid of the camp the boy's in." On these words Harmon looked the young agent in the eyes.

"I volunteered to go for him. The warrant wasn't ready, just gonna go look for him. Ask around."

"To the AIM camp, 'cause he's afraid, and he said that?"

"Not the camp, sir, he said he was afraid of the Goons who were watching it."

"Well, is that so? Have a good day, my young man, stay cool, gonna be a hot one." Then he stops to add, "Oh, by the way, Ronald McDonald, change those goddamn shoes for me, would ya?"

"Boss man, these are outstanding!" Ronnie says, lifting a brown leather moccasin boot up for a closer look. Harmon rears back as if it is too disgustingly close to him. "They can stop a cactus or a snake bite even. I don't want a walk out there," he says, pointing to the window, "without these buddies on."

"Okay, okay, California boy, wear what ya like in the field, but carry your Florsheims, with regulation polish, and wear them if you're coming into my office. I got enough explaining to do without a goddamn agent of mine looking like he's going native. Besides that," he adds jokingly, "how in hell, if you're wearing those, can ya die with your boots on?" They are both laughing now.

Agent Harmon will recall this last exchange with Special Agent Ronnie even into his old age; like an echo, it would haunt him.

Ronnie knows his boss is not too subtly referring to Ann with that "going native" dig, but on that matter, Ronnie will not compromise. Some things, very few but some, are worth being insubordinate about. He likes this girl a lot and plans to see her every day if he can. He's just made up his mind about that.

All Ronnie knows at present, as he leaves the diner, is that he is headed straight over to the small community stronghold on the reservation known as Porcupine. It is probably a blessing that he has no inkling what's coming.

CHAPTER 23

The Shirtwearers
June 25, 1975

Since late April, Leonard Peltier hadn't been left with any specific instructions from Dennis Banks, who had his hands full with his upcoming trial. Leonard had been asked to watch out over a problem he had no feel for—a camp. At times it felt more like a fishing camp in the Northwest than an AIM one. Just one a little too idle and waiting for a fight. Under such conditions, one will fight their own. Mainly tents, and open campfires, and arguments, lots of those. Both areas filled with deaths and fighting, he'd grown weary of seeing it and of attending Indian funerals.

With Herb Powless just recently arrested and likely to be gone up the river for a long time, and everyone in court or about to be, all in the Movement felt rudderless for the first time. Twenty-eight AIMers were arrested the same week as Herb. The joke made of Herb's arrest was, "Bet Powless wished his wife Dorothy had been driving through Hot Springs that day! He couldn't outrun 'em, but she coulda, I been night hunting with her!"

Leaders out of commission meant things could only go haywire. Specifically, Leonard had been called to Pine Ridge by Dennis, to work security and guard what was left in the camp. A few Navajo friends had followed him, and his Northwest AIMers, Dino and Nilak, were on-site, too. A good group if sober. Fear and terror did not help support sobriety. The kids' sneaking booze in didn't support it, either. Leonard had to be the heavy, and he was less liked for it.

Herb wouldn't have allowed it, not even of the younger ones. Norman Brown was a good kid, but some of his friends were the very ones bringing in booze. He checked the trunk of every car that pulled in. Even his close friend Dino was thoroughly pissed when Leonard broke a bottle of good whiskey against a cabin wall. Tempers ran hot with the stormy weather coming in.

Anna Mae and Darlene Banks showed up, and many ran to hug them, especially Nilak. Kola sauntered over to where Leonard was busy under the hood, making a snarky sound as he glared at the women.

"The Canuck and Kamook, pair of queens, I'm surprised they stand each other, running with her old man's snag."

"Man, brother, quit talkin' shit on a nice day. Lighten up. Women stick together, you could learn from it, ask me."

"When a woman can hurt same as a man, I stop noticin'."

"That's some cowardly shit you're talkin', just ran Doug off for talking it, keep it up. Why is it I feel good, and two words from you and I feel troubled? Why's that?" Leonard looked over at Darlene and Anna Mae and noticed they'd pulled colorful material from their sewing bags and had begun sewing. Hands always busy. They were finishing up on a few ribbon shirts they planned to use in a giveaway later that night. A giveaway was a tradition where you gave the best of what you had; in the old days you gave all.

"I hear that snitch is back in Milwaukee talking shit about you."

"I don't know how you could hear nothin'." This did concern Leonard a minute, but just because he knew Dorothy was without Herb. Doug Dunham came out as an informant, and on a radio station the weekend Herb was arrested. "Coward" was all Peltier thought about Doug. He moved his attention elsewhere as Razor popped open his hatchback and people started taking cans of beer out of it. Jimmy Eagle was handing out items that appeared to have been swiped right off a convenience store counter, by the looks of them. Honey Buns in their individual wrappers. Beef jerky. Individual bags of peanuts. Darlene Banks complained first.

"They'd knock over a liquor store on the way to ceremony, those two!" Jimmy Eagle, mocking her pregnant belly, walked behind her sloshing a large jar filled with pink vinegar water with boiled eggs. Another dead giveaway.

"You told us to bring food for the drum, so I did, now ya complain, ingrates!"

"Why ya making new clothes, wash the ones we have." Kola chimes in.

Darlene leans back over the bright material and says, "Get me a washing machine up here and I will."

Jimmy Eagle snorts at her, "wash 'em on a rock, good enough for my momma!"

"I'll wash 'em on a rock, with you in 'em." She answers, as others snicker.

Leonard lowered the hood a second time that day. Jimmy Eagle took a quick exit.

The camp seems safer now that Leonard's on-site, Anna Mae feels, as she looks over and smiles at the churned-up earth, a garden that she and Leonard had started the day before. He'd hooked up an old lawnmower engine to a horse plow he'd sanded and sharpened, and others laughed as it dragged them all over the field and made a small clearing. Hopefully, Leonard said, no one would use it to spy down on them. Ole Chairman Dickie is always spying and making stuff up on them, like that they had the cabins laced with charges. What cabins, and what charges? They have tents. It requires planning and money to do what they are accused of, and AIM has none of either. There is always the persistent rumor—or dream—of a Wounded Knee *Three*. BIA in Rapid believes it and fears it. After The Knee, money for Indian schools dried up. Other than the run Anna Mae made with Leonard back to Wisconsin for that monastery takeover, things have grown monotonous. A tense quiet, as the trial is coming. Dennis and Darlene have five acres and a cabin nearby, thanks to Cecelia and Harry Jumping Bull, and all AIM are welcomed and feel safer together. And Wallace and June Little just across the road.

Already a hot one, this day starts off pretty much as usual for Leonard, as he is the complaint department. Grandma Jumping Bull has asked to see him and won't settle for being talked down by anyone else. A big holiday is happening to commemorate the Battle of the Greasy Grass (aka Battle of Little Bighorn). A friend of hers, an elder, promises to bring out his nearly hundred-year-old flag, one that only Lakota people ever see, as it was captured at the 1876 battle and has been tucked away all these years. Torn, aging, and bloodstained, likely it rode tied to a horse's neck or a lance. Not the size that went on a flagpole, small as a bandana. *Would be exciting to see it*, Leonard thinks, as few in the world have ever captured an American flag during a battle and lived to show it off. Just the Sioux. Following World War II, elders buried the shirts of the Shirtwearers in a large hole in the Badlands, declaring an end to fighting, as they had fought for the United States.

A midday barbecue will precede the big ceremony. Seems like the baby AIMers think that since it's a party occasion they can do as they like, and Leonard is tired of hearing himself talk sense to them. Now Grandma Jumping Bull wants a few minutes of what would otherwise have been a well-earned break.

Leonard gets out from under the hood, smooths his hair, and receives her with great respect. The old ones like Leonard particularly. He hauls their water and chops their wood and answers any questions they ask squarely. He is different from some of the ones AIM was drawing in. Leonard thinks part of the problem is that they don't have any work to occupy their hands or minds and they are caged in by Goons on all sides, so no one left the area much. Well, there is work to be done, and he'll help them do it. There are plenty of cars to be fixed, so today they can take a front end off and use up some of that youthful energy.

He doesn't keep Grandma waiting. She is the landowner who gave AIM her home, and a Gold Star Mother who'd lost two sons at the Battle of the Bulge. Her voice is soft, but she is serious and highly respected, especially by Leonard.

"Them boys near drove us crazy last night with their drinking and shooting around. One point I had to get under the bed," Grandma exclaims. Leonard recalls seeing a bullet that stood out of her wooden cabin once, like a porcupine quill after it hit. They sure knew how to cure wood, these Oglala. "Now, I've told them young boys, but I need you to back it up." She and Harry are going off the ranch for a few days to see about some cattle and are imagining what might go on while they're gone.

Leonard looks at Razor and says, "Go with her and get them up now, and then bring every one of them to me. Grandma, show him which tent, and you two get them up." Leonard is funny that way—if you told on somebody, you had to be present, tell that truth and be aware of their punishment. You couldn't just tell and then back on out the door. Not even Grandma. Leonard hated tattling.

Grandma goes out over the road, as asked, her pastel scarf tied tightly under her chin and her silver bun coiled neatly at her neck. After a few minutes she returns, shaking her head as she says, "Leonard, they are just boys. I'm sorry I bothered you about it, it was just the drink that done it. They say they're not coming; they ain't up yet."

Leonard lowers the hood of the car with a thump; having removed a broom handle that held it up, he now crosses the road with it. Grandma keeps her head down, as Razor snickers. A few others come over to see what the commotion is about, Dino Butler among them. They wait as the air fills with tension. Peltier returns, puts the broom handle back under the corner of the heavy hood, and says, "They're up."

As he walks back to the Littles' cabin, he notices the large hand-scrawled banner. Battle of Greasy Grass, Remember! Rosebud River June 25, 1876.

James War Bonnet is sitting to one side of it, somber-faced and missing his good friend Herb Powless. He'd only seen Herb once or twice before he got arrested and isn't likely to see him again. Just back from Vietnam, he is wearing a bloodstained T-shirt that reads Remember the Knee with his red beret adorned with eagle feathers dangling from its side. He is busy making something on a stump, and though Leonard knows better than to ask him any questions, hot-headed Jimmy Eagle does not.

"What ya making there with that big knife, Hoss?"

"Another knife."

Next to War Bonnet, half a rusty fifty-five-gallon barrel is serving as a makeshift grill. A large elk flank hangs just above the coals, dripping fresh blood. Some splashes into the nearby water bucket.

Jimmy's aunt calls out, "Move that water bucket, it's the only one, and we need it for drinking water later."

War Bonnet reaches in, scoops up a handful of the pink water, and drinks it down, laughing. Leonard notices his eyes are a bit bloodshot; best to leave him be. 'Nam is sending these men back pretty tight. Good country fresh air, ceremony, and friends would unwind them.

War Bonnet, an Oglala, is especially bothered by all the armored personnel traveling down their roads of late. With the trial coming to Rapid, there is no way to avoid it. That this is "all for show" does not impress him. He often hears helicopters overhead that aren't actually there. He makes his feelings clear. "They'd better keep off my land. Same problem in 'Nam, why the tens of thousands of bombs couldn't break them, because it was all at a civilian level. It hasn't broken my people, either." He considers this intrusion into Pine Ridge an undeclared war. He calls out, "If the FBIs walk on your land, have a ceremony to cleanse it!"

War Bonnet will never be the same after Vietnam. Leonard is not happy he failed the physical at the marine recruiting office; it's why he never mentions it, but on reflection he knows a bum knee is better than a bum heart.

Leonard has just started to rebuild a rusted-out transmission when the pointed toes of a new pair of blue snakeskin cowboy boots make an appearance. Jimmy Eagle and his usual nonsense, Peltier muses. He also notices that they are reddish brown along one side, and something tells him it is not elk's blood splatter.

"Where's that five dollars you owe me, before I put these tools down and whip your ass, little brother?"

"What, Leonard, ya think you can get blood out of a turnip?"

"You can stop being a turnip. Move away from me."

June Little, a jovial man and their host, leans down and tells Peltier they'll eat soon. Jimmy Eagle just walks away, seeing that a few girls are arriving. June pulls a half-broken lawn chair over closer, having decided to get in a visit. Leonard asks him something he's always been curious about.

"How'd you lose that arm, brother? You don't have to tell me if ya don't want."

"I don't mind. Truth is, I was lacing up a charge and it went wrong. For a minute there, I thought I'd be meeting Crazy Horse a whole lot sooner than I expected. But it just took my arm off, I was lucky."

"Lucky huh? I don't want to be around any of that shit or your luck. Where'd it go off? Wounded Knee?"

"Hell, nah. Actually, it was darn close to where you're standing, memory serves."

Leonard says, unimpressed with the humor, "I'm serious; don't want anything to do with any of that, keep it far from me."

"Yeah, neither does the law and that's the point. It keeps everything at a distance, which is about all we can hope to do. Hell, nobody gets hurt out here but us anyway. We got quite a list of names going. Where's their list?"

"Goons are getting way out of control. Little baby over in Kyle lost a finger other night. Shot right through a window. No ambulance, nothing."

"Damn, Leonard . . . a child. No respect for nothing, not even their own."

Leonard moves from the old car, and June starts to close the hood for him. Leonard stops him.

"Better leave the hood up, unless ya see rain. That way the mice won't build nests in the carburetor and chew the wires."

Leonard looks over at Razor, who is lounging with Dino Butler, who has Nilak on his lap. The party is starting. If they're back, then Anna Mae must be, too. Leonard misses his girlfriend all the sudden. She is not a regular thing, but better than loneliness. He notices that June is still waiting for him to speak.

"Hey, June, where you think Jimmy Eagle got those fancy cowboy boots?" He's asking because he knows he'll likely have another mess to clean up later.

"These boys are just too young and too wild. We need more men in this camp, men like James, or old men even. Glad for Dino." Leonard is suddenly of a mind, while Herb is out of Milwaukee, to maybe go on back there for a while when this trial is over. Over? Not a word anyone ever used before. Time to go home, he's thinking. Soon.

June looks over at Jimmy Eagle and whispers to Leonard, "I hear it got pretty bloody the other night and a sheriff's looking for him. Bad scrape, in Porcupine."

Heralded by screeching tires and dust, young agent Ronnie and his partner Jack are speeding across the road, turning around. Dusty, a Lakota youth in a hammock, has just informed them Jimmy Eagle hadn't been there in days and they left in dust a mile high upon seeing the crowd standing at both sides of the compound. They decided to wait until another day. It angers Leonard that Dusty even spoke to them. He is also aware young Norman Brown, with his pals are walking the same road. The young AIM boys are walking to go find a shower. Leonard's sure they know better than to get in the car, if the agents spot them.

War Bonnet is none too calm, seething actually, and comments, "One day, they are gonna ride in, but not ride back out, not if it's on my land." Peltier has noticed his white Chevy sitting not far from him, with its .223-caliber Heckler and next to that an AR-15.

"They oughta get a fine for speeding, we got kids all over this road playing." That's about as much attention as Peltier gives it, it being a common affair.

He's barely gotten the words out when Jimmy Eagle's auntie hollers out the back door, "Jimmy, you git! They're looking for you now. Go, go!"

"Ahh, they aren't gonna look for me way over here, auntie. Dusty sent them off! Just BIA cops all way over in Porcupine." Jimmy Eagle knows something they don't. It isn't Goons looking for him, or Indian cops, it's FBI. Someone in Rapid has already tipped him off.

CHAPTER 24

The Porcupine Incident
June 26, 1975

Agent Ronnie is used to driving at high speed in high altitudes and is usually lost. A joke around the Bureau offices in Rapid is that Donald Harmon recruits Eagle Scouts, drops them off in the Badlands, and if they find their way back to Rapid, he gives them a badge. They also get a gun, but in Ron's three years out here, so far, he hasn't pulled it from its holster except to show it to his new girl.

Girlfriend. He loves that word. He's seen a few girls in his time in South Dakota but kept a wall up, as he always imagined he'd settle down back in California. He wanted to be near his mother. He would know he found the right girl when she understood that. He confessed that to Ann just the night before, who seems devoted to her mother, and she replied, "Of course you do!"

At that, he kissed her for real and started dreaming about marriage. He knows she couldn't easily leave the rez, but she wants four years in a real engineering college, and Cal Poly is real. As dreaming goes, he's making it a good one, it kills time. Once married, they can worry about the other details later, like whether he'd stay with the Bureau. For now, he is headed in the opposite direction of the Rapid office, back over to Porcupine in Pine Ridge. A BIA sheriff is waiting.

Arriving at the BIA office, he notices Dick Wilson speeding out of a nearby parking lot. He asks an Indian cop where Wilson's off to in such a hurry, and the guy just says, "Hiram, I think."

Porcupine is a traditional stronghold, what in hell is he doing over here rooting around? Ronnie thinks, as he makes a note in his report manual. He will definitely be mentioning it to his SAC.

The Indian cop right away scoffs at his beaded moccasins. The new BIA superintendent notices, too. "Hell, I thought a minute there Wilson left a Goon behind. Come on in." This young agent is a contradiction for sure, and he greets Ronnie by saying, "I hoped I'd see you back here today." Ronnie is aware of Ann's voice over the radio dispatch, from back in Rapid.

"The Porcupine incident? Jimmy Eagle? Aren't you back here for that?" the superintendent asks. "He eluded you boys yesterday, but he's at that ranch."

"No. I'm gonna handle it today," the BIA sheriff says. "Soon as I get up the guff to go over to Littles' ranch and then likely, God help us, over to the Jumping Bull homestead. Not a pleasant place these days."

The sheriff gets an odd look on his face.

"What's keeping ya?" Ronnie asks.

"He's an Oglala kid, ya know."

"I know."

"Angry as hell for someone so damn young. Didn't just steal some boots, a nice pair, hand-tooled—he beat the man he took them from almost to death. A real scrap ensued. I gotta go get the little bastard myself, since you missed him."

"Is the warrant ready, sir? We can go out again. Not a problem, why are you so worried about it? You know the people there."

"It's not them that worry me, like I said yesterday, it's the Goons that are watching them. People are likely still partying. Don't like truckin' near a god-damn Goon watch, they'll shoot at anything that moves them guys."

Ronnie recalls seeing Dick Wilson's car, then shakes it off and says, "I'll go. No problem, sir. I'm not worried about that group, they know me. I'll take the warrant over, and if he's there, I'll bring him in to ya. Deal?"

"Warrant not here yet. No matter, you guys don't really need one, right?"

"No, sir. Then I'm outta here."

"Blink your lights when you enter the Little ranch or Jumping Bull's."

Silly, Ronnie thinks, *it's daylight.* As trained to do, the minute he gets to his radio he lets his partner, Jack, know where he is headed. He doesn't let SAC Harmon know, as he is having car trouble and can't likely follow anyhow. Agent Jack says he'll piggyback.

Ann hears their radio messages. The voices are scratchy over the wire. She notices her boss Gail Harmon picking up the phone. She jumps back to the radio where there's a lot of activity all of the sudden. She sees Ronnie's radio signal light on. That gives her a little peace.

Agent Jack has the arrest experience Ronnie lacks, and he often says so. He'll head with him back over to the Littles', in case they do find the twerp and get to arrest him. Jack would enjoy an arrest of this kid, after glancing at the report he'd read the day before. They can bring him in to question and by that time the warrant should be in.

Special Agent Harmon is frustrated, sitting on a road nearby. He is having car trouble yet again, after just leaving the shop in Rapid. The locals are always mentioning their high-end government cars, but most of the procurement models are pieces of shit, and none of his men, including him, know mechanics. If one of them got stuck on these roads, they were just as stuck as Harmon is now, watching flies on a buffalo pie.

Hearing his radio crackle out of the Rapid dispatch, he is pleasantly surprised to hear his wife's voice, until he notices that her tone doesn't sound good. "Come in, Gail, come in." The crackling dies out, then resumes. It makes a popping sound that mimics gunfire, but he knows it can't be that. He tosses his Coke can and leans in closer. "Gail Harmon, dispatch, come in please. Over." Then he hears Ronnie's voice, agitated and, oh my God, he is calling for help. Where the hell is he? What kind of help does he need at this hour of the morning? He quickly checked his wristwatch and scribbled on his dashboard with his fountain pen: 11:45.

Then he hears Gail say she is trying to get armed backup to go to the Jumping Bull ranch. Backup for Ronnie? *Chrissakes!* Donald Harmon jumps into gear.

"Ronnie," Donald says as he intercepts the call, "Where are you? What's your location? Over." When no answer comes back, he talks to Gail. All she has is that Jack and Ronnie were investigating the Jimmy Eagle situation and are now on the Jumping Bull AIM compound. Neither Donald nor Gail know the agents are currently in a ravine below a green house and got there by chasing a red pickup that pulled down the Jumping Bull road. Gail Harmon herself noted, "sees red pickup leaving the area." They spotted the youth they were looking for in its truck bed. The men from the pickup exchanged fire with them. What happens next is purely frantic for all sides. The radio dispatch witnesses it along with spectators from both sides of the road.

Then a reply comes on to Harmon's radio, and comes in clearly. It's a frantic call from Ronnie in the field. "We are being fired on. Send . . ." is heard, then more static, ". . . get help to us quickly or we are dead! Repeat! Urgent! Over!" The wavy crackle goes in and out again. Donald responds, in case Ronnie can hear him. "Hold on partner, I'm coming!" He doesn't step away from his vehicle's radio before telling dispatch, "Get every possible man within a hundred miles to that area! Now! Over!" Gail Harmon has already dispatched that message, and every available BIA cop and Goon is ensuing. Even the National Guard, who are nearby, are pulled off maneuvers and on their way.

Next, Donald holds his badge high in the air and flags down the only vehicle in sight. A very pregnant Lakota girl pulls over her rickety vehicle, probably thinking he might be arresting her. He pushes her to the passenger side and takes the driver's seat. She is in for the ride of her young life. He is now without a radio, but at least is heading in the correct direction. The girl knows the place and points down a side dirt road he'd never have found. A few miles later she points again.

He says caustically, "This better be the right way, lady!" It was, and forty minutes later they pull up among many other cars parked overlooking an embankment. They had all arrived ahead of him. Edgar Bear Runner, known by all as a young traditional, recognizes Harmon's passenger and runs over to embrace her before leading her away from the cars. Her name is Jean, and of all coincidences she is Peltier's girlfriend.

Then Dick Wilson pulls up and gets out holding an AR-15. He is with his tribal chief of police, many of his own men, and the Porcupine district BIA police. A new and very green BIA superintendent stands by and is trusting Edgar.

Seeing them, Donald says loudly and with finality, "Who the hell are these men? This is *my* jurisdiction, so stay behind me! Those are *my* men in that field."

Dick Wilson glares at Edgar Bear Runner and asks, "Why in hell is he here? He's a goddamn AIMer! So is that woman!"

Donald goes over to Bear Runner and pulls him close, asking, "How can you help this? Can you go in there? Stop their firing?" Edgar nods. "Then *go* and come back in five minutes or I am coming in and will be after you as well. Go!"

The Indian man pulls off his T-shirt, which reads Remember the Knee, and inverts it to look more like a white flag. He holds it above his head as he moves toward the ravine. "Harmon knows his men are suffering when across the radio he'd heard for himself that desperate plea from Ronnie. It was still ringing in his head and he's ready to shoot it out to get in. He won't wait long!"

It seems like Bear Runner has been gone for hours, but it is only thirty-four minutes before he signals the men on the bluff to let him come back up.

A few hours pass and a lot of sniper fire is exchanged before Donald Harmon can get to his men. Edgar assures him it is too late to save them; this recovery will mean bodies, not souls. The National Guard has made its way over. He sees what transpired within just one hour of his last radio exchange with Ronnie.

Donald has seen a few battlefields; still, none break his heart like seeing what he does in this ravine in South Dakota. The ground is so chewed up that it looks like thirty or more shooters have had at it. The bodies of his two men are facedown in the dirt. Jack looks as if he bled to death; one arm has been shot nearly off. Apparently, Ronnie used his shirt as a tourniquet around Jack's missing arm. He turns Ronnie over. He is missing his face and fingers off one hand. One bullet wound indicates that he had been shot after he was already dead. Harmon thinks it looks execution-style—but that is incredible. *Why, over what?*

He sits back and squeezes a handful of dirt so hard, his nails cut into his palm. The pain wakes him out of his shock-induced haze, and he jumps up. Every minute counts. A BIA cop thinks he has something in his gun sights. Harmon moves to yank his gun away, but before he can, it goes off. The cop says he thinks he got one of them. Harmon notices the car radio is shot to pieces and silent.

"One of who?" Harmon says through gritted teeth.

"One of the Indians that shot your men."

Up to this point, Donald Harmon wasn't satisfied it was Indians.

Later, when Gail gives him the radio transcripts, the day's horror show gets even worse. Ronnie can be heard desperately pleading for backup that had no way of getting to him in time. Jack can be heard begging Ronnie to walk out of there, to use his shirt as a white flag and get out. Ron would never have left him, but it is clear later that he had had that option, and it had been his only one, to live. There are only a few shots at first, and then later, maybe after it is all over, there are many. Then the radio goes dead.

By nightfall, the new superintendent of the BIA had written a ten-thousand-dollar check to be spent for arms, flights, and vehicles to chase eighteen men, women, and Indian children across the Black Hills way out beyond Oglala. A costly seventy-mile route. Armed helicopters dotted the sky, and several troop transport vehicles and half-tracks, the military trucks that transport weapons, move through the area. The response is meaningful but of little use. The Indians know every backwash and gulch, and those who lived there hid out easily. They already lived out in obscurity before this and have had to escape many times themselves. They were good at it.

Through that first night and for the next weeks, distractions had the authorities scrambling around in the Black Hills. First over to the visitor center at Mount Rushmore, where a small charge had been detonated, enough to bring them to where the Indians were not. Another charge went off near the armory at the old sculptor's ranch. Days later, Harmon went into Crow Dog's paradise and arrested everyone but Dennis, his wife, Darlene, Bob Robideau (Razor), and Leonard Peltier. They were nowhere to be found. *How have so many managed to slip through their net?* Harmon thought, devastated, and working with a heavy heart.

It turned out that Darlene Banks, very pregnant, had begged her husband Dennis to stay the night at Crow Dog's paradise and let her rest, but by instinct the group's leader decided to leave right away. Razor slipped away in his hatchback and Leonard with Dennis and family in another car. Others weren't so lucky. Anna Mae stayed at Rosebud. The young Navajo boy, Norman Brown, was interrogated the very next day, along with his poor mother. Anna Mae took the worst of it until, and as in times past, Harmon intervened. Possibly it was he who asked for her release. Did he hope to follow her, as he knew where she would be heading? One could only guess, as there was no plan that was evident.

Anna Mae begged Lew to make the judge keep her in jail. Lew responded that he could work a lot of magic with a law book, but making the authorities keep her when they didn't want to was not a trick he knew.

The fleeing AIMers eventually cross the country together, but not before pulling off something remarkable: their hiding locally. Oglala families hid them before their cross-country trek began, destination Los Angeles. For a moment, Leonard thought of going over to Milwaukee, but without Herb to help that would be a mistake. He'd never take this trouble to Dorothy anyway, so he heads to Denver. Herb's sister, however, just got a new car and offers to drive him from there over to 11129 Mulholland Drive, Los Angeles, the home of Marlon Brando. That's where he will meet up with Dennis and Darlene Banks, almost full term in her pregnancy and with her sister Bernie at her side. Anna Mae leaves the Ridge and will eventually rendezvous with them at the Santa Monica Pier. They'll leave Brando's with ten thousand dollars and a motorhome. They'll stay with friendlies all along the California coast and the rather large vehicle will offer a chance to stay incognito long enough until they could circle back to Pine Ridge.

But the FBI is closing in on them as if they know their whereabouts, and soon the Bureau is aware the escapees are hiding on the Chumash Reservation. It's the last place Donald Harmon, with his men, want to stage a showdown. Not on another reservation, no way—to what, garner more sympathy? So they waited and watched.

Harmon is bitter and determined and always staring at a map. "More likely, they'll eventually turn back east from Oregon," a snitch informs him, "and if so then head out onto the sand flats. We'll roadblock them out on the Snake River. Harmon alerts Oregon's highway patrol. Far from any town; all will be better out of sight, and civilians well out of the way." An arrest would be satisfying, but it might go another way.

The FBI trails the fugitive AIMers for eight months. Harmon's hopes for the Snake River capture never materialize. Instead, a green Oregon State Trooper misreads a teletype and thinks the final word, stop, means *stop*. As he stops the motorhome.

He pulls over the motorhome to a side of the road, and it's Leonard Peltier's voice that's heard first. He tries to calm the anxious patrolman and warns him that there are children and women inside the home. "So calm down, we are all coming out." Soon a backup car arrives as the AIMers are spread-eagled on the ground. The fragile, pregnant Darlene clutches her little daughter to her side as Anna Mae covers them. Then Leonard Peltier flees over a fence. The young trooper gets off a round and luckily, he thinks, hits Leonard's shoulder.

"Does that stop him?" Harmon later asks his new partner, rhetorically, as they read the dispatch. "Of course not! He flies over a goddamn fence!" His partner reads details from the report. "Then Anna Mae Aquash and Darlene Banks are brought in, and the little Banks girl, Tashina, is sent to state care." Darlene, though nine months pregnant, is made to stand on a cement floor for many hours. That makes the papers.

Harmon continues, "Dennis Banks? Was he even with them? Oh, he was with them! The motorhome was found a few miles away, abandoned, who drove it? Or maybe," Harmon muses bitterly, "he has already flown away in a prop plane with Marlon Brando at the controls and is hidden on a Polynesian island some-goddamn-where!"

Those two are gonna pop their heads up somewhere, sometime soon, and when they do, I will be there, thinks Harmon. Razor has been caught, and Dino Butler, then Jimmy Eagle came in and was dismissed. Harmon lingers on the memory of his recent Jimmy Eagle interview. The youth had just brazenly walked into his office. Harmon had put out an all-points bulletin that he would give immunity to anyone who came in with useful evidence regarding the murder of his men. His own supervisor and Bureau chief had objected to the wording, as murder one, two, or three each carried particular charges. This had been a firefight, and little had been proved yet against the people they were hunting. Many thought Donald Harmon needed to be taken off the case. He had just up and decided to be the point man, and there was a reason US law did not favor turning the accused over to a victim's family. They just wanted a hanging, any hanging of course, and the dead agents *were* Harmon's family.

Jimmy Eagle had had the gall to waltz in wearing the stolen cowboy boots that many believed had started this whole nightmare. Donald took a closer look, as they were part of what had cost the lives of his men and ruined his own life. Sure enough, they were spiffy, and Harmon said so. The bitterness in his voice, however, escaped the notice of Jimmy Eagle, who had no idea what he was dealing with.

"Information? Ya got some, I'm told?" Harmon said casually to Jimmy, who was busy looking at the board full of photos of all the AIM members and their many supporters. Even Chief Frank Fools Crow had made the board.

"Ahh, nah, he is not Klamath Falls! Where in hell ya get that?" Jimmy said, pointing to Darrell Butler. "Dino is Rogue River, Tuni, man. And this guy," Jimmy tapped another photo, "he's Navajo, you got Chippewa. You have got to keep this shit straight. This shit is important." Then he said, "I sure know this one!" tapping a photo on the board, "he wore his ski mask all through the shoot-out, like that'd hide him! Hell bro, it just pointed you out!"

Harmon walked over and pinned a picture of the bodies of his agents in front of him. The boy recoiled. "Yeah, that one, I recognize his clothes, and he had this little trinket around his neck, his shirt was off, yeah. Which one is that again, the shirtless one? Man, I can't recall, they all look alike to me." At this last quip, he stifled a giggle, overestimating Harmon's tolerance level.

Harmon's new partner chose that moment to pop his head in and ask, "What charges, sir? We are dismissing what, exactly?"

"Uhh, some stolen boots, retail larceny, a misdemeanor." Harmon's head was bursting with pain and his nerves rattled like a snake.

Jimmy Eagle whined, "They ain't hardly much retail to it no more, they're too goddamn worn!" At that, Harmon jumped up, grabbed him, and upended him, using his weight to the floor to pop him on the head. Harmon's partner didn't dare intervene as he watched Harmon rip open a large evidence bag with his teeth, prop one foot on the boy's stomach for balance, and yank the boots off him. Slammed them in the bag, then taped it closed. Grabbing a big black marker, he scrawled on the bag James Theodore Eagle, evidence, larceny and assault. His partner added a date, then walked him to lockup. Many suspected, as they'd heard Jimmy Eagle bragging about killing the agents himself, that he had some story to tell, and likely gave Harmon his version, true or false. Harmon's new partner is shocked when James Theodore Eagle is released, *charges dismissed.* When he inquires, his weary SAC answers; I'm not interested in locals.

When Dennis Banks hears the siren and sees the blue lights, Leonard Peltier pulls the motorhome over. Leonard is first at the door, but he does not leave the driver's seat before cramming Dennis's head down and saying, "Stay put, they don't know how many of us are in here, they won't hurt the girls or the little one." Dennis follows this direction and sure enough, the single patrolman can't check out the motorhome for other occupants. As soon as Dennis hears the shot that wounds Leonard, he jumps into the driver's seat and drives off. There is too much to protect on the ground for the patrolman to follow, and he also has a wounded Indian taking off toward a populated area. Dennis slides away. Later, he abandons the vehicle and takes off on foot, then hides for several days in a barn, on a remote farmstead, slipping out just at night to get water from a well.

One morning Dennis wakes up and sees through a knothole in the barn that the farmer has just set a fruit jar of fresh water and some breakfast on the well. Dennis walks out to meet him. The man says he's seen the news and suspected he was one of the AIMers. He offers to drive Dennis to the California border, but no farther. Dennis has to trust him. And the man is true to his word.

Once in California, John Trudell arrives to pick him up. Though Dennis is later arrested in Oakland, Governor Jerry Brown himself gives Banks asylum.

Darlene Banks remains in jail and gives birth there. Agent Harmon is standing in the courtroom when the judge gives the order to extradite Anna Mae back to South Dakota. As she walks past the agent, she stops and eyes him directly. Clearly, he is a changed man.

"Remember when I asked you how many numbers there had to be before you'd investigate a killing? Now I know, the number's *two*." Then she walks off from him, never to see him again.

Even Dorothy was in the dark as to the whereabouts of the missing AIMers. All concerned friends could do was wait and hope someone gave some little hint on the moccasin telegraph. And then it came in: Peltier had made it, wounded no less, all the way to the Canadian border. Of course Canadian Indians were helping him. Dorothy didn't know it yet, but it was just Leonard who'd made it out.

SAC Donald Harmon was left to wonder until the following January, when he got intel from Vancouver, Canada. There was an Indian male whose name had been picked up on a Title III wiretap. He was at Chief Small Boy's camp; the reference used was "*Tatewikuwa.*"

Harmon knew he'd seen that name with its odd spelling before, in his own files. He found it in the last file box he checked, the one marked Milwaukee AIM. The Indian male in question was a young Chippewa, also Miniconjou Lakota on his mother's side. In translation the strange spelling translated to English, "Wind Chases the Sun." He was also Leonard Peltier. His name was in many files, including Jimmy Eagle's. "Pay dirt!" Harmon said aloud.

CHAPTER 25

Chief Small Boy's Camp, Outside Vancouver, Canada

January 6, 1976

It seems forever since the motorhome escape, as Leonard rides with his cousin Pauline to the northern border of Washington State. She wants to take him farther, but he already regrets letting her travel this far, especially in this weather. Any minute he could face capture, and the men gunning for him will be dangerous men.

"Cousin, hey, you, pretty girl," he says to her before leaving the car. "Yes, I mean you, quit bowing your head. Do something for me, will ya? Hold your head up. Listen to me now, I ain't got time to say this right, so I'm just gonna tell ya. I felt like hell leaving you behind at boarding school that day when we were kids, If I coulda done anything about it I woulda."

"Jesus, Leonard, will ya let go of that? You want to tell me? You hardly tell me anything else. You were nine years old, what do you think ya could'a done? She was your guardian, Grandma; they kept me on a technicality. You guys couldn't a taken me, she begged them, I heard her. I was there, too, remember?"

"They took ya to that school from our house, then all of a sudden we ain't kin enough to leave together. I hate those people."

"Well, hate them from a long distance, will ya? Get up there in those Canadian mountains and don't come back down again for a long time. If they get their hands on you this time, you'll never see the light a day again. Feel us with ya, 'cause we are, and no matter what you done, I love you, Leonard."

"Look at me, Pauline. I ain't done nothing but be born what you are."

"I don't need to hear that, Leonard, I ain't asking."

"I know, I just want you to know, is why I'm saying it. I want you to know and tell Ma."

"We know. We lived it with ya. Don't nobody need to tell us. Go now. And stay gone!"

"Pauline, if you need me or Ma does, call the old stone church. They'll know where to get word. I'll see ya soon."

Pauline watches him move off into the snow, and her eyes fill with warm tears. She hears geese in flight and realizes there must be a lake nearby. She prays it won't bar Leonard's path. She is glad she brought him, real glad, and only wishes their time together had lasted longer. If it was anybody but Leonard, she imagines, heading into such a deep forest and snow would be hopeless. But it is her Leonard, and she'll hear soon that he is safe with friends across the border.

She turns the old rusted-out Impala around and starts home, laughing out loud as she recalls the first words Leonard said after he'd hopped in and tossed his bag in the back seat. She started up the old car, and with 250 G-men out looking for him, he said, "Get an oil change. Damn, girl, that's the life of the car!" Cousin Leonard, always rescuing something.

Leonard, way off the main road, comes to a large metal sign on a high fence marked Warning! It also says, This is not a legal checkpoint. You may not cross here! You will be crossing into Canadian Provinces and it is illegal. Punishable by fine and imprisonment. Go back now to a legal crossing. Warning! He drags on his cigarette and listens for a second to the quiet breathing of the land. Snow hangs heavy on limbs in the primeval forest filled with old virgin timber.

He stubs out his finished Marlboro on the sign and puts the butt into his shirt pocket, then smiles and throws a leg over the top of the fence. Looking back at the sign once more he says to it, "Fu-u-ck-you" and hops easily over the fence and into Canada. Then he runs toward the green pine that seems to swallow him up.

By the following morning he is in the woods just a stone's throw from his destination. An old Indian man is fussing at his dog while digging his hand into a feed bag and sprinkling seed across the water to salmon. He has a hatchery with them inside it made out of a long wooden trough, right in his yard, and a hose keeps its water moving so it doesn't freeze up. Hours earlier, just as Leonard was almost to the man's porch, a truckload of boys back from a night's hunt drove up and so he backed off into the woods to wait for them to leave. The dog knows something is out in the woods, but oddly, it doesn't run to investigate. Then Leonard notices that a small brown bear is eating out of the hatchery with its paw. The old man is mad now and keeps fussing at the dog, pointing at the bear, but he seems to have forgotten he is a dog. "No bark, no nuthin,'" Peltier observes.

Finally, the frustrated old fellow shoots his 30-30 into the air and the bear runs off and the dog wakes up and really takes off now. *Runs his ass right past the bear!* Leonard smiles, thinking, but the old man is less amused by it, and he walks into the woods cussing and spitting. Then he stops cold, almost as if seeing a ghost, and then walks right up to Leonard, who allows it, asking, "Can ya tell me where I can find Chief Small Boy's place?"

"I can."

"Well," Leonard grins, never out of humor, "tell me where then?"

"I will."

This time, it kind of irritates Leonard. "I wouldn't take too long telling me, we might have company. And not the kind we want, if ya get my meaning? Who was in the truck last night?"

"Oh, just some boys. My people. I loaned them a wheelbarrow for a hunt, and they brought it back with some elk shank. Let's eat." The dog comes back out of the trees. "Must have heard the word eat," Leonard says, rubbing his ears. The old man says to the dog, "We ought to eat you, but you're too dumb to eat."

"What's his name?"

"Dog."

"And yours?" Leonard asks, smiling again.

"Chief Small Boy. Dog's too dumb to get a real name. Why'd you wait in the woods so long? I was waiting for you."

"I slept under your neighbor's porch, glad they had a good potbelly stove above me all night or I wouldn't be here now. You know what they're after me over?"

Small Boy just repeats, "Been waiting for you for two days. Come in and get some heavier clothes on and we'll eat. I boiled some eggs to go with that elk. Frank's already here, was just out with the hunters."

Leonard knows he means his friend and AIM brother Frank Blackhorse. He is relieved he's also made it. The warmth of the fire from the potbelly stove on the porch and the elder's welcoming manner takes the chill off and Leonard goes to sleep right after breakfast, lying on the porch with the dog's head on his chest, his warm breath on his face. He finds both to be a comfort as he falls into a deep sleep and is truly warm for the first time in two days.

For a while, others can stand watch, and he is well fed and soon well rested, Canadian style. At one point, the old man opens the back of a clock and tells Leonard to put everything he regrets into it. Then he ties it up tight with a small rope and throws it into the fire, saying, "Now that's all gone, and you need to start anew. Our home is your home."

CHAPTER 26

K'ómoks Nation, Canada
February 6, 1976

Ethel Pearson is a clan mother, a respected member of the K'ómoks Nation, and was born right on Comox Island. Comox was in English and therefore the official word for it. She'd left years ago to marry a communist, and that just did not sit right with her tribal headsmen. No matter, it couldn't keep her from being who she was, nothing could do that but the great lady herself.

Ethel still attends potlatches and ceremonies and has raised her family in the traditional way. She also keeps a long grudge list in a box. It holds the names of those who voted against her over the communist thing. After she became a respected elder and proved to be a powerful voice during the fight for timber rights, she would pull out that list if someone approached her for help, and then, once she spotted their name, tell them, "Don't even dare come on my land," then draw a pencil line through their name on the list. She'd crossed off quite a few names over the years.

On this day, her daughter Donna comes speeding into the driveway. At the sound of her screeching tires, Ethel turns off the gas burner under the supper pot, snaps open her pink vinyl purse to check for ID and keys and money, and practically trips over Donna on the porch steps headed for the car. "Momma, ya gotta come with me quick. They got this Indian man down at the jail, and they're beating him up bad."

243

Ethel doesn't ask who, or care; she'll stop any authority from beating any Indian.

"What'a they say he done?"

"Killed two agents down on the Pine Ridge."

"Good. I'll shake his hand."

"Momma!" Donna blurts out, shocked. "They won't let you see him if you go in talking like that!"

"I'll say what I please, about what I please. I buried my children with my bare hands, and I'll call the truth as I see it! Besides, we all know about the goings-on down there, the suffering those people been put through. I raised half those boys work in that jail and a Mountie or too besides. They'll let me in or know what's good for them." Off they go to Oakalla, the most notorious jail in Canada.

It had been a bit of a boast, but sure enough her mother is allowed to meet with this Leonard Peltier. She walks a long dark hall to his cell and notices large locks welded onto his cell door. She hits a nearby guard on the arm with her purse, saying, "What if there's a fire? Cut those off! Do it now while I can see you do it."

"Mother, we didn't have the right specs for high enough security for this one. Government men made us do it."

"What government men? None ours, not Canada? You just do whatever those ones tell you? Better go ask; go now! 'Cause there's gonna be hell to pay for this. You'll see. You know me!"

The young Indian guard disappears and leaves them alone. Ethel pulls a rickety metal folding chair over to the bars and sits down, folding her large, wrinkled hands over the purse in her lap. Leonard leans into the bars with a smile on his face; he'd heard the exchange.

"Son, are you okay?" she asks, her voice far sweeter than her kids ever heard it, unless they were sick. She notices Leonard has evidence of his beating above one eye and on his cheekbone.

"I'm okay. Are you okay, Momma?" He goes on to tell her he's heard all the ruckus and is shocked she's been let in. She must be mighty important. Then he gets down to business, knowing someone will pull her out soon even if she is the queen of England.

"I can adopt you," is part of her proposed solution. "We can. The locals.

We are the First Nations of Canada. I'm gonna give you a name and you need to learn it and say it correctly. It was my grandfather's name, and we will potlatch for you and get you land and citizenship. Then they can't take you back. Laws run differently up here than where you come from. We been doing this longer."

"Doing what longer?"

"Surviving. Getting our rights back; we're timber people. Here's your name: 'Gwarth-ee-lass.' The great lady thinks of her grandfather, who is in a portrait on her bedroom wall. He was a brave man. She is of the Musgamakw Tsawataineuk nation, from the traditional lands of Vancouver Island.

Leonard labors to pronounce it, with the same guttural sound she used, until she is unsatisfied and reaches through the bars to move his chin with the sounds. "Gwarth-ee-lass."

"What does it mean?"

"It means He Who Draws the People to Him. And you will be doing that, Leonard *Pel-ti-a*, from all over the world. But I'd a come to help ya even if you were just one Indian tied to a floor, remember that."

Why in hell would the world care? Leonard wonders, though he is glad she did. With that, he swears by the name and the land and accepts dual citizenship. The strength of it makes him even more determined that the FBI cannot take him.

Later, Lew Gurwitz calls, asking if he recognizes the name Myrtle Poor Bear.

"Who? Never heard of her."

"Well, Leonard, she's the fabricated eyewitness they've come up with for this illegal extradition," Lew explains. "Worse, she's out of Pine Ridge."

In a Canadian courtroom three weeks later, one government would face off with another trying to own Leonard Peltier. But Special Agent Harmon himself had found the small, plump, and very frightened Myrtle Poor Bear and sequestered himself, and her, into a hotel room for three weeks until, weary to see her kids and sisters, she finally agreed to say anything he wanted her to. This sealed Leonard's fate, and there was nothing his First Nations friends could do to save him. Harmon had an open checkbook to close this case. Myrtle was taken out of a former file, having given the exact same type of testimony in another Indian's case, unrelated to the Pine Ridge shoot-out. The judge made prosecutors work on the affidavits three times, like he was sending back homework. If Peltier's case started winning the judge over, a long break was called to break the momentum. Extradition was inevitable.

Sitting in solitary, Leonard recalled his final free days and thought that if the worst happened, he'd at least get to go home to North Dakota. He'd be locked in a hole, but a hole at home. He thought of Chief Small Boy and was grateful for his courage and help during his days inside the old schoolhouse, a final hiding place the chief had moved him to, right before the Mounties showed up flanking Special Agent Harmon. They said even the South Dakota governor took a horse and went on the hunt. And what jurisdiction did he think he had in Canada? Leonard had heard the Mounties coming and he and Frank Blackhorse ran out the back door to high ground, where they could observe the lawmen from a safe distance. Frank suggested, "maybe we should just turn ourselves in."

Leonard whispered, "Maybe, but let's watch and see how they handle things down there. They think we're still inside, that's why they're still in their cars. Waiting to see what we will do." So they watched from the hill.

They waited a good fifteen minutes, and then the law all at once hopped out of their vehicles and just opened fire full force on the little cabin, which quickly burst into flames and was allowed to burn to the ground without any efforts made to save what was inside. Leonard now knew without a doubt that they had no intention of even trying to take them alive. Afterward, they could tell any story they pleased. The two Indians ran deeper into the woods.

A month later, the door on the small schoolhouse Small Boy moved them to came crashing in, and before anyone could move, the Mounties had guns to every head except for Leonard Peltier's. Two just held him down while Special Agent Harmon, who'd come up to join the hunt, put his own gun to Leonard. He spoke the words he had been dying to say for many long months, "You are under arrest for the murder of my federal agents. Slowly put your hands on your head. Now!"

Lew saw him in solitary, but not often, even as his counsel. The last time Leonard had seen Lew face-to-face was a few months earlier, when Lew had come to Leonard's cell to break the terrible news that Anna Mae's body had been discovered in a ravine, in Wanblee, South Dakota, where someone had killed her.

Leonard went down on one knee and wept with true grief. Lew mentions he'd never seen Leonard weep before, telling Hippie Jack, later by phone, his friend and paralegal from Boston, "despite all he'd seen him endure."

Lew explained that her body had been found a month or so ago, and the autopsy said it was an Indian Jane Doe who had died of exposure. But the AIM lawyers had demanded Jane Doe be exhumed, and when a doctor was brought in by AIM to do a second autopsy, it revealed it was her.

"What a tragic end to a beautiful lady," Lew said. "Her family is devastated, and with so many of the leadership on the run, her traditional reburial had very few leaders in attendance."

Leonard said, softly, "She should have stayed close to me; I wouldn't have let anything ever hurt her. She didn't trust me no more."

Lew knew it was truly a cruel end to an era, a vicious and tragic circumstance that would reverberate. Her memory forever wrapped in the beauty of the Black Hills and the love of a people she had only sought to help save. As many said about her in the end, she was Indian all the way. A loving mother, a good friend, and a dedicated AIMer.

For its part, the Bureau scoffed at the rumors that they were in any way accountable. "Though it was well known that the snitch had helped spread damaging things and then managed to turn the focus elsewhere," Lew said, bitterly. Thinking like the lawyer he was, he added, "I wonder how many fingerprints can fit on one gun. Give me those thousands of documents they're withholding, unredacted, and we might know a lot—they recorded it all, and I do mean all."

Leonard is brought into the Canadian courtroom in body chains for his final extradition hearing, the sound of all the dragging chains preceding his entrance. The room goes silent in horror as they wait. His Canadian mother, Ethel, claps her hand over her mouth and keeps it there. Leonard smiles at her, of course, hoping to send her some comfort. It is inhuman to drag him in this way, and she'll have a word about that with the judge.

Clan mother Ethel follows Myrtle Poor Bear out of the courtroom and talks the authorities into letting her have a word. She asks the most important question first. "Have you ever seen Leonard Peltier before?" Young Myrtle nods yes. A surprised Ethel asks, "When?" Earnestly, Myrtle says, "Here, today."

Ten days later, Leonard stood by a waiting helicopter, and Ethel could see him shivering in the cold. After she voiced a few harsh words to his guards, they unchained him and let her help him put on a thick sweater, white with a design in black markings of Ethel's tribal symbols. It was beautiful and warm, real wool, and designed to last forever. That's Canada.

CHAPTER 27

The Explorers Club, Manhattan, New York City
June 1979

Peter Matthiessen, a lean fifty-year-old with wavy, silver-streaked hair and the chiseled features of his Danish ancestors, stands in the lobby of the Explorers Club on East Seventieth Street in Manhattan. The walls are lined with the heads of polar bears, tigers, antelope, and all manner of wild creatures, relics from a time before film and camera could prove the existence of such exotic creatures. A plaque declares that Explorers Club members had accomplished many firsts—they were first to the poles, scaled the highest of mountains, and plunged to the deepest depths of oceans. First to the moon. Peter himself is no stranger to firsts. The *New York Times* declared him "America's most important naturalist since the 19th century." The minute Peter walks into the room, everyone present gets to their feet.

A friend, a German-born zoologist named George, joins his side. They've recently returned from a journey of 250 miles on foot into Tibet. Their goal was to find the Crystal Mountain, the Tibetan blue sheep, and, they hoped, a snow leopard. This almost mythical leopard graces the cover of Peter's latest book, which all present believe is a shoo-in for the prestigious National Book Award. Peter's friends have gathered at the club to celebrate him.

George toasts Peter and mentions their "trek back in time, where few have ever ventured"—he's quoting from the book's cover. A member calls out, "What's next, Peter? What can possibly match it?"

George opens Peter's book and reads aloud: "In the land of Dolpo, unknown to Westerners, even today, we've seen the last enclave of pure Tibetan culture left on earth. The last citadel of all that present-day humanity is longing for, either because it has been lost or not yet been realized or because it is in danger of disappearing from human sight: the stability of a tradition, which has its roots, not only in a historic or cultural past, but within the innermost being of man."

Peter listens and thinks back to that difficult and beautiful trip that he laid out in his book with these words, "where they could travel a hundred years back in time in just a day's walk." And he was about to do it again—in America.

After the toasting and a little fraternizing, Peter and George end up together in their usual corner. "Where are you off to next?" George asks. Peter mentions a pristine wilderness that his friend would never guess. "The Badlands," Peter says, to George's disappointed expression. "Indian country." He speaks of a people who have maintained their culture while avoiding the modern world, who are happy, even as they live in conditions that we call poverty. George knows there is no place for him there, and he's not interested anyway, given the chaotic times and political turmoil. *It's no place for Peter, either,* he's thinking, but he just raises his glass and says, "Here's to a short trip!" Peter had lived with the Hopi and traveled the Florida everglades all the way up to Canada, staying in traditional communities the whole way. That said, the Badlands were different.

Weeks later, Peter Matthiessen finds himself moving fast in a dilapidated Indian truck that's being buffeted by harsh Dakota winds and peppered by a mixture of blowing snow and sand. The driver is a Lakota Indian elder named Oscar Bear Runner. In the middle seat sits Bob Robideau, and though known as Razor, Peter calls him Bob. Bob announces he is from the Defense House in Los Angeles, as if it is commonly known, is thirty-six years old, and keeps his oversized black cowboy hat with its dangling eagle feathers on, even in the small cab.

Peter thinks him charming and well-spoken and that he has acquired quite an education from somewhere. Likely, AIM brought him that education, if not the discipline that goes with it. Reading in jail. The great author knows why Bob is here, and Peter is not interested in his offers. Bob hopes to persuade him to write a book on his perceived infamous cousin. Peter has noticed the partly concealed handgun between his legs but is unimpressed. The author has spent many a weary hour chasing armed poachers and isn't easily rattled. He is, however, impressed by the landscape. The prisms of light cutting the Black Hills are spectacular.

Past the steep, ruddy hills a path appears, not much bigger than a goat could crawl. Matthiessen asks, "Will we make that climb without a road?"

"We'll make a road," Bear Runner says, turning suddenly into the tall grass. Gripping the armrest, Peter notes the yellow scrag-grass, or needle grass as locals refer to it, standing as high as their truck and tipped with a fine layer of new snow. It looks like they're driving through a birthday cake.

The Sioux, he imagines, would have traveled here in mile-long caravans of horses and travois carrying their elders and supplies during warmer times on the plains. How beautiful it must have been after they left their winter camps to see them returning here in spring to find the water sources renewed and the grass replenished. Every two years or so, they'd choose a different area along the rivers, always following the game. They knew preservation, and the whole country could learn a thing or two from them before it was too late.

To break the ice, Peter, cleverly turning the tables, asks Razor if he is going to take him to meet his famous cousin.

"It takes a senator these days to get someone in to see him, lawyer ain't enough. You coming to Point Conception though, right? California?"

"Yes, I'm getting John Trudell at the airport, then out to your Defense House."

"Well, be prepared for a wild ride when he gets in. Last time he flew into LA my girlfriend picked him up and she said he made her drive three times around the airport first with him diving into the floorboard while she did. He was afraid of being followed." Razor laughs heartily, then stops. "Everybody wants to be me."

253

An hour later, after a fine lunch at the Bear Runners', Peter hopes his next ride will come soon, though the best they can do now is a quick run out before sundown. Every point of call is the journey getting there, all remote. On that thought, he turns to pretty Nilak Butler, who has joined them for lunch. Nilak had escaped that fateful day on the rez, with Peltier and the others. Peter's nature is curious, as he camped himself out in the Badlands just the night before and knows the terrain, just recently staying under the stars at the top of Harney Peak. He always prefers a tent and a lean-to to a hotel, often armed with nothing more than a pencil. "How did you get out of that ravine that day and across miles of wilderness in the dark? Not one escaping Indian was caught or killed."

"The Loud Hawks found us first, Kenny and his brother, on horseback, dug us out of a drainage ditch and then we were right here where you sit," she says with a giggle. "Edgar's parents' house, yeah, you're sitting where Leonard sat." She giggles again in a shy way.

"You surely outfoxed a lot of smart people in that wicked pursuit."

He is feeling a little foxed himself, at the moment.

"We stayed here a good while, didn't we, Edgar? First we were at old man Noah Wounded's house. Mainly outside. Then Morris Wounded and barely the next morning FBIs and Goons came speeding up and pouring out of a bus. It came up out of nowhere. Anna Mae had just showed up, fact I rode out in her car. She'd guessed where we'd be. Poor girl, that same shit seemed to happen whenever she showed someplace, cops came in behind her. It didn't mean nothin', but people read into it."

Peter is quite enthralled as the young Inuit lady relives the night. After all, they'd eluded hundreds of law enforcement looking for them. It was not long ago enough to speak about it as casually as they are doing. But it seems they are determined, quite fearlessly, to help Peltier yet, if ever they could.

"Hell, the helos were on us once in the hills, ants crawled up my nose and I couldn't move! Everyone was terrified and trembling, but Bro, he was calm and in charge then." Edgar calls Peltier Bro, as he's gotten used to not using his name. They are still evading something, never sure of the listener. Nilak speaks next.

"He ran at the back of everyone else and we'd made it to the hills and hunkered down when we heard this helo, blowing sand on everything. Suddenly, he just stopped and curled up inside his jacket almost like a ball, he'd dusted it quick, and when they pulled low, he looked like a rock. Helo just pulled off and we jumped up and started bookin' it again. Little Navajo girl running with him. She kept up, too. He stayed behind her."

"You say you hid at Morris Wounded's home, and the FBI came there and missed you? How's that?" Peter asks as he finds Nilak sincere, and very detailed. The young Inuit lady continues her story, with obvious affection and respect for Peltier.

"We all ran and crammed into a back bedroom to hide when we heard this bus speed up. All of us trying to fit under one bed. Leonard and one of the Loud Hawk brothers sat outside the front of the bed. I start pulling at Leonard's pants leg, begging him to cram under, that he'd be shot sitting out front like that. He said, 'Yeah, and they'll get it out of their system. Then crawl on out from under the bed.'"

After a brief pause, Edgar adds, "Well, that's Leonard."

CHAPTER 28

Point Conception, Chumash Coastline, California July 20, 1979

A month later Peter stands with Lew Gurwitz at Point Conception, waiting for a sweat to begin.

"What in hell are they thinking, destroying this perfect coastline with a refinery? Why does Washington back policy that makes bodies of water used for nothing more than to make a big corporate toilet?"

Peter will be writing another letter to his editor friend at the *New York Times*, and Indians will be part of the narrative. John Trudell has driven out with him and arranged an important radio interview to follow the night's sweat.

He stands a little outside the circle of men when he hears a loud, piercing yelp right at his back. By instinct he crouches a little and turns. The young Indian man behind him is laughing as he says, "Used to be if you heard that sound, I was on you, and it was only out a respect for the living you got one second left to make good with your maker, cuz you were about to meet him!" A few laugh at Peter's discomfort, while others just keep on smoking, as if this merited little notice. Just making fun of the new guest, or being a jackass, or letting outsiders present know not all are so easily welcomed.

Razor and Archie Fire Lame Deer arrive and prepare to enter ceremony, framed against the crashing Pacific. A man with a thick auburn ponytail is chopping wood for it. Razor calls him Hippie Jack. Peter sees him as a warm and well-spoken middle-aged man from Boston, one of the many paralegals Peltier's attorney has on board, albeit unlicensed. Peter notices that Lew usually makes his way cross-country using free labor, given that he is free labor himself, and a lot around here is unlicensed.

Gurwitz is on a brief that might get Peltier's Fargo trial thrown out and a new one brought in. Not much hope for that, Peter's been told. They all have a fighter's mentality, though. Some of them real activists. The Indians on board are giving it their all, and a new voice is being heard across America. Even members of European parliaments are starting to listen. "They get to enjoy our colonial sins for a change," Matthiessen says to Lew, with a smile.

For now, Peter just stands and watches the Pacific churn every color from turquoise to deep purple toward the cliffs. He is glad he came.

Late into the night, in mid-sweat, Hippie Jack comes running with news he heard on a nearby car radio. Leonard Peltier has just escaped Lompoc prison! Peter expresses his amazement that Peltier is even in such a low-security prison. Razor sets out at a run, shouting, "'Cause they wanna kill him!" Peter is close on his heels when Razor says, "Well, Professor, you may not need a senator to meet my cousin after all!"

All scatter, and Peter knows they want to enable the escape. Even the medicine man comments, "If he makes it to Canada on foot this time, no one in America will have ever even heard of Leonard Peltier!"

Trudell is determined to get to the radio station to keep that interview appointment and convinces Peter to join him. They dash to a waiting van as local Indians all around have sprung into action. Indian women hurry to towns around the prison with instructions to pull down any wanted posters; old women organize to put food, blankets, and water jugs outside near their woods and barns. When trucks of migrant workers are pulled over and searched, most all of them will know to claim to be Peltier.

Peter thinks they recognize something in this situation that is old and familiar—the romance of the warrior returned to protect the people. The romance of the one that got away. They are Peltier, and he is them. Peter feels the romance of it himself, but as always, the calm, cool head of reason prevails. He is not one to get too caught up in anything emotional.

Their ways are the story of man and by their very definition mean unbroken. But these people have been broken on the American wheel, and all has changed—land lines, languages, customs. To Peter's mind, nothing can restore that. Still, he is increasingly curious about this famed urban Indian—if he's still urban—and if not, what is he? *After four years of harsh prison life, what is he?*

Hours earlier, in the sweat, Fire Lame Deer said, "I saw a face in a dream, the face was bloated and fat and his words that came out of his mouth were a noise like a screech. I still dream in my language and because of that I see things in a different way. The spirits know my words in my dreams. This face became my face but not my words. The wind blew hard against him and replaced him with another's face. This face was lean and taut and skin barely over its bones. He was starved to death. Starved for the wanting of his people."

Watching the medicine man closely, Peter wondered, *Has something returned, stirred up, born out of anger, out of loss, or separation?* Returned for some, he knew, but for others it never left. Fire Lame Deer called out, "We are still here! If you are listening to me now, I am still here!" Peter was caught up in the sincerity. The idea was a powerful one, the dream, too. Sometimes prayers had to be said out loud, in a sweat lodge, or even in a courtroom.

Peter had asked Archie Fire Lame Deer, "Weren't these urban Indians a trouble to the rez, yet another burden?"

"Oh, yes. Trouble. You see, we'd been marginalized, Peter, beaten down years ago, we were of no trouble, not any longer. AIM came, and there was trouble, all right. They became the face of what *no* looked like. They were our beautiful trouble—now yours."

He is actually warning me, Peter thought, *also an Indian way. They let you know what you are in for so you can turn back.*

"Anyone who helps our brother Leonard will feel the wrath," the medicine man continued. "Chief Small Boy, who helped him up in Canada, was later turned away from a place to sleep and died of frostbite sleeping outside in the cold. Chief, medicine man, or blue blood, it don't matter. It won't to them."

As he heads for the radio station, Peter is increasingly sure he'll be staying on, and that he'll meet Peltier, too, if the Indian survives the night.

Leonard Peltier is recaptured five days after his escape, and without a single shot being fired. It is worldwide news. He will be tried for escape and other charges. The Lompoc escape trial starts five months later on a bright, sunny Los Angeles morning in January 1980. It lasts weeks, during which time Leonard is moved from maximum security to the LA County jail.

On the first day the LA police are out in full force, and they catch Hippie Jack in a tunnel spraying graffiti that reads Free Leonard Peltier. This happens just as Peter is waving to him from his rental car. Peter keeps driving, musing that the hippies have the same vision as the Indian, they've always been a natural pair. He is all for it and proud of the damn lad, though he might have finished sooner. Peter, despite Yale and a home in the Hamptons, is frequently referred to as a hippie himself. He knows he likes them. He definitely shares a common vision with the Indians! What environmentalist doesn't?

Hippie Jack is going to miss the first day of the trial and also give his friend Lew another person to bail out, and that's a shame, Peter thinks, because any Leonard Peltier trial will be a show worth attending. Sure enough, Indian communities from all over the country have sent representatives. Old buses and rusted-out Indian cars are parked everywhere. The blanket crowd, as the LA police refer to them. Peter watches as Diné (Navajo) elder Roberta Blackgoat, with several other elders and a large number of young people, emerge from an old school bus painted with Big Mountain or Bust! Thomas Banyacya, Keeper of the Hopi Prophecies, is already in the courtroom, sitting beside Oklahoma medicine man Phillip Deere, whose colorful beaded hatband displays his Creek Nation colors. Other traditional Native people fill the courtroom to overflowing.

Peter is held up on the courthouse lawn as Crow Dog is preparing a buffalo altar right out front. The smell of sweetgrass is intoxicating. Many pipes are tied to a full-length buffalo robe. The Lakota prayers are mesmerizing to hear.

Peter finally enters the courtroom and is shocked to spot Hippie Jack. He grabs a seat beside him. "You beat me in here! How did you get out from under those blue lights, my friend?"

"Don't say that so loud, brother, they'll be calling me a snitch if they hear I slipped away so easily. They have to drive Leonard through that very tunnel on his way to court every day, that's why I picked it. Ahh, some of them are good boys—I found me an Irish cop and told him my dad is the chief of the fire department back in Boston. It worked!"

"Solidarity always works," Lew says, walking over, slapping Hippie Jack's back, and nodding his approval. "I also mentioned I was the paralegal for the defense counsel. One of them, anyway, and I needed to book."

"We were almost one short today," Lew says, laughing in his stilted way. Excited, the lawyer says, "They're gonna allow it, argued it hard, they're gonna allow it!" He walks on up to the bench and opens his files. Peter notices he's cleaned up nicely.

"What are they gonna allow?" he asks Hippie Jack.

"Oh, the pipe, they can swear on the pipe today instead of the Bible."

Peter knows that even for liberal California, this is unprecedented. "All wins count, and it is also why so many distinguished are here today. Voice of the people."

"I broke a fundamental rule for graffitiing. I shoulda left my ganja weed out of it. I couldn't smoke during the trial, so you know, but now I have more for later."

"Then I'll see you later!" Peter says, moving over to make room for a familiar face—Bill Hazlett, the *Los Angeles Times* court reporter, who returns Peter's nod of greeting. Bill is never in a good humor. He is stout, with military-style razor-cut hair, and looks every bit a former army sergeant. Peter notices that a few FBI in the room exchange a nod with him as well. None of them smile.

"See Phillip Deere over there, Peter?" Hippie Jack lowers his voice. "With the black hat on and Creek colors. He's promised some entertainment today. He sprinkled the courthouse windows and thresholds with some substance just before we got here, he told me."

Hours later, Lew Gurwitz is busy arguing his finest to the judge, as it seems the judge forgot about his earlier promise to the lawyer about allowing Indians to swear on the Sacred Pipe during the proceedings, rather than on a Bible. Lew had won this argument in court before, with the Mashpee Nine of Cape Cod, Wampanoags outside Boston. He was determined to win it again. Indian people were being denied their religious rights, a Bible was not theirs to swear on, a Sacred Pipe was. You could not hold the pipe and tell a lie. It was unthinkable. Although all tribes in America did not have pipe-carriers in their way of life, many AIMers did. The judge's voice is raised, threatening Lew as he is unsympathetic and doesn't want to recognize them as spitiual people, and therefore sympathetic to the jury. Lew begins citing his case law that supports the precedent, for he is a brilliant legal mind and is determined to win his client's this right, if he can win them nothing else this day. And he succeeds!

Lew is representing Roque Duenas, Peltier's codefendant, and Leonard is represented by a popular young AIM lawyer named Bruce Ellison. To make matters worse, no one stood, when the judge entered the courtroom, although that was courtroom decorum. The gavel sounds and the judge turns; his face appears somewhat disgusted as he looks toward the Indians as they walk toward their table.

"Here come the perps," Bill Hazlett says.

"Look again, brother, they're more than that!" Hippie Jack corrects him.

Hippie Jack has his gaze trained on Peltier as he enters the room with Roque Duenas and Bobby Garcia beside him. Bobby had engineered the escape from Lompoc and poor Roque (pronounced Rocky), is charged with leaving the weapon in the drainpipe. He was in such a hurry to help, it being life and death for Leonard, he left a weapon registered in his own name. He would be sent up the river for that. Peter had been permitted a short interview with Leonard the previous day, and he is most curious to see him in this setting. Peltier is nothing like the other Movement leadership Peter's met or read about, and nothing like his dear Cousin Razor. He doesn't have the ego; he seems earnest, genuine, and bright. Brave, with quite a sense of humor. The courtroom atmosphere and his imminent fate don't seem to faze him.

The jury is seated only a few minutes and sure enough, there's some entertainment. Every one of them starts scratching as if they itched. It makes quite a stir before they're removed. The old Creek medicine man, Philip Deere, laughs out loud, and Hippie Jack turns to Peter with a look that says, *See, I told ya!*

The jury ends up staying out for hours. Their seats are wiped down, but the bailiff can't find the source of the itch. Since Leonard is already in the room, he gets to enjoy waving to his many friends, new as well as old. Steve Robideau, a handsome stately Indian and cousin to Razor, has accompanied a traditional elder to Leonard's side. Roberta Blackgoat takes a beautiful hand-woven basket right up to the defendants' table, and no one moves to stop her. She lifts out three ribbon shirts, and to the shock and dismay of the FBI in the room, she re-dresses the defendants. The judge looks on as if to say, *What can anybody do about a grandma?* Already today, grown men have been bodily thrown out onto the street, medicine men arrested off the lawn, and Native women's bras searched, yet this stately elder has gotten away with ribbon shirts. Yes, Peter is again glad he came, as are many others. This won't be just a trial; it's becoming a statement. Suddenly a ruckus starts up outside and Hippie Jack jumps to his feet. Peter and Bill Hazlett follow.

"They have a permit!" Hippie Jack yells into the face of an LA cop. Apparently, a duly permitted buffalo altar on the front lawn of the federal courthouse has offended and it has been ordered forcibly removed. Three busloads of riot police arrive. Brule Lakota medicine man Leonard Crow Dog and his Indian entourage are told to "get off." A young Lakota translates from his native language, instructed by Crow Dog, into English. Crow Dog explains to the young Lakota the medicine has already been laid down, he can't leave. Then the young Lakota attempts to explain the dilemma to the member of the LAPD. The cop simply says, "move it!" So the young Lakota gets under the buffalo robe, all two hundred pounds of it, and it becomes a roving altar as he walks around the sprawling facility, followed by a drum and dozens of Indian affiliates from across America.

Hippie Jack continues to yell, as if it means something, "Hey man, they have a permit!" The cop tells him the Indians are going to hurt the lawn. Razor boldly answers back to the LAPD cop.

"Indians hurt the grass! Really?" Razor steps in to interject. Then he turns his attention to Hippie Jack, glad to see his presence. Few knew it by looking, but Hippie Jack is a strong man, and it didn't hurt he used to be a bouncer in a bar in Harvard Yard. An all-around cool guy.

"Bro, why is it when you show up trouble starts, and not the good kind?" Razor goes on, this time speaking to his friend as they line up together, suspecting what's coming. They try to keep it casual, for it calmed the nerves. "Hey, I'm, sorry if I'm on your turf." Razor says. "Better move that piece of shit red Subaru you and Lew pushed out here. Damn lucky ya even made it."

"We made it because Kees was in the back seat praying!" says the hippie, his thick red ponytail glinting in the morning sun. He's referring to the distinguished Wampanoag medicine man, "Kees-Ah-Taan-a-Muck," who hitched a ride with him and lawyer Lew all the way from Boston to the trial. "Crossing the Rockies, the car stalled a few and Kees got out and prayed and the car started! Now that's some real Rocky Mountain high for ya!"

"Look at you, talking to cousin now, so now you're a regular industry guy with press following ya and lawyers. Good for you. Just remember, Jackie my boy, there are two lists. One where everyone kisses your ass, and then there's the short list of who don't give a fuck about what you say. Go ahead and put me on that short list right now," Razor says.

"Hey, brother Bob," Jack says wryly, "your name heads that list." They join as one, as if rehearsed, and are pushed off the lawn by cops with outstretched billy clubs, and Hippie Jack tries to block the blows to Bob. Real friends, though no one would know it by listening to them. Bob runs the Defense House in LA, and Hippie Jack has been sleeping on his floor since his arrival. Lew, too.

During the entire first week of the trial, Peter makes a point of staying close to Bill Hazlett. The reporter confesses to Peter that he, too, has been drawn into the mystique of this perp, Leonard Peltier. "I always liked the FBI agents I've known, and I'm considered a friendly, and this is the first time they've shown me the door! Hell, even the *LA Times* tell me they won't print my dispatches from this trial, and they paid my ticket here!" Peter offers to intervene. He, too, has good friends at the top at that newspaper.

Peter goes off to make the necessary phone call and returns shortly, chagrined. He, too, has been put off. This has never happened to him before. "What is in your daily notes that could cause such offense?" he asks Bill.

"I'm not sure, maybe because I said Peltier might be innocent?"

Razor's been sitting nearby and interjects, "We ain't innocent, Professor, but we ain't guilty neither." Peter scribbles down these words.

Driving to LAX to fly home the following day, Peter passes from his hotel near the courthouse through the same tunnel as he had every day attending the Lompoc escape trial. He notices the now-elaborate graffiti, thinking his new acquaintance Hippie Jack would sure be proud of this monstrosity. A huge eagle now looms over a portrait of Peltier, and underneath the head are the words Honor the Earth! on a ribbon with US flag colors.

Beside him on the front seat are files from his friend Bill Hazlett. He plans to read them on the plane.

CHAPTER 29

Red Shirt Table
May 1980

Ann Richards is a little surprised to see Gail Harmon at her door after five years, even though she'd called ahead. "Proper" is Gail's middle name. She is still the same warm, correct, friendly lady she had always been to Ann when they worked side by side as transcribers in the Rapid's BIA radio dispatch office. Maybe she'd aged a bit, not quite the perky, quick-stepped Methodist she had always seemed. Though Ann has agreed to go with her on this day trip, she is a bit suspicious; but she cooperates, just as she'd fully cooperated with Donald Harmon's investigation after the shoot-out. Government matters on the reservation had grown quiet rather quickly, after the years of violence. The FBI had pretty much abandoned their Lakota country. She was rather surprised to hear from the Harmons.

The two women drive to Ellsworth Air Force Base, right outside of Rapid, and right through the gates like they own the place. Gail parks near an orange and tan Cessna. Donald Harmon has his head inside it, testing the gauge lights, but then hops out with a jovial smile when they arrive, as if he and Ann Richards have known each other a lifetime. In fact, she only formally met him in depositions.

"Hello. Are we having lunch off the ground?" Ann asks.

"Ahh, we'll picnic later. Thought we'd show you a magnificent sight first, climb in!" Though she has noticed that Gail is not joining them, it is Ann's custom, being well-trained in law enforcement, not to question authority. Besides, she knows why. They've assumed she'll do as she's told and just follow directions. Nothing new to her, really.

After a period of talking only to the tower, once at high altitude Harmon speaks directly to her again. "Isn't it magnificent up here, like I promised?"

"Oh yeah, I can see the whole treaty from up here. There's Montana."

Harmon is not amused. She is reminding him of her traditional roots. It's not lost on him. His tone changes with the next question. "You were the last to see him? Ronnie was a pilot, did you know that? A good one, too. Flew this very plane." She sat stunned.

"No, sir, he saw others after me that day, and talked to others. He radioed in. I told you all this, years ago now. There's nothing new, sir."

"Why was he mixed up in that warrant business in the first place?"

"He was being nice, that's all it was, helpful. Ronnie was like that. You worked with him every day, you must have noticed. He was kindhearted. The sheriff didn't want to go over, so Ronnie volunteered. He was volunteer-minded, otherwise he'd have been an engineer, like I am."

"Yes, you've done well. Good, good. Considering your circumstances, you're one of the lucky ones. Did you warn that camp that day?"

"No, I did not, sir."

In silence Donald flies in a big circle above the glorious view, in the perfect sunlight. She imagines this is all being dug up again because some famous author is in town asking questions.

"You know, sir, I don't mean to be impertinent, but when you start the blame game, you can go around in circles 'til one day you pass a mirror and finally find that blame you're looking for. We all feel guilty about that day. I miss him, too." She hadn't expected to tear up. "All of it happened to all of us, ya know? You can realize in a single moment you've hated the wrong thing all your life."

At those words, Donald Harmon plunges the plane sideways so fast she wonders if he is going to dump them both out. He lands, and she never sees him or Gail Harmon again.

Another driver is there to pick her up at the gate, and she is relieved to see it's Dana Moves Camp, a friend from her old office over at Rapid City. They do not discuss a thing about it, and they do have a real picnic. Just sandwiches stuffed into a bag, and some lemonade in a cleaned-out mayonnaise jar. Their friendship and the lemonade are still warm. After they've eaten the last soggy potato chip, they head back to Ann's mother's house in Porcupine. She is glad to be there, as she is due at Haskell the following week to begin her teaching job.

Ann Richards has no idea that the old truck they fly over as it bounces past Mount Rushmore early that afternoon holds a tribal council member, Tom Poor Bear, and the distinguished author everyone's talking about. She makes a habit of not minding anyone else's business. She'll be glad not to be interviewed about the day of the shoot-out ever again—or about any other day, either. Whenever she looks at a slide ruler, she thinks of sweet Ronnie from California.

Peter Matthiessen is relieved when his escort, Tom Poor Bear, finally arrives at the Bear Runners' to fetch him. Peter overhears the driver saying, "He fig-ured we'd come over here." That'd take expert figuring. *No wonder they just show up when they show up,* Peter thought. No phone in any household for sixty miles. Old Ones out walking long stretches, few running cars, no cabs, no bus system.

That said, the traditionals' home is a beautiful place to wait for a ride, to wait for anything. *In fact,* Peter thinks, *it's the destination.* They all sit together in the modest wood-framed house, half a dozen children of various ages crowding around as Mrs. Bear Runner brings the best they have to the table, despite having little, to put a stranger at ease.

Tall, robust Tom Poor Bear comes to the side door wearing his beaded necktie and traditional black hat with dangling feathers—all Movement attire, now a new tradition. He will escort Peter to the Badlands as he says, "Climb on up into this old war pony, my friend." Peter is anxious to check out some caves, and Tom implies that he'll see places that likely might be seeing their first human in a very long time.

Tom is a calm driver, and the passing scenery seems to blend with his rhythm and his speech, or his lack of it. His demeanor is warm and sincere, though his brown eyes are serious. An all-around comfortable man to be with. Tom fills in a few blanks when Peter hears he was also in AIM. Peter had stopped by the shoot-out site before going to the Bear Runners' home, so he mentions the Jumping Bull's ranch to Tom.

"Hell, nobody's happy to be around that place," referring to the Jumping Bulls. "Grandma herself had to be hospitalized for a nervous condition after all that. Who wouldn't? A wonder I ain't bonkers myself. Maybe I am!" he said, jovial, but not meaning it. "Take a lot of medicine to lay down, we still pray for those men lost that day and our people, too, they threw women in jail, and babies born to them. Dennis named one of his 'Little Iron Door.' Ya know, Peter, killing ain't our way." Peter understands that out here, a certain agenda has been in play, but now, with Poor Bear, he feels his back relax against the broken leather seat as he inhales the fine air and thinks that if he weren't so enthralled by the beauty of the Black Hills, he might have slept for the first time in days. Then the wind hits the truck hard, moves it over. Tom just laughs it off.

"Looks like we're in for a bit of a blow," Peter comments, his eyes on the darkening sky.

"What, that? Nah, just headed to the same place is all."

"Where's that, Tom?"

"Where the thunder lives. Don't you head home come a' evening and let your voice be heard a little loud when you get to the door? Well, this is its door." Peter knows he means that all weather comes and goes from this spot, as does everything else. Oglalas call it *the center of all that is.* From the look of the storm pushing near them, they may be right.

They turn into the wind and the ride gets bumpier as they fight it. No cause for worry, however—this is not wilderness to Tom Poor Bear, it's home, and as tame as he is. After twenty more miles of scraggy grass and dirt roads, they emerge onto a big slate table-rock. The afternoon light breaks beneath the passing storm and casts colors across the ancient rocky tops that surround them. Peter realizes that they are driving on table, not road, and he sucks in his breath at the completely unexpected and magnificent sight. Tom pulls over. And mentions they are at "Red Shirt Table". It's a meaningful spot to his people, Tom explains to his new friend, saying Crazy Horse himself on horseback addressed many nations here, that'd come to help him exit Custer from the premises, on June 25, 1876.

Stepping out of the truck, Peter is amazed to note that they are actually standing inside a rainbow. All the colors are present, deep, clear, and radiant, as brilliant as a new form of heaven made of nature's light.

Peter has had the feeling for a while that Tom has something he wants to say, but being a respectful man, he waits until the truck has pulled far away from the glorious site.

"It wasn't like it is now, Peter. Just a few years back you had to shoot your way out just to go to a grocery store. The Movement men, those ladies, and their families all came in to help us. They brought everything they had and just put it on the line. They weren't much more equipped than we were. City people, most never even seen a gun. Teachers and mothers, and they were making peanut butter sandwiches on the courtroom steps before it was all over, still are. There was this one sweet kid, Navajo, named Norman. I can still see his face, sweetest smile, a lot of pity in that one. We pulled up to Sioux Nation Supermarket, we was on the way to take him to Leonard and the others, and he says, 'I'll go in!' Ya see, we didn't dare go in, cause we know all the establishments are owned by Goons."

"What happened to him, the Navajo boy?" Peter asks, not taking his eyes off the hills.

"Well, he shops all right. Minute he says he'll go in, we empty out our pockets and fill his hands. Cigarettes, pop, oatmeal, man, pancake flour. He nods to us, trying to remember it all, and hops out of the car. Well, they let the kid get all the way back out to our car with it, brown paper bags up to his eyes, him and his long hair, and then they start poppin' at us. Looked like we'd staged a holdup just to wheel out of the parking lot after shopping." He laughs at the memory, but then his face goes somber. "That same kid was at that firefight, ya know? Good boy, traditional Navajo. Little boy there, too, he wudn't but ten, maybe eleven years old, little Zimmerman kid, and his older sister, Jean, them were two of ours. Thanks to Leonard they got out alive. They was all good people, Dino and Nilak, too—couldn't find better friends. I guess the word traditional and Navajo's the same word. Seems lately ever' one's an enemy, fussin' all the time, pointing fingers. That's the plan, ain't it?"

The truck bounces through a pothole big as a buffalo wallow, but Tom doesn't miss a beat. "We don't believe in killing, Peter. It's not our way," he said for the second time that day. "We prayed for all the lives that were lost that day. And plenty lost leading up to that day. Richards's family suffered, too." Peter wasn't sure, but imagined *Richards* referred to a Goon family name.

Peter sits in silence and lets the peacemaker finish. No one could doubt his sincerity. Peter doesn't have any questions, though he does wonder why a Navajo kid was so far from home. They were a peaceful lot as well, sheep herders.

"Tom, many say AIM was an outside influence that was another burden. Were they just outsiders, bringing in the trouble?"

"Whatever ya can say about it, Movement arrived, and despair turned to hope. It didn't happen like, *kaboom!* 'Oh, AIM is here so we're all set.' Hell, I'm AIM, we all joined, sure. Glad I did, would do it again. We're canceling drilling leases on our own now, no protest, just a little sovereignty. What they call progress, we call dirty water. Our call to make. Our boundaries again."

"But for how long? Who knows what's next, who'll get what now that sovereignty is strengthening?"

"Out here they say, Crow got the land, Sioux got the glory, and the Cheyenne got the fight. Serves 'em right, damn outsiders." Both men laugh out loud.

Just as dusk is emptying out its last light, Tom pulls up to a little flat-roofed motel. It's in the middle of somewhere, but a somewhere that hasn't passed a gas station or a restaurant or any building in hours. Peter's grateful Mrs. Bear Runner had pushed a few newspaper-wrapped bologna sandwiches into his tote along with two large clean-scraped carrots and a jar of lemonade made from a mix.

Peter steps out of the old jalopy and before pulling out his gear he goes into the small office and retrieves his key to room 107. Its plastic fob is shaped like an arrowhead. The white owner had acknowledged his arrival with a nod from the check-in window, but with no smile. Peter notices three cars in the dirt parking lot as he is walking back out and a small RV camper off to one side that looks as if it has been sitting in the grass a long time. He holds up his key and calls out to Tom.

"Thanks, Tom my boy, that was a magnificent ride. I think it may have been one of the most beautiful sights I have ever seen, in this country anyway, and my feet didn't even have to leave the ground."

"No. But the ground left your feet a few times," Tom says.

Peter laughs, because it's true. "A rare eagle's-eye view! Out of this world!"

"I brought a hippie gal up here once, pretty, redhead. She called it Utopia. 'Utopia?' I says. So, I look it up, it means nowhere, just a place in your noggin. Maybe the ground moves under your feet out here to remind ya, you're somewhere real. Ahhh, she left me. Guess it was too real for her. I know I was."

"You coming inside?" Peter asks, hoping Poor Bear says yes, as Peter lifts his gear out.

"Nah, got a pile of hungry kids waiting on me, and uncle's *takojas* [grandchildren]. He's a grandfather now! Just seeing ya get in your room okay. If anyone gives you a hard time out here, brother, just call me. I'll come back and introduce them to a man's world."

"Call ya how, Tommy Boy?" Peter's trust and affection for this man are very clear.

Tom Poor Bear puts his large hand out to the wind and swerves it up and down like a bird's wing. Peter interprets this to mean *just put the idea on the wind, I'll hear!*

"Goodbye, brother, goodbye, my good friend," Peter says, watching Tom Poor Bear's truck disappear, leaving a mile-high dust cloud in a wake behind him.

Unlocking the room door, Peter notes that both the key and lock are pretty scratched up, but then, everything out here is more than a little worn. He pulls off his dusty boots, then goes in and sinks down onto the small, thin mattress, his back against the headboard, missing the mattress frame by a foot. He reaches for his sandwiches and out of habit begins to read the newspaper they are wrapped in.

He's startled when the phone rings. "Yeah?" he answers warily. He hasn't told anyone where he is staying. Maybe Poor Bear wanted to say something further, but he couldn't have reached a phone so quickly. The other end is dead quiet. Peter knows his new friend's silences, and this one is not his. "Hello," he says again, very officious this time.

"Peter," the anonymous voice says, "you're asking all the wrong people." And then a dial tone.

Pulling on his boots quickly, Peter runs to the office, pushes through the door, and blurts out, "Who was that?"

"Who was what? What are you asking me?" the night clerk answers.

"The call you just transferred to my room. Did they ask for me by name or by room number?"

"I didn't get any call. Not to you. No calls to nobody. Phone ain't rang."

Peter waits for the man to say more and examines him as if he were a poacher. His guard is definitely up.

"No call just now?" Peter repeats. He knows how to ask questions: be direct, repeat. The South Dakota cowboy behind the desk, with his sweaty hairline barber cut, also knows how to answer. "Look, buddy, no one called this desk, I tole ya the first time. Only way a call can get past me is if someone is staying in the motel. They can enter your room number direct."

Peter pauses at that sobering thought and steps back out of the office into the broken concrete parking lot. He walks back to his room, aware of every step, his eyes on the still-visible dust cloud that had risen behind Tom Poor Bear's truck. Even his dust is a comfort, for in this vast emptiness, Poor Bear's his only friend out here at the moment, and he knows it. Good people know good people. It's a human thing.

A day later, Peter's plane lands in New York, and even in the crowded airport, he feels that he is being followed. The promised harassment is becoming all too real. Any means necessary to persuade him that this story should never reach the American people, and especially not while a pending appeal might yet free Peltier. Peter knows that they know it'd be better to dissuade him early on. He is beginning to itch like a member of the jury. He drops by the Explorers Club for a drink with George, and when he enters, nobody stands up.

CHAPTER 30

11129 Mulholland Drive, Los Angeles, California, Brando Residence

His early comment to Lew was, "I tried to hook the Indians up any way I could. I said 'hey, go take your own damn names off the endangered species list!' Would do it again. Money, motorhome, whatever." Marlon said this from a lawn chair near his swimming pool. Lew pulled a stadium chair over that made him sink so far down into his knees; they were practically at his chin. Not very glamorous. Lew had been alerted by the authorities that the motorhome loaned to Dennis Banks by Marlon Brando had been released back to its owner, with the occupants' belongings still inside, Lew's clients. Many hoped to get Peltier a new trial, or an appeal. Something in the motorhome might help. The aging movie star greeted Lew graciously; that was rare for a lawyer, because such a visit usually came with some questions.

First, they exchanged some insider unpleasantries while sitting beside the actor's rather dirty swimming pool, more like a scum pond. Though LA royalty, Brando had to be on watch himself now, rarely even letting someone in to clean. Lew offered to clean the pool, saying, "Other places I fixed furnaces, stoves, a car, one poor bastard let me try that, never again."

"Hey that pool ain't just ripe because I'm paranoid; I can't afford it, all I give away this year, and not getting hired as much, either."

"Shit, bro, you got ahold of enough of that filthy lucre you can give it away!"

"Oh yeah, I heard that about you, only New England lawyer broke."

"And you the only movie star." They share a knowing laugh together.

"Well, sleep on my couch anytime."

"No thanks, I might get bugs."

"No, you *will* get them! Ain't the first I let do it."

Then Lew grew serious-minded. He pointed out straight off that Brando himself "was never charged." The onetime Godfather smiled at the notion. "Hell, I went to that monastery takeover and got shot at, don't that count? Leonard Peltier did a cat and mouse with the National Guard, and damn, what's his name?"

"Herb Powless?" Lew offered.

"Yeah, him. He makes the guard stop and give us a ride! Beautiful Indian woman was around to perform that night, in Milwaukee. Weather colder than shit, man, and the Oneida fella says, I ain't walking, they got jeeps, it's our land, let's show 'em! Sure enough, they truck everyone back to the monastery."

Lew noticed the ugly black tarps with peeling tape at the corners that covered every possible fence and window, anywhere that could be used for spying. A fat yellow cat dove onto Brando's lap from an unknown location but didn't seem to startle him. Lew's questioning didn't, either.

"Charge me? Oh, I asked them to, begged them to charge me. That was the point of my goading them publicly, but of course they aren't that stupid. About gave my lawyers conniptions. Fuck 'em." Then his face lit up when he began talking about the Indians, showing real admiration. He had seen from the vantage point of the true insider, knew the system and what they were facing.

"Dennis was standing in his own grave taking on all that government, and he knew it, too," Brando said. "Took it on anyway! Hell, they all did!" He smiled widely, activating those famous eyebrows. "And in doing so, he exposed them! Not like we don't already know in this country. But exposing it like that? Now we *got to* know!" His tone conveyed the equivalent of a good old secret handshake. Lew did know. All haves knew, and more than a few of the have-nots.

"Simple enough equation, they wanted to help them as long as they made the cities red and the rez white. However, Nixon did give the Taos back Blue Lake, and all that acreage up in Alaska, just in time, too, before parachuting out. Just eight months before leaving office he reversed the Menominee termination. Surprised even the Menominee, though they'd fought for it for years. But that Coast Guard land deal was a stand-alone affair."

"I stay there whenever I'm headed anywhere. Told Dorothy, Herb's wife, I felt safer on her kitchen floor than the best hotel," Lew said, smiling and shaking his head at it all. His life had been hard, living out of his car, following this never-ending road all these years.

"They gave that land to them, an AIMer, not a tribe. The AIMer passed it to a tribe. Herb told me that Nixon gave some advisers unlimited choices for the Indians, for a while, until AIM embarrassed him with that Washington DC takeover. Then nobody would take his calls again, especially not after Wounded Knee." Lew said, nonchalant as he stretched his back in the uncomfortable chair.

"Hell, no one will take mine. No more help from Washington, that's gone." Marlon replied, with the tone of *easy come, easy go.*

"Gave them," Lew commented, thinking of the irony. "Help? God help the poor when the rich show up."

"That's a good one, you say it?"

"I think Eleanor Roosevelt did."

"The look, the smug look on those blocks of ice when Sacheen Littlefeather walked up to that mic."

"Oh yeah, biggest show in town. One beautiful lady, too. Navajo, right?" Lew is referring to the night of the Academy Awards on March 27, 1973. On that day, Marlon Brando sent Sacheen Littlefeather onstage at the Academy Awards to decline his Oscar for his celebrated film *The Godfather.* He was bringing attention during the Wounded Knee takeover. Lew regales the movie star with a story he heard from Russell Means about that night.

"She had that letter from you nobody heard; her voice was so low, respectful, and the booing was loud. News said she took the stage ranting and raving," Lew begins.

"They must a' not been there. Any booing is a shocker in that hall." Marlon says, not smiling and without his usual charm.

"Russell Means tells a great story about it, he's at the Knee and says he hears this Indian granny yelling 'there's an Indian on TV!' It was a night spirits were low," Lew continues.

"I bet' cause food and ammo were low, and attention had dried up." Marlon adds.

"Yeah, sure, sure. Well, they all ran into the little church where they'd wired up a black-and-white TV; it's blaring. They come running to see what the fuss is about. Russell himself yelled, 'An Indian is on TV! She's talking about us!' He hugs Anna Mae, everybody hugged everybody." Lew paused with a wry look, "Now the world knew!"

"Knew what? They didn't listen. She was beautiful and she's not Navajo, she's Apache. Bastard press leaks she's an actor paid to do it and not even a real Indian, even when she's standing there in traditional regalia! Friend of mine, he was the presenter, brought the Oscar over to my house that night and the studio, I guess it was them, sent these armed guards over to get it back." He smiles and then his smile trails off again.

Lew suddenly admired this man very much. He put his hand up to a statue everyone in that room wanted badly, but all he could think about was the desperate plight of those Indians and that was heavier to him than any statue. It wouldn't be without consequences and he knew it. The young beautiful Apache lady likely suffered for it, too. But they went ahead and did it anyway.

Lew gets a serious look on his face, as he's thinking this. "Imagine for a minute if I was told I could have the whole American dream, all of it, just have to pull down every synagogue in every city in the country, no more Hanukkahs, no bar mitzvahs, and definitely no Hebrew; just one way. Imagine that offer for a minute."

"You got it, man. No way, right? You already turned down that deal." Lew knew his implication and it was heavy; it was also accurate. "This country is turning into a triangle, man, rich at the top, and Constitution at the bottom. Nothing angrier than a confused American. Someone just spoiling their fun. Think they'll get this, now? I doubt that Indian client of yours ever walks out of there alive. They intend to anchor this story to dead quiet, my friend. They aren't ambivalent about it."

"Motorhome out back?"

"Yeah, it is, took them this long to return it. I found some unique items in it. In a little beaded purse, there was a hand-drawn map on the back of a café place mat, all folded. I think they were planning a return to Pine Ridge, you know?"

"For what? It would have been the most dangerous place to go."

"Another Wounded Knee. Round two, or round three, that'd be. I wish they made it!"

"Was Peltier here?" Lew asked.

"This ain't an investigation, is it?"

"No, just curious."

"One day I come home and see someone sleeping on my couch; I could see this back and long dark hair through the window. I have my girlfriend bring me my pistol, from out the glove box. Dennis comes running through the house, his voice all raised, 'No, Marlon! He's with us!' I'm thinking I have a break-in. We all laughed. My son Christian asked him to share a bong, and they were sleeping it off. Son was across from him in a chair, I couldn't see him from the window."

"You pulled a gun on Leonard Peltier, that's funny as hell."

"He just laughed. A good-natured fella. I don't think he knew this was coming down on him. Just a hunch, but he acted like there wasn't anything weighing on him, to me, just an observation. Some Indian woman from Milwaukee drove him over. He was here. Anna Mae was, too, earlier, but not then, they could've picked her up outside somewhere. Poor kid, my maid said, when she came last she asked to borrow some scissors and was busy cutting tags out of her clothes, said when they found her, she didn't want them to be able to recognize her. Chopped her hair off with them, too. What was bearing down on them kids could drive anyone loco."

"Well," Lew says, "let's see that motorhome."

"Sure, sure," Marlon says and lifts his heavy frame from the chair, dumping the yellow cat as he goes. They begin a walk through the house.

"It wasn't new or fancy or anything like that," he said of the motorhome.

Lew walks behind him and then comes to a stop. He surveys the living room ceiling. "Ya let that dry rot and mold set in much further, ya might be living in it."

Marlon laughs and says, "Only good advice a lawyer ever gave me." He opens the door to the garage.

Then, almost as an afterthought, he turned around and says, "Hey, stick around, Lew. That Oneida kid, what's his name, Charlie Hill, is opening for Richard Pryor tonight at the Comedy Store. You should go. He's a laugh riot, really talented."

CHAPTER 31

USP Marion, #89637-132
June 1980

Peter Matthiessen arrives at Marion at the expected hour of 8:00 a.m. As he drives up to the prison on this fresh sunny morning, the looming grayness of the buildings in the distance floors him. *What an ominous place to call home*, he thinks, *like some ancient gloomy castle.* He knows there are three stories of cement underground. The surrounding quiet of the bucolic countryside just adds to its horror.

Walking toward the entrance, he's approached by two men in flak jackets with their arms out. "Go back. Get in your car and back away from here now!" Hard to argue with a man cradling an M-16.

One guard turns his back on Peter and points to a narrower road that leads to a small "observation area" with another guard gate with far more personnel. It is the only visiting facility and is off from the main grounds. It has tunnels underground that bring the inmate to the visitor. How can there possibly be any oversight to what goes on in such a place? An ominous atmosphere rife with indications that there's no way to check on these lost souls, those with no appeal left and no habeas corpus coming. Hence the label by prisoners "the end of the line." He's at a place now where few questions will be allowed, and little openness in answering them. Possibly Peltier will become inaccessible forever.

Peter Matthiessen is no stranger to watching something endangered disappear. In this spirit, he determines to act boldly and mentions this impending doom to Peltier, meaning his own possible extinction. As they talk, Leonard lets his shield down a little and describes USP Marion in southern Illinois, America's darkest hole. Here, he will not be lauded as he's been in LA but met by flak-jacketed tough guys who are a breed unto themselves. Peltier smiles in his usual brave way and describes his predicament as a federal lifer, "Ya know, Peter, almost everyone you meet in my predicament hates the FBIs. But the exception in my case? FBI hates me back. Makes my circumstances a little different." Peter knows Peltier will face the hardest time one can do.

But Peter has gotten a visit in, for now anyway, and soon he and Peltier are sharing a good laugh as Peltier, handcuffed, announces that he has been nominated for the Nobel Peace Prize. "Well," Peter says in retort, "you sure won't get it!"

Peter quickly inquires as to how Peltier has been faring. Peltier goes on to describe the containment units called "the hole" by inmates that seem to be his fate, though undeserved. He is arbitrarily put there for no reason. He's the reason. "It can begin to drive a man crazy in just twenty-four hours." He is left in this hole for weeks at a time. "They kept telling me I could lose my mind and forget who I am, so I traded my last tobacco for a pencil and wrote down who I am under my bed. In case I forgot, I could read it back to myself."

Smiling as usual, he tries to put Peter at ease.

Peter fears his welcome mat will not be out long. Every visitor, and that includes families and friends, entering one of these harsh institutions feels like it is a miracle when they are finally seated before their loved one again. A visit can end arbitrarily as well, no notice, with no explanation given.

Although Leonard is now housed in dramatically different circumstances from the LA County jail, he seems little changed—at least to Peter, who complains about the endurance test of getting in to see him. Leonard reminds Peter that Dennis Banks and company, hundreds of Indians, had recently camped just outside Marion so close that he could hear the drum all the way into solitary.

"Ask Hippie Jack if ya don't believe me, they were all here. It was real, man!"

That last is a common expression of Peltier's, as the constant behavior modification makes a prisoner doubt that anything they say will be believed. It is only true if a guard or warden says it. Every phone call is listened to and every bathroom break is monitored. How could one stay human in such conditions? Yet here is Leonard, laughing as if it's old home week.

Peter lowers his head, as he has something weighty to share. He'll wait another moment for it. Leonard wants to hear about a few things, his attention still lingering on some *New York Times* articles. "Man, you talk, Peter, and America listens, man!" Peter hesitates, then decides to ask Leonard about the Lompoc escape.

Peter starts with the farmer Jeremiah, mentioning he walked into the LA courtroom with dirt beneath his fingernails and wearing blue jean coveralls. Probably just a generation from the dust bowl transports.

"Yeah, the real thing, like me!" Peltier smiles. "Farmer had a small farm near the Santa Maria city limits. He ran this watermelon outfit I stopped in. There was an Indian cop with a sheriff that figured out my route. Ain't no one ratted out and told him; my friends were too dedicated. Hell, poor Roque, he left that gun for me so fast he didn't account for the fact it was still registered in his name! Damn. Now he's in jail. As for Judge Lydick, for a Nixon appointee he acted as expected. Judge was typical. At least that Asian judge let me marry Carlotta right in my cell downstairs."

"Yes, I saw her, she is a beautiful girl, Leonard. However do you manage it? Hard to have a life with her this way, though."

"Yeah, beautiful, Nez Pearce, well, no, you can't keep something going on with life on a telephone, or behind the glass, it just puts them in here with you, and you don't want to do that. It was real nice for a while. That's about all it is."

Peltier is still young, still handsome, and he looks a little mournful as he says this. He married this girl because he's still hoping to get an appeal and get out in a year or two. Peter can't shake off the feeling that Peltier has a good heart. Of all the candidates to carry AIM's torch, why this man? Not an egotist. Not yet. And with guidance from so many good people who are pulling for him on the outside, he might make good use of the time, too. It is still a dreadful price to pay, a human sacrifice, really, for a landscape that so many, on both sides, laid out.

Peter gets down to it and asks Leonard about the farmer Jeremiah, who had supposedly come to court that day in LA as a witness for the prosecution, but it didn't go down that way. He testified that he'd spent that morning in his truck, looking for work outside his farm, and he hadn't had any luck that morning so returned earlier than usual. He'd said this on the stand.

"Way off on his land he could see me, I was up against a backdrop of trees, just a man squatted in his garden." For the moment, Leonard and Peter are transported back to the courtroom, where this witness said more than he knew he had.

As Peter recalls it, the farmer had pointed to Leonard and said, "That man, the one sitting right there." Bruce Ellison started to object but Leonard grabbed his arm as if to say, let him speak. The defense team went still and Farmer Jeremiah went on. The farmer continued: "He appeared to be eating something and I realized it was one of my melons. I didn't make the connection with the radio broadcasts I'd heard all morning," alluding to the high-alert regarding an Indian escapee from Lompoc. "I just didn't make the connection. I'd never had any trouble before 'cept a little theft, maybe. 'Cept a lot of theft." Now the whole courtroom went quiet and still, including the judge.

"Most aggravating for me was when it was my tools. I'd lately made my living more from them than farming. The gardens weren't that giving as of late, and now this migrant man was stealing my melons! Well, I'd had just about enough of this aggravation, so I went back to my truck and took down my rifle from the rack and aimed careful and shot just to the left of him. Well, things got big real quick, and I can't for sure explain all the details that led to what happened next. For one, the thief had a better rifle hanging on his back than I did, I hadn't even seen it. I'm sure he'd have a better aim."

The courtroom stifled a giggle at this, though Lew Gurwitz was not amused and a little stymied, as they all had to let him finish now, the judge included. "Before I knew it," Farmer Jeremiah went on, "he had both the rifles in his hands, and I can't for the life of me explain how that happened. It happened fast, is how." It sounded right out of a picture show to an LA audience, and Creek Indian Phillip Deere threw back his head and laughed. Many followed suit. The lawyers and judge did not, nor did the Bureau men present. It was excruciating testimony, as the farmer had taken on the tone of a character witness. Neither side knew what he was about to say.

"Then," the farmer continued, as if telling a tall tale around a campfire,

"I got the seriousness of the situation and put it together he was the Indian they were all looking for, and I said so. To his face."

He demonstrated for the court by putting his hand over his mouth and wagging a finger in the air. Leonard remembers that the man had pirouetted in a circle, too, with a gun trained on him and all, and said, "You're that Indian they are looking for. And now you're gonna kill me. Well, go ahead and do it and get it over with."

Leonard was a little taken aback at such a statement, at the time. It would never have occurred to him to do such a thing. He was just shaken and more than a little pissed at this man for landing a bullet so close to him. "No," Jeremiah said, repeating Leonard's response for the court, "I ain't gonna kill you, though I feel like it, if I ever felt like killing someone. You gonna shoot a man just because he is hungry? Damn, mister, how's that a reason? But no, I'd never kill you, I'm a workingman just like you. I am gonna take your boots though, take them off and hurry. And I'm gonna take that El Camino."

Jeremiah went on to say that he dropped to the ground in a hurry and pulled off his boots. He was feeling a little safer in what this Indian had said to him. He'd said it like he really meant it, and the farmer thought he did. So he said earnestly, "Please let me get my tools out the truck bed. I make my living with them and can't replace anything right now. It's why I was mad about the melon, son. If I stick so much as a lawn mower out in the middle of my yard lately, a hand will come up out of the ground from nowhere and just take it!" This, too, he illustrated with gestures, making a fist and raising it up before his face as if it were rising out of the ground.

Then he went on to report that Leonard said, "Ya ever wonder what stole everything around that fist? Ever think of that?"

The farmer said he repeated, "I need my tools, sir." He reported that Leonard's reply was that he was ready to go and couldn't take time for that, he had to move fast, but he promised that every single one of his tools would be right where he left them. "And they were! Every single one!"

When the farmer left the witness chair and passed Leonard, he nodded, at which time Peltier called out, "Would've been nice to have a second gear. I wouldn'ta blown your clutch!" Everyone who heard it laughed outright again. Leonard was being kinder than anyone knew to the man whose phone call triggered nothing short of an agent-style assault and arrest.

Leonard sat on high ground watching them come up the hill toward him, and though his rifle was fully loaded, he never fired a shot.

Peter reminded Leonard the courtroom went into stunned silence when that farmer finished.

"Yeah, I remember, sure-sure, but what everybody there don't know is that the sheriff saved my life. I heard them talk about just shooting me, and he said he didn't sign on for no killing. If he had gone along, we wouldn't be sitting here today, brother." Peter finds it odd to hear Leonard speak up for the sheriff.

This confidence reminds him of the delicate nature of sharing. There is an intimacy to it. In order to get to know someone, they also have to get to know you. Peter mentions his impressions of the agents in the courtroom, and it is obvious to Leonard that Peter is sympathetic to one of them. Leonard flares up a bit upon hearing his name and refers to him throughout the next exchange as "the coward." He's speaking of Donald Harmon.

They continue on the LA trial, remarking that the FBI agent had fumed at the circus-like atmosphere the trial had yet again become. "Charming as a goddamn rattlesnake," had been Harmon's muttered comment, staring over at Peltier. As hard as stone now, Agent Donald Harmon had become bitter as gall. He wasn't the only one present who felt that way. The FBI attended in full force.

"Goddamn," the LA prosecutor had complained openly when the farmer became a character witness right in front of their eyes.

"You'd think you could depend on a man to object to someone holding a gun in his face! In his own backyard!" the prosecutor said to his assistant prosecutor. It had about taken his breath away the first time he saw the route of the escape. Peltier had practically run right through his new suburb, rifle, bundle, wind band, and all! "The Bureau just couldn't get a break!" Peter thought to himself, recalling the day. "Bureau men had openly cried at the verdict at Razor's and Dino's Cedar Rapids trial. Dennis was beloved in California, made an honorary professor, and other trials exonerated AIMers. The only win they ever had was against Peltier, and it was becoming painfully obvious how they got it, so it gave them little moral satisfaction."

A man named Standing Deer got up and says he was offered a reduced sentence if he set Peltier up to be killed in Lompoc. The Indians swearing to it were a few who'd been moved to Lompoc at the same time Leonard was. It was a new prison, they had the room, that was justification enough. But, funny thing, the main Indian spinning the plot did have his sentence reduced and then was moved from state prison to a federal one to wind down the reduced sentence. That doesn't happen. It never happens! Lew Gurwitz had mentioned to Peter. "You don't go from state prison to federal to wind down anything!"

Peter puts it out of his mind and goes back to what is before him. "Well, the FBI got a few breaks in California," Peter says to Leonard, "and this farmer running to a phone was one. Or you," Peter says to Leonard, "would likely be in Canada this very day." Though it was not likely Canada would allow being lied to and tricked a second time.

Peltier asks, "Did you see the coward speak to me?" Peter nods yes. Donald Harmon had gotten his turn, and he would not be moved to pity, for damn sure. On a break he walked right past Leonard, since everyone was allowed to be so casual, and whispered his own remarks.

"I wish I could get just ten minutes alone with you, Peltier," he said, and eyed him closely.

Leonard lifted his eyes to Harmon's. "It'd take me ten just to catch you." Hate had become banter, and Leonard knew the language well. He also knew that no matter what the truth was, he'd never deflect their hate now. Why try?

Leonard looked around the courtroom and caught the eye of the Chumash cop who had arrested him. He knew he likely owed his life to this man, so he stared for a beat at him who'd discovered his trail and knew not only to look toward the ceremonial grounds, but also to not cut across them but go around instead. And then the farmer's call came in and all the law with guns drawn.

It was said through the moccasin telegraph and repeated that some sheriff had declared he wouldn't just shoot Leonard, and Leonard was pretty sure this Chumash had had something to do with that, them being in such close quarters. It all happened in five short days. He had felt every hour of them; even in his desperate state he had breathed in the clean, dry air and enjoyed the tropical sun on his back, and especially the candlelit flicker of stars at night.

After the arrest that day, in the sheriff's car rolling back over the hills, Leonard is handcuffed and belly-chained at the waist. He is sitting behind the cage that runs between the front and back seats. Leonard listened to the Chumash cop remind him that he was likely headed for the deepest, darkest hole they could put him in, so he ought to give up the man he knew shot the FBI men. If he did know. Leonard didn't say one word, in his own defense or otherwise. He just breathed.

He knew enough by now that if he did talk, they would not free him but just put everyone he mentioned inside with him. Good people, people with family, men and women, friends. No, he would never explain or give them any information. It would never occur to him to do such a thing. Never.

As if the Chumash cop sensed his determination and that he had very little time in which to break Leonard's resolve, he shared a piece of information. He did so as he poked a cigarette into Leonard's mouth through the cage hole. Peltier took the Marlboro and was glad it was already lit. It also afforded him the only opportunity to look into this brother's eyes, likely the last Indian he'd see until trial. The Chumash cop took his shot. If he could help this man at all, getting him to break and let go of that shooter's name was his only chance. Draw any information out of him, which wasn't looking likely.

"Another friend has been lost, did ya hear? Someone you couldn't protect. Did you know Dallas Thundershield was killed after going over that fence behind you?" Leonard was caught off guard—he hadn't known, and he lowered his head as best he could with the belly chains around him and began to cry. The sound of his weeping would haunt the Chumash cop for the rest of his life.

CHAPTER 32

"In the Spirit of Crazy Horse"
August 1980

When it came to Matthiessen's visitor forms—those had gone missing three times before his first visit to Marion, though not for today's. Once you were processed in, you could count on staying on the visiting list for a while, and this being his second visit it appeared he was in! Leo Peltier, Leonard's father, was leaving as Peter walked in. He had the look of the World War Two vet, and of a loving dad.

Peter sits across from Leonard, alone now, and has decided to say something he's never shared with anyone else, not even with those closest to him. Peter is a disciplined man, a Buddhist, and he knows this is something he needs to mention before things go further.

Peltier can sense there's something heavy on Peter's mind, and it is not the usual buildup to asking, "Who did it?" or "Did you do it?" Peter has won him over one hundred percent, and clearly, he is now about to go all in himself about something. Picking up on Peter's hesitancy, and aware of the growing brotherhood between them, Leonard approaches in his naturally open way.

"Whatever it is you have to say, just say it man. I won't be mad."

Peter can't help smiling warmly. It's as if they were ten years old again in a schoolyard somewhere. Leonard's obvious sincerity melts his reserve. "I did something when I was a young man. And I want you to hear it from me."

"You did something? Well, so what? You damn sure won't be apologizing to me for it, if that's what you're worried about, whatever the hell it is. I'm serious."

Peter is feeling unexpectedly vulnerable, and says by way of preamble, "I want to write this book. No, I need to. And I will."

"Well, good then. That's good for me, brother; got about a million people praying you do." Then Leonard stays silent, in the respectful way that implies, *take your time to say what you want, and if it turns out that's never, that'll be okay, too.*

After a moment or two, Peter begins. "I was traveling, in China a lot, and on many other foreign soils, as they say. It was after the war, and we were all very patriotic. I was. A man came to me when I was stopping over in Paris. He asked for my help. That's how he put it, anyway, and I was a greenhorn, young."

Leonard smiles, knowing he's been that a few times himself, more than a few. He swirls a finger in the air, reminiscent of a pipe ceremony gesture, and says, "Well, something about these walls brings out the confessing in people for damn sure." They share a deep and genuine laugh over this. "I have heard some damn unreal things in here, man. This one guy killed his whole village in Alaska, or so he says. Weren't many people, but he got all of them. Hell, Peter, I wouldn't let half of these people out of here myself!" Peter nods and then continues.

"It was in the aftermath of the war, and many Americans were traveling to places not allowed before. This man wanting help was in OSI, that was . . . is . . ."

"I know what that is. Was." They are talking about the CIA, and Leonard is alert now, engaged and poised for the unexpected.

Peter looks Leonard in the eye, man-to-man. "I helped him."

Leonard does not ask how. Instead, he thinks, *Prominent family, a genius, and yet he was coerced by the same organization as a lot of naïve abroad have been snookered by!* He appreciates Peter's confidence more than he can say, and he'll keep it. He was always good for that. He does ask if Peter had shared the information with his friends in Paris, who likely got eavesdropped on for it, and can tell by his silence that it pretty much means "no." What a burden to carry all this time, impossible to explain, even harder to live with.

This good brother, Leonard thinks, *who would take such risks for the most helpless, all those birds and land, and would do so much for me now. There are species of birds that would have perished off this earth if not for him, and chasing down poachers would be scary as hell.* He feels as if at last someone has come his way, whose voice would be heard above his, and he was willing to risk to do it and say, simply, "Wait a minute, wait! He might be innocent!" And now many would listen. It might not make any difference, but they would have to listen. That means everything to Leonard and will to anyone captured and voiceless.

Peter's confession is heavy in the air until Leonard clears it, saying as their visit ends, while being re-chained, "Look at it this way, brother, when you do tell all your friends, remind 'em you made friends with me and so now people will be listening to your every piss! So, there! They got ya back! You got no apologies to make to any goddamn body!" Peter notices that Peltier is laughing so hard as he turns to go that he is almost bouncing. It wasn't that funny. The topic is never mentioned between them again.

Peltier hates parting from a friend, and Peter is surely that. Peter hates to go as well, and squeezes in one last question, aware that this is a rare moment. "Dick Wilson ceded off a hundred and thirty thousand acres just after AIM left the reservation. Did you know that?" Peter is referring to all the land leases that were going out the back door to corporations, energy corporations, getting Indian land that was supposed to be held in trust. He was curious if Peltier knew about it. Peter was aware of it, and far worse.

"No. But then, we stopped a lot of things we didn't know. I guess something knew, brother, so we didn't have to." Still smiling, he turns to leave for real this time. Instead of his familiar parting word, *doksha,* which means "see ya later," today he says, on a more serious note, "In the spirit of Crazy Horse." He is still smiling as he's led back through the heavy metal doors.

Relieved of one burden, Peter is taking on an even bigger one, whether he knows it or not. Leonard has always been on the side of a friend, right or wrong. It is his nature to fight off the bully and draw the heat to himself. But this time someone will be taking the heat for him, so a new day has arrived for Leonard Peltier.

Once back to his cell, Leonard recalled his last memories of being on the outside, when he was recently zigzagged across the entire country in transport to Marion. Anything to make the walls in front of him disappear. Prison transfers were blind travel, but occasionally he'd been able to catch glimpses of what was outside the various transport vehicles. His favorite was passing Amish people on some highway, riding in a horse-drawn wagon full of their harvest, little kids on the hay.

Skies changed colors and fresh air was gulped in like a last breath during the transition from one vehicle to another. He had been grateful for every minute they were made to stop their movement. Often facilities did not meet the security requirements imposed for him, so he was locked down hard to a metal seat before being loaded onto a plane. He saw the moon more than the sun.

Most of the time his own family was not notified when he was transferred in the night to another facility. Not even his lawyer knew if or when he had arrived until, eventually, Leonard got to make a call. Or he found a stamp and wrote from a hole. The moccasin telegraph would buzz across the country with two words: "He's alive!" When he could call, allies who once ran to take his call didn't even answer now, not after the Lompoc escape. Except Dorothy, she always answered. She always would. *So would Dennis if he could find his ass near a phone*, he thought. A prisoner couldn't schedule a call, you had to get lucky.

During the final days of the transfer saga, he found himself in a common stopping place before the end journey, and that was South Dakota State Prison. He was not far from Fort Totten, North Dakota, where his sister lived, and his mom. He had the legal right to be imprisoned close to home, but as usual was put a thousand miles or more away with his eventual arrival to Marion.

For now, he was close by, but due to solitary confinement he was denied any visitors. Just more torture to be so close, and yet not be able to see anyone from home. The cost of a thousand miles, travel would work an unbearable hardship on his family. Rules didn't apply to him, even when it was theirs. This one particular day, he was killing time by sketching an eagle on the cement floor. He'd had a week or two to perfect it. Not sure how long it had been, as time got away from you in solitary. It was coming along nicely, looked just like the proud thunderbird.

He was glad to be in one transition for so long now: hard to mess with him until he was in the final place for good, which would be Marion. He'd become a good sketcher while in Canada, always using what he had. Here, he only had a lead pencil and a gray cement floor. He saved all his cigarette butts and used the ash for shading. His fingers were stained gray.

At first, he was allowed to order a small paint set that came with a brush and a paint-by-numbers drawing on a canvas-lined board—like something for a child. The guard in charge of this privilege had given him two choices, the Stations of the Cross or the Last Supper. He chose the latter. Another guard, who, in spite of himself, had become Peltier's friend and even sneaked him pizza, had seen the colorful painting and scoffed. "You ain't going religious on me, are ya, Peltier?" To which Leonard replied, brush on canvas, "F-u-c-k you." Peltier knew he'd miss him after his South Dakota State Prison stint, which must be drawing nigh.

A month later, still in what was called "Super Lockdown" for South Dakota State Prison lingo, the same guard seemed animated as he came to the far end of the hall that led to Peltier's cell. Leonard had learned to move like lightning when he heard the metal door slide open to the hall that opened solitary. He had only seconds before whoever it was went back out the other end and the timed lights darkened the hall again. Even a glimpse of another breathing human being was a relief. Even if it brought unkind words, he was a human, and it was good for Leonard's mind to glimpse one. Only this friendly guard lingered.

Usually the guards left a tray of food and were out the other end of the hall before the light flickered out. Today the guard walked toward his door and paused. Likely it meant bad news. They never brought good, but he prayed it was a message from his lawyer. From anybody, about anything.

Leonard glanced at the tobacco he'd left high up at the corner of the windowsill. It was still there after all this time, next to a windowpane that had a cement ledge to it. One day he'd seen that a bit of the black paint had peeled away from this top corner glass to reveal the outside, as if nature had peeled it away. He could see a tiny bit of a nearby treetop through it. It was a gift of life-giving force just to see that little bit of green. Or a raindrop rolling past it. Oh, that was a good day.

The guard seemed to be excited, and Leonard called out, "What, man? Tell me quick, what's happened?" He told Leonard that another prisoner, an inmate he knew, was on the other side of the wall from him. "Right there," the young guard said, pointing. "He was told you were here. He wants to try and meet you in the law library if you stay here long enough to get out of solitary. Or he does. He's a famous hard case! From Milwaukee."

Leonard, exasperated, said, "Well, bro, who the hell is it? Are you sure I even know him?" Likely it was a trick, Leonard thought, likely someone sent inside to talk to him for the Justice Department. Wouldn't be the first time.

"Leonard, I'm telling ya, it's a man you know, a friend or someone . . . *Her-bret* Powless." Leonard blanched, and then his eyes moistened so fast he couldn't stop it. The guard, used to his humor, took a step back.

"Are you sure? You ain't lying to me, are you? Herb's here? That's the name they said?"

"Yeah, man, right on the other side of your wall." The guard pointed to it.

Leonard turned away, from the guard and from the whole world, as he walked up to the wall and laid his outstretched hand full on it. The cement block was cool to the touch and prickly-rough. He felt his palm on it first, then his fingers and fingertips, and then the bones inside his hand, as he pressed as hard as he could, thinking he could almost push through it if he concentrated hard enough.

"Does he know I'm here?" Leonard said, without turning around. "I mean right here, on the other side of this?"

The guard answered softly, as if he were suddenly standing in a church, witnessing a very human moment. He wondered who this man was to Leonard, maybe like a dad or something. Maybe he'd have reacted the same if it'd been anyone he knew? No, this Powless from Milwaukee was someone special.

"Sure, Leonard, he knows, he was told first. They say he is such a handful it took a few days to get him to even roll over and listen to the guard. He keeps his back to everyone. He stays in solitary almost by choice. A real hard case. An inmate friend of his came by, this Italian celly, and he mentioned it to him. Then he listened. Jumped up even, like you did!"

Leonard smiled at this information, thinking Herb would more likely have just said "Christ" at the sound of his name and then rolled back over.

"Then he, well, passed a twenty around until they found someone who eventually told me. They knew I might get it to you, the message, that is. I sure did when I heard it'd matter so much. Uh-huh. Her-bart Powless, there he is."

Leonard stood there and stared for a long time, hardly listening to the young guard, who eventually walked away softly. Leonard didn't know or care. He just stood at the wall, breathing. And he did so the next day and then the next. He didn't know it, but on the other side of the wall, Herb Powless was doing the same.

CHAPTER 33

Determination,
South Dakota State Prison Library
One Month Later

"I wish I was doing all my time with you," Leonard said, grasping Herb's hand tightly, elated they had both been released from segregation isolation, and were now standing in the same room.

"Well, I damn sure don't!" Herb replied, though he, too, is almost smiling at seeing Leonard again.

It was a lucky moment when they hooked up, a miracle really, as Herb was almost through with his sentence. Herb still doesn't like the words "miracle," or "luck." He remembers this and remains cautious. The only spot an inmate was allowed to go, when in super lockdown status, was the library. They couldn't deny them this one place.

Herb looks quite different, but he sounds the same. He just walks into the law library as if he owns it. *Given his friends in Washington*, Leonard thinks, *maybe he does.* As usual, Herb gets straight down to business. Leonard is unaware Herb no longer has those same friends. They are both on their own.

"We don't have long, and we can count on every word being heard. They send in lip-readers for the likes of us, so don't trust even a visiting room. Ya know that? And quit that goddamn grinning."

Leonard breaks out in genuine laughter, and Herb looks like he wants to club him with a law book. "Christ, Peltier, quit bouncing up and down in that irritating way you do and grab a book. I wanna show you a few things I been thinking about. Or we can just cross-leg it and shoot the shit and wait for the guards to come back and get us."

Miserable or not, it is great to see Herb.

"Let's start at the beginning." Herb pulls a book on due process.

"You know I didn't do what they're having me do time for?"

"I don't need you to tell me that, and you know it."

"Yeah, I know that; it's why I'm telling you. I just want you to know."

"Well, don't want me to know. Don't get in that habit. You and the Creator are the only ones that need to know a goddamn thing. Look at this statute, here. Lew mentioned it to me. Says you can add good time to your years, and to Canada seven years is already considered a life sentence. You've done five years already. Somebody up in Canada is calling up about you, from Montreal I think Lew said, a man by the name of Warren, I think that's his first name."

"How's Dorothy?" Leonard asks. "Was Lew with her, when'd ya hear from him?"

"She's Dorothy, that's how she is. Pissed at me half the time."

"Be good to her, you're a lucky man."

"I don't feel lucky at the moment. Stay off the subject of my wife."

"We were all admiring of her; half the guns were in her name."

"Maybe that's why they didn't work half the time."

They share a knowing laugh.

"Don't talk so much, or get too sentimental, makes you soft. You ain't headed where being soft will help you none."

"You act like I hadn't been there before. My old lady doesn't even know where I am right now, and likely won't visit me again when she does."

"Maybe you getting married at Lompoc upset her. Don't get some woman on my mind. And which old lady might she be, while you're remembering my wife? Shit, Peltier, you just got married, *again*? What happened to that Ho-Chunk gal from Pine Ridge? Jean somethin'?"

"Again? Like it's happened a lot? I married Audrey and thank God I kept her far from me, too much dangerous shit 'round our camps."

"Yeah, I know. Seems leadership kept away, too."

"Does it look like we had any leaders there?"

"No," Herb says, and they laugh again.

"She had two babies for me, did you know that? Beau-ti-ful kids, sweet. A little boy and a baby girl. I had to book it out of there without even saying goodbye. Not gonna lead anyone to them, for damn sure."

"Yeah, seems I heard something about it. If I can keep up. Ya had another kid in the Northwest, too, Lew mentioned that. And another after the monastery takeover. Hell, if we can get you free, you and Banks could double the whole Indian population. Let's either talk shop or just fold our arms till the guard comes back and ask him to bring us a Coke."

Leonard knows Herb hates too much sentiment; he is a sensitive guy is why, really. Came from a war thing, the not talking. A Herb thing. "Nah, okay, no man, I want your help. Just such a relief to see someone from back home."

"Back home? I'm Oneida and you're Chippewa, our home is a thousand miles from each other. Pay attention now, we can be sentimental when you're out. Get in that habit. Even with your old lady, make the visits count for something."

"So, I write to this guy in Canada, you got his address?"

"No. It's fucking Canada, find it."

"It's a big place, I'll need his last name at least."

"You ought to know how damn big it is. To hear tell it, you walked half of it. Maybe flew over it, too."

"Yeah, well, I shoulda flown out of it while I had the chance."

"Could ya have?"

"Yup. To Nicaragua. This one guy offered to take me, had this little prop plane. I'd probably have been labeled some damn mad fighter down there in the jungle and be dead by now. Not interested. Milwaukee's the only place I ever missed that wasn't home."

"Got in nothing but trouble in Milwaukee; don't know why ya like it so much."

"Had work to finish there. That employment agency was starting to cook, man!"

"Now let's look at the books. I marked the place. Their chain of evidence starts with your skipping out of Milwaukee."

"Yeah, but that was a chain of lies."

"You did jump bail. Do the crime, do the time."

"You think I give a damn about running out of Milwaukee? Said I was gunning for something, because scared over Milwaukee! More lies, I had to stop and remember what they were even talking about. If I was so worried about it, why'd I come back to Wisconsin and help you and Menominee at that takeover? That came after I jumped bail. Cops looking for me all over Wisconsin, right?"

"Menominee's termination ended! Nixon shocked us all and reversed that. Had his own hair on fire, leaving office, and stopped long enough to sign those papers." Herb Powless wasn't as surprised as others. He'd pointed Brad Patterson to it many times, but he doesn't mention it now.

"Who was that movie guy came in with Dennis?"

"You don't know who Marlon Brando is? Biggest star on the planet, man. He really helped us, bro."

"I don't trust nobody I don't know."

"You don't trust anybody ya do. Look at you."

"I'm standing here, aren't I? I'll pay time, said I would."

"They ought to name a statue after you, man. In Milwaukee, at least! Where's our people's statues or street names?"

"You'll see them, day ya see a Reverend Black Elk or Reverend Red Cloud." They share a knowing smile. "Some hot day, right!"

Their laughter is deep, and it feels good. But Peltier's face goes somber when he says, "Not everybody jumped in their damn melting pot. Shit, our people, they'd melt first."

"Almost did a few times. Shit, I got blisters in Crow Dog's damn lodge," Herb says. "This one *Uwipi* ceremony I tied Crow Dog up, I mean tied him tight, man. I tied the knots, used navy knots, and tied each individual finger. Tied inside a star quilt, he looked like a mummy, his voice all muffled. Ceremony ends and later the lights come on, and him just sitting there in a chair and his voice is clear. We saw some things, didn't we?"

"Damn. That's heavy, hunh?"

"How in the *Helena Montreal* did you go wounded and bleeding all over the place and still get all the way to Canada?"

"Motivation," Leonard says with a smile. "Everything got fun once they took me to Oakalla. Just chain me up in a wet cave next time. Rotting old place."

"It's always hard when it's your first time, by any measure. You had a few nights in county jail, but that was the real thing for a first one. Shit, Peltier, who in hell would ever dream it'd ever be you they'd hang it all on?" Leonard just raises his eyebrows, brave to the end.

"Yeah, you always remember your first time, because it's the beginning of many last times. Cold, dank blank place, as blank as my life was about to be. I decided right then, scared as shit man, I was gonna take all that greyness they got planned for me and bring in my own color. Ya know? This hateful guard started taunting me about looking scared, too, sayin' 'You just wait till we slam those big heavy doors down on you, son, you just wait. You'll know.' I wish he knew that the minute that cell locked down that night, I slept like a baby. Finally felt safe, 'cause they were locked out."

"Who's the real mad dogs?"

"Later, I just wanted out of there. The lawyers were pissed off about the extradition from Canada, but the one good thing was I was getting my ass out of that old decaying prison. They loved to play tricks on me there, hand me a rusted metal cup of milk as my only light bulb goes out. Roaches crawling all over my hand minute lights went out. If you think Indians are treated better in Canada, then stay a few months in one of their prisons. *Shee-it.*" Leonard lights a cigarette and hands it to Herb, then lights his own, inhales, and looks down at the law book.

"And there are some strict rules attached to your vacating documents, Lew says." Herb flips another book open, and Peltier looks over his shoulder. "Fargo provided a damn nightmare of paperwork that violated every goddam rule they got in the US Constitution. Hell, Peltier, don't ask for a new trial, ask for your first one! By the description of what one is in this book, you ain't had one yet! Lew's working on getting his hands on those documents."

"Yeah," Leonard says, sarcastically, "They can stonewall. They musta held a railroading convention over me with every expert in the country. It'll take forever."

"That might be how much time we got," Herb says, sharing an uncomfortable laugh this time.

"What about who you know, your friends in Washington?"

"What friends?"

"They helped you, man."

"Helped me to stay put, ya mean."

"You got money out of them and land, for real! You stuck their feet in the fire!"

"They were playing us, just like a tribal chairman, no difference to them, recognizing us as those 'successful urban Indians' they promised to produce, ya see? Ask yourself why they give us anything, back or otherwise? I asked myself. Kept rolling over why I didn't feel good about it when all youz were slappin' me on the back. Had a lot of time to roll it around in my head. They were gonna terminate everything out on the land. Look at this," Herb says as he writes something out in pencil and shows it to Leonard. "What do you see?" He has scribbled out the words *self-determination* and then lays his forefinger across part of the words until all Peltier can see is "*termination*."

"Can't have one without the other. Determination means termination. I looked it up, get a dictionary and keep it in your cell, it's all about the words. 'De' is Latin, ya see, and it means 'back from.' Determination, back from termination."

"Damn. Never believed we'd swing back the other way."

"No, they didn't. They knew we weren't gonna ever play ball and so they gave it to the Justice Department."

"They weren't expecting us to swing the other way around."

"Nope. Patterson was told he could give us anything he wanted, which was saying 'anything we wanted,' just don't embarrass the president. Problem was we just wanted the same one thing. Always will."

"You know they'll never listen to a single thing we say again." Leonard's eyes are steady as he says it. Herb goes somber a minute.

"I don't have anything left to say," he confesses to Leonard. "Thought I'd never get a tribe to take that damn land once they did give it!"

"Shit, you say? In Milwaukee? Not take land, our land? Who'd not take it?"

"Nobody, Menominee. Took five tries. Offered it to Ho-Chunks."

"Jesus, I'm just hearing this. Even your brother Percy didn't want it for your people?"

"Especially not him. No one liked the way we got it. Afraid of it, thought it would bite 'em back later. I went to Potawatomi, who ended up saying yes. Oneidas, no, didn't wanna touch it."

"Shit . . . land?"

"Potawatomi said they weren't worried about anything biting them, they were so damn dirt poor nothing could hurt 'em worse." They both nod with a laugh, knowing what that means. "I say, you been hungry. You been afraid? Take it!"

"Hey, you said five times, that's just four tribes you named."

"Because I asked Oneidas twice, they were first and fifth. Poor as shit, Potawatomi got it, heard they're gonna start bingo games."

"Not poor long." Leonard smiles as he draws in a long breath. "Herb, those government men weren't caring about that, it wasn't for a right reason, or that treaty, it was dealing with you, man. You held out, you wouldn't quit on that Coast Guard station and it was the real deal. Dorothy just walked right in the damn back door, remember? She's a trip! Yeah, Herb, you did it, man. It was cold as shit on that lake."

"So what, you said you don't mind the cold, remember?"

Leonard looks up and straight into his eyes now, like the time he did on the fateful day he first met the AIMer from Milwaukee in that parking lot in Los Angeles and he says to him, sober, "No, I don't mind the cold, I told ya that."

They grow quiet, lost in memory, and then their smiling stops.

"It wasn't me they gave that land over, Peltier, it was us. All of us."

"Yeah sure, all seven of us." They huff out a knowing laugh at that one.

"Hey man, your wife was brave!" Leonard insists. "We're standing one night out front of the Station House, you weren't there, and these marshals pull up, and she ushers us all out front, including her, to make it look like we have more than we did. Spider was there, Stanley started shivering, it was obvious, and it weren't from no cold, he's shaking like a leaf, and I'm trying not to crack up laughing, and Dorothy's shushing us like schoolkids, and Stanley up and says, 'Dorothy, I gotta have a drink, woman, come on now, I can't get shot sober!' She says, 'If I can take a bullet sober you can! It took me six months to get you sober, Stanley Morris, so hell no, ya ain't drinking now!'"

Herb raises his eyes again to Leonard, a rare and beautiful thing when it finally happens. "You came in there with us, ya know? You did a lot there. That employment for Indians was a good idea."

"Year later."

"Don't matter when. They staked out that diner just to get you cuz of it."

"Yeah, dumbass." They laugh again, this time like brothers who've shared a familiar fate.

"Leonard, listen to this. It weren't never about any one day. But all them days that lead up to it. It was gonna happen someday, bad shit comes down, they push it. They want us all off the land, any way they can manage it, helping us, not helping us. Why ya think our people used words in those agreements like 'as long as there's water in that riverbed, or the sun shines,' our promises will hold? They connected it to things they know are forever, 'cause their word was gonna be! Break your promise, man, but they aren't going to. They held on."

"Nobody expected anything out of us."

"No, they didn't. Nixon loved those words, self-determined, well, we was, exactly that." He stops speaking. The so-called "urban outsiders" had used their individual worth to become a line of defense. So their people, those like them, those they might have been, those desperate to stay communal, might have a chance. Because it was right with their souls and good for their land. And it was the law.

They smoke in silence a minute or two, then Herb opens a law book titled *Due Process and the Constitution* and pushes it toward Leonard.

Herb speaks fast now, as he hears the guards jangling keys. "Make some real friends at Marion, make sure we know and can check 'em out first, talk to their families. Alan Iron Moccasin will be waiting for you, soon as you get out of the hole. If they won't sweat with ya, then you'll know. We will do what we can to get a sweat in there, minute you get there, whether you can join it or not. Have the presence, ya know. Crow Dog is already working on it. Lenny Foster has started to sweat in prisons, officially."

"He's a good man." Leonard says, as his voice trails off.

Leonard and Herb end things that day the way all Indian brothers do, with a good laugh and an inside handshake. And moist eyes. Nothing could ever come between brothers in the Movement. Not really. Not for real. Leonard hadn't remembered that Herb once started every recruiting speech with the words, "I'm going to prison. If you get in my car, you'll need to know how to do time." It wasn't like Leonard to remember such a thing, but today the words do occur to Herb Powless. Leonard had gotten in his car.

An unwelcomed silence falls when Peltier leaves the room. Herb usually treasures silence, but at this moment, he doesn't welcome it all that much.

CHAPTER 34

Green Bay, Wisconsin
November 2012,
More than Thirty Years Later

A mix of colorful wallpaper and generic Indian motifs decorate the walls of the new grand Oneida casino in Green Bay, Wisconsin. Dorothy Ninham still has her wit and beauty and doesn't miss a trick, not even at seventy-one, as she still moves quickly as a teenager down the long hall of the Radisson Hotel, her long neatly tied ponytail swaying to and fro behind her, always in charge. Still.

The banner over her head reads WELCOME IN 2013 WITH US! She held the position of a tribal judge years earlier, but now, well into the new millennium, she is a property shift manager at the casino. She is trusted with the property and is called to oversee large payoffs when jackpot winners are paid out. She turns around and heads down another hallway, as her name has just been called over the intercom and she needs to backtrack.

Passing the Duck Creek Café, the smell of wild mushrooms steaming in rich butter, mixed with the aroma of roasted mutton simmering in garlic atop a bed of fresh onions, permeates the air. Always on the side would be black wild rice and stewed red apples.

A tobacco shop can be spotted in the short distance, its neon light bouncing off the window. One of the last places where communal smoking could go on indoors. But not alcohol. Never that. You'd have to sneak that into your room, and some endeavor to do it.

From over a loudspeaker the voice of a familiar local is heard.

"We wanna welcome the Wisconsin Smoke Dancers and their friends visiting up from Clearlake, better catch 'em tonight, or you will have to wait until State Fair!"

Even at the early hour of the day, many are milling about. Mostly seniors.

An Oneida Indian security guard spots the beautiful, small-framed Dorothy. The handsome young Oneida with his severe haircut puts in a lot of effort to try to make his errand look casual as he endeavors to catch her.

"Dorothy, good, hey yah, Herb's lookin' for ya at security desk. Dorothy, the other way, hey?"

Dorothy raises her hand in the air to him and waves as she passes, as if to say *I already know.*

Flanking her from yet another direction, the Oneida box office manager runs up.

"Dorothy, there's a property shift management meeting, where ya goin? Wrong direction, sister."

Dorothy blows her off without even a nod.

Dorothy quickens her way back to the security desk. It is vacant until she looks down around the corner and spots her young granddaughter Nolu Powless running toward her, with hair that is almost as long as she is. Dimples and a grin greet her grandmother as the young, strong girl, just turned six years old, quickly leaves the ground and lands in her grandmother's arms. You'd think they'd been parted for days, not hours.

Dorothy says directly, "Where's Grandpa?"

Herb Powless saunters up from between the clanging machines as if he has all day. He wears a slouched tan wool cap and carries a cane. He acts casual and sure of himself, as always. In charge. Why shouldn't he? Wherever he is, he was.

He pats young Nolu on her head, reminding her they have a secret, but his eyes don't leave Dorothy's as he does it.

Dorothy blurts out, frustration in her voice; "You didn't call me, Herb, I almost landed in a meeting." Casually his eyes roam the empty security area as he takes her words in, but you'd never know he's paying attention.

"Security desk unattended. Yeah. That's us," remarks Herb, matter-of-factly.

Dorothy responds, "What's unattended is my granddaughter."

Herb says back, "Gotta drop 'em. Sonny and Abi." Their two other grandchildren are in the car. Casually, Herb says, "Call the girls." He is referring to their daughters and grown-up granddaughters.

Dorothy is mad now. "'Takin' 'em for the day' does not mean noon, Herb, christ! Council members have come over—they're watching—"

Herb interrupts as he pats Nolu's cheek: "Hell, this little one could take care of the whole tribe better than that damn council. Watch is all they do. They're all out on the golf course anyways, we passed them on the way in, so nothin' to watch. They're what ya better watch, around here. *Hee-hee.* I gotta be someplace."

Dorothy, in her usual fluster with him, says, "Jessica is in class, and Cheryl's working, it's why I asked you!" She's referring to her granddaughter and daughter. Dorothy is exasperated but knows not to bother asking twice. As tart as she could be with him, it was not her way to pressure anyone into doing anything; she'd rather manage than have an ill-spirit about her. She waves him off.

Maybe she can call Gina, she thinks. No, not Gina, not today. Her beautiful, hot-tempered little Gina, still a fighter, now works in the tribe's legal department, and likely has her own granddaughter, Nyah Bear, sleeping in a low crib beside her. Catrina, her daughter, has just started nursing school.

Over the loudspeaker the announcer is heard again.

"*Eagle Butte Seniors, come get your buffet tickets now. Buffet has a few special items today, I won't tell ya, just come on over and see for yourself! A good ol' Wisconsin feed with baked apples at every meal and the best fresh-made cheese you'll ever taste!*"

Herb's listening, but Dorothy is not, as Herb says, "Ol' powwow caller, I recognize that arena voice, ol' raspy-tongue devil. He found a new job."

Herb looks Dorothy over in a glance as he says, his voice raised, "You said it was a slow morning." Dorothy replies, "It was when I came in at five o'clock, then we had an OTL call in and I had to go run the cage." The loudspeaker finally stops.

"OTL? What's that one again?" Herb asked.

"Over the limit; this one was a ten-thousand-dollar payout."

"*Christ.* I knew better than to ask anything around here," Herb says as the loudspeaker cranks up again. He raises his face up to it this time, as if the announcer is speaking directly to him. Might be about another ten thousand.

"*At three o'clock don't forget the drawing for the Chevy pickup in the lobby, swipe your rewards card for extra points and dining, it'll give ya more chances at the truck, too!*"

Herb laughs outright. "I could sure use a Chevy pickup, a free one. My word!" he says as he turns quickly to Dorothy, as she is often off like a puff of smoke. "Hey shorty, I need thirty dollars and some cigarettes."

"Thirty dollars won't buy you some cigarettes. Where's your check, ya just got it?"

Herb looks sheepish. For a hard man he can still play innocent as a small boy when he wants something out of her. "Ask these guys where it is, these machines are rigged!"

Dorothy crosses her arms. "Then stay away from them. I just give you fifty dollars."

Herb scowls at the casino floor, "Great plan, poor Indians giving it all away to poor Indians."

"You're not poor, Herb," she says as she starts to walk off. She turns back just long enough to lift her beautiful little great-granddaughter Nalani, who has joined her cousin Nolu's side. Effortlessly, Dorothy raises her to her hip.

Herb continues, "Those machines show no mercy, and as usual I got nothin' for it. I oughta shoot it!" He leans forward and kisses Nalani's mussed dark hair, as Nolu is busy trying to smooth it out and make the little girl look more presentable. Obviously, she's been pulled right from naptime for this excursion with Grandpa, as she is still in her PJs and wearing an oversized little boy's coat.

"There's senior housing and a nursing home—" Dorothy says as he cuts her off.

"Shoot me before you send me over there, will ya? I went over there, only old people inside! Getting on a bus to go to some damn mall, I reckon. Not me! If I gotta come all the way over to Green Bay, then take me to Longhorn's and get me a decent T-bone at least for the trek."

Dorothy settles the collar on the worn coat around the baby girl's neckline. Giving Nolu the eye, she says, "Does this mean Sonny is sitting out in the car without a coat on?" Herb joins in. "The only one who stays, when I say 'stay,'" he says, eyeing his granddaughter just as Abi, his third granddaughter, walks up.

Dorothy, turning to leave, says, "Why would any of them stay, they know you're bringing them all to me anyway!"

His voice follows Dorothy, but he does not. Herb Powless would never follow anybody, that much had not changed, not even for her. But his voice does easily as he continues, "Took 'em to McDonald's, and they all ordered double-trouble somethin' or 'nother and drank milkshakes like it was coffee."

Little Nolu looks back and nods to him, making it clear she will keep her agreement with her grandpa, whatever it is, it will never be known. Grandpa had given all the kids long talks about agreements, and sacred trusts, and how they could never be broken. Being young was no excuse. It was a special day when Grandpa trusted you. He was big on trust.

Dorothy pulls Nolu's hand from hers so she can point with her index finger.

"Only double trouble you ordered this morning was me, Herb Powless," she says on a turn and starts off for real this time.

Herb calls out again, and almost like an echo reaching her, Dorothy hears, "Oh yeah, Dennis called, he wants you to call him."

That stops her. Likely he wants something from her; he is not calling to chat. Dorothy half-turns back and says to Herb, "You can do me another favor. Go pick up the meat. For ceremony tonight."

Herb smiles. "Okay, get the casino to loan me a truck and I will, hell, why not, they got so many they're giving 'em away."

Dorothy shakes her head. "We never needed no truck to do anything before. Just forget it, I'll send Geronimo," referring to their son.

There is a pause between them as Herb is finding it hard to say something else, and there is something he wants to say.

Herb looks up from his feet to her eyes as he says, "Those Potawatomi ought to give us a truck if we need it. Their lobby's gonna be a mile long in that new tower they're adding. Just loose talk maybe, but then, maybe not. It's the big town. Milwaukee, ya know?"

"Well, they won't give you one," Dorothy says, always direct.

Herb smiles. "No, they won't. Those running it now, why would they give me a truck or otherwise? They sure could afford to, though . . . now." Dorothy chuckles with him and lets him take it as far as he needs to.

"Yes," she said. "Now."

Herb, with a look of pride, says, "You sure run a beautiful fireplace, lady."

"I'm not the one running it." Then, with her usual quick stride, she heads off.

Always to have the last word between them, though divorced now over twenty years. He lets out a laugh as he calls out his last: "Tell Banks I don't make a good errand boy, never did, but then he already knows that. Good thing he calls you!"

She knows the words were meant more for her, a reminder that the old lion may lose his teeth, but he can still roar. If Herb Powless hasn't earned that respect, then nobody has. She hurries to her office, the hustle and bustle of bells of a thriving casino ringing out down her path as she goes. She passes another Oneida woman in security clothes who also calls out to Dorothy, "Must be important if it's Dennis calling, probably about Leonard, want me to take the kids?"

Hours later, back home in De Pere, a dark pink early twilight was setting in against a fallen snow as Dorothy sat in her comfortable ranch house. She owned her home outright now, and never took the feeling for granted, especially when a hard snow was blowing outside. The early fall white sat in clumps, and peeking from under it was a hint of greenish brown apple leaves and shrubs that lined a gravel stone drive. A barn was filled with lawn chairs, folding tables, a large smoker, and a new riding lawnmower. Dorothy's new Chevrolet SUV was sitting in the drive.

She sat in her burgundy night robe on the living room area rug, her blue jeans still on underneath. With company coming soon, she couldn't get too relaxed. She'd prepped all day for the breakfast and then noon meals that would follow ceremony. It would all begin when it was completely dark outside, around 9:00 p.m.

The snow was peaceful and blowing and quickly gathering up on the corners of the windowpanes in its usual fashion. Wouldn't slow down the ceremony tonight; it wouldn't even be noticed, and would never be complained about or called bad. No weather was bad; it was Mother Earth doing what she needed to do. The boys were outside stacking up the wood near the tipi and covering it with a tarp.

The lodge was a grand article that stood high with as much as a thirty-foot ceiling. People traveled to her Wisconsin home from as far away as Canada and New York, with some friends coming in regularly from Arizona. Just as many others often asked her son Buddy or Geronimo to make a fire for them, to run a meeting, and when they did, they would all do the traveling.

Rarely was a request refused by her son Buddy Powless; he was a medicine person who typically ran the ceremony, with his younger brother Geronimo at his side. Geronimo was handsome with short-cut brown hair and always with a somber expression, even at just thirty-seven. Although soft-voiced, his words carried the same import as his father's. His beautiful wife Michelle was devoted to him, at his side, and she was an Ojibwe girl.

Tonight would be Buddy Powless's fireplace, and with a few variants it would be run the same way as from his first teachings, having been mentored by Ellis Chips himself, then later Leonard Crow Dog. Buddy, now in his forties, had a stern, quiet expression, and a little silver showing on the sides of his pulled-back long dark hair. His wife Linda was Oneida, and also always at his side. He was seasoned and very adept at what he did, a good counselor, and a good son. Dorothy would never forget their lowering her son into that deep hole, many years ago now, and how his power came to him. This was part of the making of a medicine person, deeply spiritual and what went on was private, not even mentioned to her. She did know he could talk to the fireplace and when he did, it talked back, and that was all she needed to know. Leonard Crow Dog had had Buddy Powless, at the young age of twelve, run a passing ceremony for a boy who'd been shot in the back; his name was Dallas Thundershield.

Both he and his brother Geronimo were prolific now in language and song and traditions of a few nations, not just their own.

Dorothy recalled the day when there were no ceremonies; they were just busy trying to find food to put in their mouths. The Movement changed that.

Dennis Banks and other leaders wrote books to record some of it, and

Herb was told he should, too, while his memory was good. After all, he'd retired years ago. Herb laughed at the idea and told Dennis, "I didn't take no pictures for no book, what I was doing ya don't take pictures of and ya try *not to remember*. And how in hell do you retire from being Indian?"

The ceremony wouldn't be for many hours yet, so for a few minutes longer Dorothy could lounge. She pulled a leather satchel out of the bookcase near her. It was packed full of weathered memorabilia. She sat down on her plush area rug.

She noticed on the wall a grand oil painting of horses running, against the orange sunset of a mesa of squared mountains, a stronghold. Neatly in the corner was a small painted arrow and the name Leonard Peltier.

She glanced at the black and white photos that were haunting to her. Though young men and women in the pictures, their faces all looked old beyond their years. Dorothy recognized most all of them, give or take a few.

Nolu walked in and sat close beside her on the rug. The little girl was careful not to sit on her own long, wavy brown hair. She had on a little pink robe over blue jeans. She lifted one news clipping as gently as if she were lifting a snowflake, respecting her grandmother's obvious reverence for them. The article's photo showed the long body of a boy as he lay twisted off in the distance. He was half-covered. The little girl knew at first glance he was dead on the ground and didn't ask unnecessary questions of her grandmother.

"That is little Joe Stuntz," Dorothy said. Nolu smiled back at the oval framed picture of the youth inserted above the photo of him slain. It was of the smiling boy's face from an earlier time, likely a school picture, as she asked, "What does this word say, Grandma?" Dorothy glanced over at the little girl's finger, and she moved it to see what she was pointing at. "That's not a word, Nolu, it's a tribe. It says Coeur d' Alene. His people were originally from Idaho, I guess. Hunh, I don't recall knowing any of them. We're here," she said, as she put her index finger on the rug and then slowly moved it left, "and they're over here."

"Grandma, why'd they kill someone who's little?" Dorothy just shook her head. "In those days, they were killing a lot of Indian people, people were killing people. It was a tough time. He was called little because he was only twenty-three, and a sweet and good boy I heard. I didn't know him. Grandpa did."

Nolu popped her small head up under her grandmother's arm to see closer. "Twenty-three, that's old! I hate it when I'm called little. Bet he hated it, too . . . Joe . . . *Stunze Kills* . . .?" Dorothy looks at her face and repeats, "Joe Stuntz-Killsright, that is his name. He was part of Northwest AIM. The Klamath tribe took them in. Maybe his people were relocated there."

"I wish we could be relocated, don't you?"

Dorothy answers directly. "No, I don't. Traveling and seeing new things is a good thing, but when the government relocated you, you came home and didn't know how to communicate with your own no more, you forgot your language, or your way was strange. That was terrible on people."

"Did they do this to you and Grandpa?"

Dorothy smiled as she pulled the young girl into her arms. "You think anybody can make your grandpa do anything he didn't think of?" Nolu giggles and shakes her head; Dorothy hugs her and they both say repeatedly. "No no . . . no!"

"Was that when you were my age, Grandma?"

Dorothy smiled down at her and lifted her small chin up with her forefinger. "I was never your age."

Dorothy paused on a faded newspaper clipping dated July 23, 1979. The headline read: "Leonard Peltier escape continues into the week . . ."

"Grandma, why does ceremony go on all night, why not in the daytime, and can I go in?"

Dorothy took her chin with a finger and lifted her sweet face up to hers a second time. "It's out of respect to the Creator; late into the night it becomes as quiet as earth can be, most all living things are asleep, and he can hear our prayers easier. By sunup it's through. You can come in, but you have to stay."

"Wish it'd stop snowing."

"It will, eventually; spring will come and the blanket that warms the mother will melt and become a washcloth that comforts her, and then underneath it all, that which is living will start to be born." Her granddaughter listened intently.

Snow suddenly blew in the door just as her youngest son, Geronimo Powless, opened it. He struggled with two large metal pots, one scraping the side of the door. Nolu and Dorothy ran to help him. Their manners were in actions, not words.

They headed toward the stove, as it was time to put on the prepared meat. First, they seared the buffalo chunks and then added the broth and spices and then the beans. There'd be a hearty stew simmering all night to be ready for noon meal on the following day, for the next day's feast. The beans had already been washed and were sitting ready. Freshly made fry bread would go with it, both light and hearty. A little sweet, too, depending on the oil.

Dorothy's mind wandered back to the vintage news clipping, with its high-desert background of scenic Lompoc, California. She could still see the scrub trees in it, and in her mind a lone figure of a strong lean Indian man was running through them.

Suspended forever now in timeless memory in a newspaper clipping, and though not visible in the picture, Leonard Peltier was the man running. His freedom forever just a touch away. The photo might be a still life, but its memory would never be.

From the kitchen window Dorothy noticed the fine, somber orange glow of the tipi canvas. A small star hung in the sky nearby and its small brilliance could be glimpsed now that the snow was receding. All was right with the world on such a night. Her world, anyway. From the open door of the tipi she could see the white-hot glow of the wood that fed the flame, which promised a warm strong fire would soon follow. Ceremony was coming.